Leisure Policy and Planning

Other leisure titles published by Longman include:

Sport and Physical Recreation (2nd edition)
Leisure Operational Management Volume 1: facilities (2nd edition)
Leisure Operational Management Volume 2: people (2nd edition)
ILAM Guide to Good Practice in Leisure Management
Law and Leisure Services Management (2nd edition)
Research Methods for Leisure and Tourism
Finance and Leisure
Leisure Marketing
The Economics of Leisure Services Management
Developing Partnerships in Sport and Leisure: A practical guide
Case Studies in Leisure Management Practice
Marketing Tourism
Customer Service Training Pack for the Leisure Industry
Quality First: Quality Management for the Leisure Industry

For further information contact SAM COX on tel: (0279) 442601

LEISURE POLICY AND PLANNING

by

A.J.VEAL
University of Technology, Sydney

LONGMAN

Leisure Policy and Planning

Published by Longman Information & Reference
Longman Group Limited, Westgate House, The High, Harlow,
Essex CM20 1YR, United Kingdom.
Telephone: (0279) 442601
Facsimile: (0279) 444501

First published 1994

A catalogue record for this book is available from the British Library.

ISBN 0-582-23820-X

Typeset in 10/11pt Souvenir medium by York Publishing Services.

Printed in Great Britain by BPC Wheatons Ltd, Exeter

CONTENTS

FIGURES

TABLES

PREFACE

This book is based on the experience of teaching leisure planning and policy in the Universities of Birmingham and North London in the UK, and the University of Technology, Sydney, in Australia.

Some of the material in the book draws on papers previously published or presented at conferences. In particular, chapter 6 on planning techniques is a development of a paper which was originally published from the then Polytechnic of North London (Veal, 1982a) and subsequently appeared in various forms (Veal, 1982, 1984, 1986); it is satisfying to be able to update the material and present it in a more developed and permanent form. Part of chapter 2, on the concept of need, was developed from a paper originally presented at a World Leisure and Recreation Association Congress (Veal, 1988). Chapter 7, on forecasting, is adapted from a chapter originally published in *Leisure and the Future* (Veal, 1987). Chapters 3, 4 and 8 have had a long history as draft papers inflicted on long-suffering students at UTS. I am grateful to Simon Darcy and numerous other colleagues and students who have read and commented on the earlier versions of this work and prompted me to produce, I hope, clearer and more relevant material for this book.

AJV
May 1994

1 INTRODUCTION

Introduction

This book is concerned with the roles and activities of the state sector in leisure. The state includes governmental bodies at national, regional and state levels and their many agencies. Another term used to refer to this phenomenon is the 'public sector' – in contrast to the private or commercial sector and the voluntary or non-profit sector. Substantial parts of the leisure industries lie within the public sector, including urban, country and national parks, many sports facilities and events, the arts, public broadcasting, heritage, and tourism promotion. In addition, a great deal of leisure is regulated and/or heavily taxed by the state, including the consumption of alcohol, entertainment products, and gambling. In western countries governments at various levels spend billions of pounds a year on leisure and tourism services and also garner many billions in the form of duties and taxes on leisure services.

There is apparently a deep ambivalence in people's attitudes toward the state. Nearly everyone wants the government to do more for them: if they are parents of pre-school-age children they want more child-care facilities; if they are parents of school-age children they want more money spent on education; if they are motorists they want more and better roads; if they are environmentalists they want the government to intervene more to protect the environment; if they are state employees they want higher pay; if they are farmers they want more subsidies; if they are elderly they want higher pensions; everybody wants better health services; large numbers want more resources devoted to law and order; internationalists want more spent on overseas aid; the tourism industry wants more money spent on tourism promotion; sports enthusiasts want more money for sport; and arts enthusiasts want more generous grant-aid for the arts.

However, despite the apparent enthusiasm for more government activity (and therefore more expenditure), few of the advocates of such activity appear to have a worked-out position on the role of the state in society as a whole: they are merely partisans in their own limited cause.

While many might advocate an increased government role and increased government expenditure in a number of the areas outlined above, the question arises as to whether they have a clear idea of the aggregate consequences of such 'shopping lists' for overall government expenditure and taxation and the role of government in society generally. No-one, it would appear, wants to pay more taxes; in fact most people probably believe that taxes are too high. Many believe that government is too big, too bureaucratic or both. Many people have a poor opinion of politicians, who are ultimately responsible for the activities of the state. Many believe that state agencies are ineffective and inefficient. Generally, it would seem, people want governments to do more – but not with their money. There is therefore an inconsistency between the widespread demands for more government services and the equally widespread suspicion of 'big government' and opposition to high taxes.

The ambivalence of many people's attitudes towards government is further exemplified by the common belief that, on the one hand, 'they' (meaning elected members and paid officials of government) make the wrong decisions and do so without consultation with ordinary people, but on the other hand few people take any great part in the political process which *leads* to such decisions, beyond voting in elections every few years. Membership of political parties in the western democracies is minimal. In countries where voting is not compulsory voting turnouts are often very low – for example only half the eligible voters in the USA vote to elect the president and often less than half the electorate vote in local council elections in Britain.

Why the state?

In a primarily capitalist society what is the role of the state in the field of leisure? Is there a *rationale* for the particular pattern of state involvement which has evolved? What are the competing philosophies concerning the appropriate role of the state? Why do some fields of leisure apparently merit state involvement while others do not? Why should taxpayers as a whole subsidise some people's leisure-time activities? Why should taxpayers pay for the promotion and market research costs of a largely privately owned industry, such as tourism? How are decisions made on these matters? These are the sorts of questions which are examined in this book.

The role of governments in leisure, as in other fields, has evolved over the years, and continues to evolve. Sometimes change comes about gradually, for example by means of an Act of Parliament authorising a new piece of government expenditure or establishing a new government agency. At other times change is cataclysmic, as in Russia in 1917, when the Communist Revolution resulted in the wholesale takeover of economic activity by the workers' state, and the almost equally cataclysmic return to private enterprise in the 1990s. But even when change is gradual, it is rarely achieved without controversy – some groups gain and some lose, some see the change as fulfilment of political promises, others as a betrayal.

The development of the public sector of leisure has not been entirely the result of the political acts of elected government, although they provide the framework and background to what happens. The professionals involved in the area have also been influential. Professionals work as public servants at national, regional and local level, and for the private and non-profit sectors, and in academe. They conduct the research and produce the reports and policy recommendations which are the basis of political decisions. Then they are responsible for implementing the decisions and managing the facilities and services, or imposing the regulations, which ensue. Considerable power is therefore exercised by such professionals (Henry, 1993:110–37; Coalter, 1988:177–80; Bacon, 1989). This text is concerned with the skills which such professionals bring to their tasks. A number of texts exist which are concerned with leisure *management* – that is, the efficient and effective operation of facilities and services once they are established – but this text is concerned with the prior stage of formulating policies and plans, and evaluating the implementation of such policies and plans as an input to further policy and plan formulation.

In chapter 3, a wide range of views is explored concerning the appropriate role of the state, from complete state control to a minimalist, 'roll back the state', view. This book, however, is predicated on a 'middle-road' perspective: that the environment in which leisure professionals in the western world work is a basically capitalist one, but with a strong and essential role played by the state; that part of that role is legitimately concerned with community leisure services; and that that role can be enhanced, and society benefited, by the exercise of certain analytical skills which are directed towards a better understanding of community leisure needs and demands and their more effective and efficient satisfaction.

Three topics of importance to public policy are *not* covered in this book, partly for reasons of space and partly because they are adequately covered elsewhere. The first of these is the question of history. There is no doubt that the current patterns of public, and non-profit, leisure services and the values and practices that surround them, are the result of particular patterns of historical evolution, particularly dating from the industrial revolution. This history has been well documented in a number of texts, to which the reader is referred, including Henry (1993), Coalter (1988), Bailey (1979) and Cunningham (1980). The historical perspective alerts us to the fact that public policy has been as much about *controlling* leisure, through laws and regulation, as it has been about *providing* for leisure and, further, that decisions on what to provide and what not to provide and what to regulate and what not to regulate reflect the relative power of various interests and classes in the political decision-making process and have ongoing consequences in terms of which groups have access to facilities and services of their choice and which do not.

The second area of omission is any outline of the constitution, powers and responsibilities of existing public agencies, particularly in Britain. Again, such outlines are provided in numerous other texts, including Torkildsen (1986), Coalter (1988), Elvin (1990) and Adams (1990). The sheer complexity of the institutions involved in leisure in Britain (which is by no means exceptional in this respect) is conveyed by Bennington and White (1988: 6–7).

Thirdly, the book does not consider political behaviour in any detail. While political ideology and the role of public participation and community consultation are considered, the role of pressure groups and parties, the relative powers of national, regional and local government, and the processes by which political decisions are made, are not addressed. For coverage of these important topics, the reader is referred to other sources, including Henry (1993), Coalter (1988), Bramham *et al.* (1993) and Limb (1986).

Rather than consider specific institutions, an overall framework for viewing the leisure service delivery 'system' is presented here, in Figure 1.1. The framework consists of five elements.

Figure 1.1 A social/political framework for studying leisure

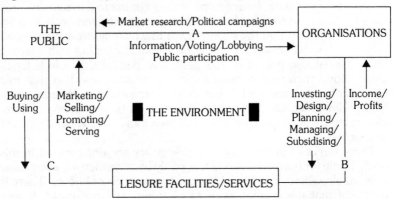

a. *The public* – individuals/households/communities.
b. *Organisations* – public and private sector organisations involved in the provision of leisure and tourism facilities and services, including voluntary organisations, commercial companies and governments and their agencies, including elected and appointed members and senior and strategic management personnel.
c. *Leisure facilities/services* – facilities and services, including line managers and 'front-line' staff.
d. *The environment* – the natural and built, physical environment.
e. *The processes* – which link these various elements, including planning, marketing, political processes and the use, purchase and consumption of services.

The essence of the framework is the linkages between the elements. Between any two elements there is a two-way flow of influence. The nature of the processes, or at least their names, varies, depending on whether they relate to the public or private sector.

Along Link A, between *The public* and *Organisations*, the flows are:

- in the case of the *commercial sector*: the process of market research and the provision of information;
- in the case of the *public sector*, and to some extent the non-profit sector, this is where the political process takes place, including political campaigning, voting, lobbying and public participation.

Along Link B, between *Organisations* and *Leisure facilities/services,* the flows are:

- from *Organisations* to *Leisure facilities/services*: the processes of planning, developing and managing;
- to *Organisations* from *Leisure facilities/services*: income and profits (or losses).

Along Link C, between *The public* and *Leisure facilities/services*:

- here the process of selling and promotion takes place and, the process of using or not using the facility or service provided.

The (physical) *environment* is represented as a background, but all-pervasive, element of the system and includes the urban, rural and natural environment. It is there as an entity in its own right; it is the object of policy, a constraint on activity and a resource which is used for leisure and tourism. When a part of the environment gets taken over and managed for leisure or tourism it becomes part of the *facilities/ services* element.

The uses of the framework are, firstly, to demonstrate that leisure facilities and services are not just 'there' – they arise as a result of interaction between the public, as users and as political/social groups, and organisations and their activities; secondly, to illustrate the idea that both public and private sector provision exist within the same basic framework, although the relationships between the elements vary; thirdly, to show the interconnectedness of the elements in the system; fourthly, to provide an, admittedly simple, link between the various applied subfields which are studied in leisure and tourism courses, namely: politics, planning, design, marketing, market research and management.

Structure of the book

Among the most widely accepted roles of governments is the duty to uphold and protect human rights and to ensure that the basic needs of their citizens are met. In chapter 2, therefore, the status of leisure as a right and a need is examined. In chapter 3 competing ideas about the right and proper role of the state in society, and particularly in relation to leisure, are examined from the point of view of various political ideologies. In chapter 4 the ideas of 'mainstream economics' are examined, since they underpin much of the thinking of the centre to right of political thought, and provide the basis for economics-based analysis of state activities. Chapter 5 examines the planning process, both in a traditional sense and in the context of contemporary ideas concerning strategic planning and management. Chapter 6 considers a range of specific techniques and approaches which can be utilised in preparing leisure plans. Chapter 7 is concerned with leisure demand estimation and forecasting techniques. Chapter 8 presents an overview of two economics-based techniques used in leisure planning and decision-making, namely cost-benefit analysis and economic-impact analysis. Chapter 9, on performance appraisal, is concerned with evaluation of policies and plans once implemented, and how the information generated from such a process is utilised in further rounds of policy formulation and plan-making. Throughout the book there is a tendency to deal with leisure as a whole and with the public or the community as a whole, whereas, in fact, leisure consists of a number of very different activities and sectors and the community consists of numerous groups, with differing resources, needs and tastes. The final chapter gives specific attention to these sectors and groups.

2 LEISURE RIGHTS AND NEEDS

Introduction

It can be argued that the reason why governments must be involved in leisure provision is that leisure is a *right* or a *need* and it is the job of governments to ensure that the rights of its citizens are protected and the needs of its citizens are met. In this chapter we examine the two concepts of rights and needs and how they relate to leisure and leisure policy.

Rights

The *Shorter Oxford English Dictionary* defines a right as a 'justifiable claim, on legal or moral grounds, to have or obtain something, or to act in a certain way'. Thus a right is seen as something which must be claimed by an individual or group and, in turn, be recognised by others as legitimate. *Human* rights are those rights which can be claimed by all human beings and which, through various national and international legal instruments, have been widely recognised, particularly by governments.

The modern idea of human rights arose in Europe and North America in the eighteenth century as a reaction against the arbitrary exercise of power by rulers. One of the most famous declarations of human rights was contained in the 1776 American Declaration of Independence, which stated:

> We hold these truths to be self-evident: that all men are created equal; that they are endowed by their Creator with certain inalienable rights; that among these are life, liberty and the pursuit of happiness.

The reference to the 'pursuit of happiness' is perhaps the earliest indication of a recognition of leisure as a human right, although, of course, leisure is only one means by which people might pursue happiness. In the Universal Declaration of Human Rights, adopted by the United Nations in 1948, leisure received explicit recognition in Article 24, which declares:

> Everyone has the right to rest and leisure, including reasonable limitation of working hours and periodic holidays with pay.

Rights in relation to the arts and culture were recognised in Article 27, which states:

> Everyone has the right freely to participate in the cultural life of the community, to enjoy the arts and to share in scientific advancement and its benefits.

Of relevance to tourism, Article 13 states:

> Everyone has the right to leave any country, including his own, and to return to his country.

The general statement on leisure was reaffirmed in the International Covenant on Economic, Social and Cultural Rights, adopted by the United Nations in 1966. Article 7 deals with leisure, but in the context of the 'right of everyone to the enjoyment of just and favourable conditions of work', which includes the right to:

> Rest, leisure, reasonable limitation of working hours and periodic holidays with pay, as well as remuneration for public holidays.

Since all the members of the United Nations are signatories to these declarations, it might be assumed that all national governments recognise leisure as a right and accept a responsibility to uphold that right. However, as Cranston (1973: 5) points out, rights can be divided into *positive* rights, which are enshrined in law, and *moral* rights, which are not so enshrined. Cranston uses the example of violations of Article 13 of the Universal Declaration of Human Rights, relating to freedom of travel, by the United States, the then Soviet Union and South Africa, to make the distinction.

> Clearly, therefore, the right to leave any country, which the United Nations Declaration says 'everyone' has, is not a positive right. The intention of the sponsors of that declaration was to specify something that everyone *ought* to have. In other words the rights they named were moral rights. (Cranston, 1973: 6)

The declarations on leisure and culture could similarly be termed *moral* rights, since the declarations do not specify the *amount* of leisure time which is considered acceptable, or what constitutes 'reasonable' limitation of working hours, or the amount of paid holidays or public holidays. Only some of these matters are codified in the laws of some countries and the details vary from country to country. Indeed, some critics have suggested that declarations, such as those of the United Nations, are not in fact universal in application, but relate primarily to developed countries with the resources to implement them.

More detailed declarations exist in relation to leisure and to different aspects of leisure. The *Charter for Leisure* (see Appendix 2.1 on page 18), drawn up by the World Leisure and Recreation Association (WLRA) in 1970 and revised in 1981, declares, in Article 1:

> Leisure is a basic human right. This implies the obligation of governments to recognise and protect this right and of citizens to respect the right of fellow citizens to leisure. This means that no one shall be deprived of this right for

reasons of colour, creed, sex, religion, race, handicap or economic condition.

The charter goes on to extol the virtues of leisure and to exhort governments to make provision for leisure as a social service, but it stops short of declaring access to leisure facilities and services as a right.

The *European Sport for All Charter* (see Appendix 2.2 on page 19) was adopted by the Community of Ministers of the Council of Europe in 1976, and declares that:

Every individual shall have the right to participate in sport.

As with the WLRA charter, subsequent articles envisage a major role for governments in co-ordinating, planning and providing for sport. Unlike the WLRA charter, however, the Sport for All Charter has received the formal endorsement of the member governments of the Council of Europe. Individual member countries have generally adopted 'Sport for All' policies and the Council of Europe monitors progress through the activities of a permanent committee.

The 1989 United Nations Convention on the Rights of the Child, in Article 31, states that signatories will:

1. ... recognise the right of the child to rest and leisure, to engage in play and recreational activities appropriate to the age of the child and to participate freely in cultural life and the arts.

2. ... shall respect and promote the right of the child to participate fully in cultural and artistic life and shall encourage the provision of appropriate and equal opportunities for cultural, artistic, recreational and leisure activity.

Are these declarations of rights of assistance in determining the appropriate role of governments in relation to leisure? Yes and no. The declarations of rights refer to rights to *leisure*, in the sense of leisure time, but not to facilities or services. As *moral* statements, they indicate a broad consensus that governments should be concerned about leisure, but since the statements about leisure rarely translate into *positive* rights, they provide little guidance on the nature or extent of government involvement necessary to secure such rights.

The idea of need

While statements about leisure rights are made in an international context, statements about leisure as a *need* are more common at national and local level. The idea of need occupies an important place in the lexicon of leisure studies and leisure service provision. Iso-Ahola has said:

In a way, the future of the entire field of leisure studies as well as the recreation profession depends on the construct of leisure need. That is, if it could not be shown that people have a need for leisure and recreation, professionals and practitioners might as well give up and begin searching for new jobs. (Iso-Ahola, 1980: 227)

Providing a link with the international discussion on rights, in 1987, the then Secretary-General of the United Nations declared:

> One of the primary needs of the human person is leisure and such use of it as will provide psychological strength and refreshment. (Perez de Cuellar, 1987)

Reflecting the government White Paper of the mid-1970s (Department of the Environment, 1975), and the government-funded 'Leisure Provision and People's Needs' study (Dower *et al.*, 1981), the Chairmen's Policy Group, the committee of chairmen *(sic)* of a number of British leisure Quangos, stated, in a 1983 report:

> Leisure provision has become accepted as a major element of social policy, aiming at enhancement of the quality of life of all citizens. This calls for a change of emphasis, away from catering simply for leisure demands, to understanding and meeting of leisure needs. (Chairmen's Policy Group, 1983: 61)

Such statements are not merely saying, in effect, 'people desire leisure'. If something is a *need*, in the sense used in these statements, then the implication is that society as a whole, and particularly government, has an obligation to ensure that it is provided for all. Societies or social systems are condemned as inadequate if they are unable to meet these sorts of need. The terminology of the Chairmen's Policy Group suggests that this obligation should be fulfilled by the state, since 'demand' is seen to be something dealt with by the market. However, none of these sources deals explicitly with the question: 'what is a need?'

A major problem in discussing need is that the word is used in a number of different ways. Taylor identified four different uses of the term.

(1) To indicate something needed to satisfy a rule or law; e.g. 'I need a sticker to park here'.

(2) To indicate means to an end (either specified or implied); e.g. 'I need a watch (in order to tell the time)'; 'He needs a doctor (in order to get well)'.

(3) To describe motivations, conscious or unconscious, in the sense of wants, drives, desires, and so on. So we speak of people having a need for achievement, the need to atone for guilt, needs for status, security, etc. Needs in this sense constitute conative dispositions.

(4) To make recommendations or normative evaluations. These are sometimes difficult to distinguish from (3) which are intended as purely descriptive statements. So, for instance, it is asserted that men have needs for affection, identity, self-esteem, the esteem of others, etc. But what is meant by such claims when they fall into this category is that men have these needs, whether or not they actually feel them, or whether or not they in fact count them as needs. This category also covers those more obvious kinds of recommendations such as 'what this country needs is good fighting men', or 'people need freedom', etc.

(Taylor, 1959: 107)

It is need in Taylor's fourth, normative, sense which gives rise to a public policy response. Needs of types (1), (2) and (3) are technically and empirically derived; as such they imply nothing about the obligations of society to satisfy them: it is only when some external, collective evaluation of these needs takes place that a collective, government response may be called for. The question arises as to which needs are subject to such collective evaluations and why. The literature which is commonly referred to in discussions of leisure and need tends to avoid this question, concentrating instead on various ways of assessing type (3) needs. This literature is considered below in five sections: the Bradshaw/Mercer typology, Maslow's hierarchy, motivation theory, neo-Marxist views and the work of Doyal and Gough on 'universal' needs.

The Bradshaw/Mercer typology

The typology of need put forward by Mercer (1975), based on the work of Bradshaw (1972) on 'social need', consists of four 'categories': felt need, expressed need, comparative need and normative need. Felt needs are those which individuals themselves are aware of but which are not formally expressed in any formal or active way and are generally unmet. Expressed needs are those to which individuals give active expression, for example by using services or joining a waiting list for some desired service. Comparative needs arise from comparing one individual or group of individuals with another. Normative need involves external assessments made, in Mercer's view, by experts. The typology leads to the suggestion that assessments of need for policy purposes should be made using measures related to all four categories and that policy should be based on evaluation of all four measures. The latter evaluation process, though only briefly explicated by Mercer, seems to involve taking action in areas where the various measures of need are in agreement, but provides no solution in situations where the various measures are not in agreement.

Of the four Mercer/Bradshaw categories only 'normative' needs correspond to Taylor's category (4) needs, the others being versions of category (3). But normative need assessments in recreation are viewed with suspicion by Mercer, because the 'experts' who make them are generally seen to be a 'small elite group in our society – the well-educated, well-to-do planners, politicians, engineers and academics' (p. 41) who are unlikely to truly understand the needs of people in general. But, in his conclusions, Mercer suggests that:

> ... it would be of considerable value to focus much greater research attention on the *normative* aspects of need; more specifically, on the decision-making processes associated with the formulation of normative standards and measures of adequacy. (Mercer, 1975: 46)

The Bradshaw/Mercer typology does not therefore provide an answer to the question of how or why particular needs – including leisure – might come to be classified as normative needs.

Maslow's hierarchy of need

Maslow's well-known hierarchy of need is even more widely referred to in the leisure literature than the Bradshaw/Mercer typology. Maslow's theory posits that human needs are arranged in a hierarchy from physical needs for food, drink and shelter, via needs for safety/security, love/affiliation, and social and self esteem, to the highest level: self-actualisation (Maslow, 1954). As the needs lower down the hierarchy are satisfied, so the higher needs become relevant and the individual is motivated to satisfy them.

Leisure can be seen to be related to most levels of the hierarchy: for example, rest, relaxation and exercise are physical needs; friendship groups and youth sub-cultures, based largely around leisure activities, reflect the need for safety and security; much family leisure, leisure activities related to sexual partnering and team sports can be said to relate to the need for love and affiliation; the exercise of skills in sport and cultural activities reflects the need for esteem; and many of those same activities, engaged in for their own sake, provide for self-actualisation. Since it is involved at all levels of the hierarchy, the argument goes, leisure is a need, or a need satisfier, in the Maslow sense. However, this does not make all leisure needs normative. For example, holding a party could be related to three levels of the hierarchy – rest and relaxation, affiliation, and esteem – but the provision of parties is not usually seen as something for which there should be a collective concern and government responsibility.

As presented above, the Maslow hierarchy refers only to Taylor's type (3) needs, equivalent to the Bradshaw/Mercer 'felt needs'. However, one aspect of Maslow's theory which is often omitted in popular summaries is that the hierarchy does *not* apply to all needs but only to what he calls 'basic needs', which are defined as those desires which, if not satisfied, would produce psycho-pathological consequences.

> Thwarting of unimportant desires produces no psycho-pathological results: thwarting of basically important needs does produce such results. (Maslow, 1954: 57)

'Basically important needs' are those whose denial produces psycho-pathological consequences: the rest are 'unimportant desires'. Since many would accept that there should be a collective concern to prevent psycho-pathological conditions, it is simply a matter of identifying these needs/desires whose denial would produce psycho-pathological results (and agreeing on a definition of psycho-pathological) in order to establish conditions for collective – ie government – involvement in preventive measures; and such measures could well include leisure service provision.

This implies that society can avoid difficult normative decisions about which needs it should and should not meet collectively. It implies that needs can be 'read off' from empirical facts: that if people are likely to behave psycho-pathologically if certain needs are unmet then such needs must be met, by the state if necessary. However, if this approach to providing state services were to be accepted *without qualification,* society would be hostage not only to potentially unlimited calls on its resources (Chapelle, 1973), but also to all sorts of potentially socially unacceptable behaviour. Thus people who are liable to become neurotic unless they can engage in behaviour which humiliates or annoys others (for example to satisfy their need for esteem) would have to be humoured. There would be no control on drug use or firearms if these were required to satisfy some people's 'basically important needs' for self-fulfilment. While society might respond in such a manner to 'lower-level' needs in the hierarchy, such as for food, for the higher-level needs, particularly 'self-actualisation', it is impossible to exclude a normative dimension: society must make choices. It cannot be assumed that society must satisfy particular self-actualisation needs simply because they exist in an empirical sense. As Fitzgerald puts it:

> Human selves have many potentialities ... If by 'self-actualisation' is meant *whatever* the individual can be motivated to act out or express, it provides us with no standard whatsoever for distinguishing between desirable (or appropriate) forms of self-expression and undesirable (or inappropriate) forms. This, of course, Maslow and those theorists using his scheme do not intend. Manifestly the murderer, sadist, fascist, rapist, incendiarist or machete man do not fit in with Maslow's notion of a person developing his potentialities or expressing 'what he has in him', even though there may well be harmony between basic motives and overt behaviour . . . 'Self-actualisation' cannot be rendered empirical. Maslow must, and by implication does, set up standards of what the individual in his freedom ought to become or express, and what he ought not to become or express. (Fitzgerald, 1977: 49)

Clearly, every society has moral codes which override any simplistic, mechanical approach to need satisfaction. Indeed religion, moral codes, ideology, education, the whole panoply of civilisation can be said to be aimed at providing a system of rules and codes of behaviour about how and to what extent needs should be satisfied. In a more positive sense these codes are devised to socialise individuals into *not* seeking to satisfy their needs in socially or personally destructive ways. But these codes vary and are adopted as a matter of faith, conviction or socialisation: they cannot be 'proved'. It follows that views on acceptable ways of satisfying needs will vary, depending on the moral code adhered to. It therefore follows that needs-based public policy must be based on such codes and cannot be based on 'value-free' needs assessments of the sort which the Maslow hierarchy appears to offer.

Motivation theory

Iso-Ahola has provided the most comprehensive expositions of psychological motivation theories of need, including Maslow's. Among these approaches is the idea of the need for 'optimal arousal and incongruity', which suggests that 'too little or too much stimulation is damaging to the individual, both physiologically and psychologically' (Iso-Ahola, 1980: 229). This type of need therefore has much the same basis as Maslow's conception – the idea that the *denial* of the need would be damaging to the individual. But the same cautionary arguments apply as regards their relationship to public policy: the *means* of satisfying the need for optimal arousal and incongruity cannot be accepted without reference to sets of values. This much Iso-Ahola recognises when he concludes that the '... social nature of leisure motivation is also manifested in behavior prompted by normative and comparative recreation needs' (1980: 249).

Iso-Ahola also explores the idea of 'intrinsic' and 'extrinsic' motivations for participation in leisure activities, and 'leisure needs studies', such as those by London *et al.* (1977) and Tinsley *et al.* (1977), which seek to analyse the satisfactions reportedly gained by participants in various leisure activities: here needs are seen to be merely the corollary of satisfactions. By definition, these theories relate to Taylor's type (3) conception of need, or even type (2). The fact that leisure activities provide satisfactions does not justify their designation as type (4) needs.

Marxist and neo-Marxist views

The idea of human need is at the core of Marxist thought, which sees the failure of capitalism as its ultimate inability to meet human needs, while a socialist or communist society would be based on the principle 'from each according to his or her abilities, to each according to his or her needs'. Under capitalism, however, the Marxist view is that needs are corrupted by the economic and social relationships which the system engenders – giving rise to 'false needs' (Springborg, 1977; Heller, 1976). Marx argued that, while capitalism has demonstrated that human needs are not static, but develop in accordance with the technological and economic capabilities of a society, at the same time it shows how the very nature of that society shapes people's needs. Thus, under capitalism, people develop 'false needs', for money and for the commodities which capitalism delivers.

While Marx himself envisaged that under capitalism even the basic needs of the masses would eventually be denied to them, causing the downfall of the system, neo-Marxists have developed the idea of the generation and continued satisfaction of 'false needs' to explain the longevity of capitalism. Marcuse defines false needs as:

> ... those which are superimposed upon the individual by particular social interests in his repression: the needs which perpetuate toil, aggressiveness, misery, and injustice ... Most of the prevailing needs to relax, to have fun, to behave and consume in accordance with the advertisements, to love and hate what others love and hate, belong in this category of false needs. (Marcuse, 1964: 5)

According to Marcuse, under the conditions of capitalism, it is impossible to discover which needs are true and which are false. True needs will only emerge when society is transformed.

> In the last analysis, the question of what are true and false needs must be answered by the individuals themselves, but only in the last analysis; that is, if and when they are free to give their own answer. As long as they are

... indoctrinated and manipulated their answer to this question cannot be taken as their own. By the same token, however, no tribunal can justly arrogate to itself the right to decide which needs should be developed and satisfied. (Marcuse, 1964: 6)

Under capitalism therefore, in this view, human agency is denied: human beings are passive objects, their (false) needs being entirely manipulated and determined by the system. We have to take it on trust that 'true needs' will become apparent under socialism, once social conditions are transformed. But the socialist or communist society would not escape the problem of defining need any more than can the state within a capitalist society. Such decisions require, as Soper puts it:

... a criterion of needs, a concept of value, and thus, in turn, political decisions about what is 'good' for society and its individuals to consume, and therefore what it is *worth* it producing. (1981: 208)

Doyal and Gough and universal needs

Doyal and Gough (1991), in a major study of human needs, refer to relativist theories of need, which state that only individuals or particular groups of individuals can know their own needs and that, since needs vary across individuals, groups and cultures, no 'universal' needs can be identified. The Bradshaw/Mercer typology, although it raises questions about 'real needs', can be classified as 'relativist' in the reliance it places on individual statements of need and the suspicion of 'normative' assessments. Similarly, the Maslow hierarchy and other psychological motivation theories, in their reliance on individuals alone, and denial of the collective, normative dimension, can be termed relativist. They are relativist in a very extreme way, in that they imply that only *individuals* can assess their own needs. The Marxist and neo-Marxist conceptualisation is relativist in its contention that 'true' human needs can only be determined by citizens of a socialist or communist society.

The criticisms of existing needs theories advanced above suggest that, to make Taylor's type (4) statements, sets of values/beliefs are required – a view of the good or moral life which may be threatened by the denial of certain requirements, which can then be termed needs. However, such a position can itself be seen as relativist, in that it suggests that all value systems have equal weight in assessing needs: for example, the Hitler Youth were provided with a comprehensive set of values to establish the 'need' to persecute Jews.

Doyal and Gough (1991) point to other forms of relativism. The acceptance of the liberal tenet that individuals are the best judges of their own interests has led to the rise of New Right policies which have given more emphasis to the market and have 'rolled back' the state, resulting in reductions in state services. The trend has been accelerated by 'relativists' of the left, including, for example, anti-racist and feminist activists, who argue that only ethnic groups or women themselves can know and judge their own needs.

Doyal and Gough set out to develop a theory of *universal* human need to rebut existing 'relativist' theories. They argue that, without some normative idea of universal needs, which are common to all, we are in no position to judge the success of any social or political organisation, since the main criterion for such judgements must be their success in meeting people's needs. Their approach is to start with 'values' as the basis for the establishment of a theory of human needs, rather than starting from the biological, as is the case with the psychological approaches discussed above.

Beginning with the minimal moral propositions that any human society at least has the obligation to prevent serious harm to its members and to optimise its members' ability to operate effectively as members of that society, Doyal and Gough argue that universal needs consist of *health* and *personal autonomy*. Health refers to physical health and therefore coincides with the lower orders of Maslow's hierarchy – but it is based on the idea of the individual's *right* to health rather than just the desire for it. Autonomy goes further; it means that the individual, to be human, has to be able to be a competent and dignified participant in society. This entails being educated to at least the minimum level required for the society concerned, being mentally healthy (as per Maslow), and being accorded and able to exercise certain civil and political rights. This set of needs is *values-based* rather than biologically based; as such it can be accepted or rejected by individuals, groups or organisations but, if accepted, is universal in application. In fact, Doyal and Gough's resultant list of needs is close to the various *rights* discussed above. However, through consideration of international data, they develop the case for converting moral rights to positive rights in the social and economic area.

While Doyal and Gough do not include leisure explicitly in their detailed lists of needs, it could be argued that adequate leisure time and the resources to facilitate physical and cultural leisure activity are a necessary part of the conditions necessary to ensure human health and personal autonomy, that is, they are needs satisfiers in Doyal and Gough's universal sense.

Conclusion

While human rights, including certain rights in the area of leisure, have been the subject of attention at international level, at national and local levels the focus has been on the idea of leisure as a need. Public figures have been prepared to make normative statements about leisure needs, but leisure researchers and planners have, in the past, attempted to devise scientific, objective and empirical bases for need assessment. While the research entailed in such approaches is important in understanding and interacting with individuals and groups in society, it has been argued in this chapter that, in establishing public leisure policy, values cannot be avoided. In that sense statements of need are similar to declarations of rights.

Further reading

Human rights: Brownlie, 1992; Cranston, 1973; MacFarlane, 1985; Kamenka and Tay, 1978; in relation to tourism: Edgell, 1990.

Needs: Bradshaw, 1972; Chappelle, 1973; Coalter, 1988; Dower *et al.*, 1981; Doyal and Gough, 1991; Fitzgerald, 1977; Heller, 1976; Iso-Ahola, 1989; Maslow, 1954; Mercer, 1975; Paddick, 1982; Soper, 1981; Springborg, 1981; Taylor, 1959.

Appendix 2.1: World Leisure and Recreation Association: Charter for Leisure

Article 1: *Leisure* is a basic human right. This implies the obligation of governments to recognise and protect this right and of citizens to respect the right of fellow citizens to leisure. This means that no one shall be deprived of this right for reasons of colour, creed, sex, religion, race, handicap or economic condition.

Article 2: *Recreation* is a social service of similar importance as Health and Education. Therefore, opportunities must be provided on a universal basis, reasonable access ensured, and appropriate variety and quality maintained.

Article 3: Ultimately, the individual person is his/her own best leisure and recreation resource; the primary role of governments, private agencies and groups are of a supporting nature, consisting of the provision of services where needed, with prime emphasis at the local level.

Article 4: Leisure and recreation opportunities should stress self-fulfilment, the development of interpersonal relationships, the fostering of family and social integration, international understanding and cooperation, and the strengthening of cultural identities. Special emphasis must be placed on maintaining the quality of the environment and on the influence of energy demands on future recreation resources.

Article 5: The development of recreation leaders, animators and/or counsellors must be undertaken wherever possible. The main tasks of these must include assisting people in discovering and developing their talents and helping them acquire desired personal skills for the purpose of broadening the range of recreation opportunities.

Article 6: The wide variety of leisure and recreation phenomena, including personal and collective experiences, must be subjected to systematic research and scholarly inquiry, with the results being disseminated as widely as possible to enhance the individual's knowledge of him/herself, to provide a stronger rationale for policy decisions, and to provide a more effective basis for program development and operation. All citizens must have access to all forms of information relative to the various aspects of leisure and recreation.

Article 7: Educational institutions at all levels must place special emphasis on the teaching of the importance of leisure and recreation, on helping students discover their leisure and recreation potential and on ways to integrate leisure and recreation into their lifestyles. These institutions should furthermore provide appropriate opportunities from which recreation leaders and educators can be developed.

Appendix 2.2: Council of Europe: European Sport for All Charter

Article I: Every individual shall have the right to participate in sport.

Article II: Sport shall be encouraged as an important factor in human development and appropriate support shall be made available out of public funds.

Article III: Sport, being an aspect of socio-cultural development, shall be related at local, regional and national levels to other areas of policy-making and planning such as education, health, social service, town and country planning, conservation, the arts, and leisure services.

Article IV: Each government shall foster permanent and effective co-operation between public authorities and voluntary organisations and shall encourage the establishment of national machinery for the development and co-ordination of sport for all.

Article V: Methods shall be sought to safeguard sport and sportsmen from exploitation for political, commercial or financial gain, and from practices that are abusive and debasing, including the unfair use of drugs.

Article VI: Since the scale of participation is dependent, among other things, on the extent, the variety and the accessibility of facilities, the overall planning of facilities shall be accepted as a matter for public authorities, shall take account of local, regional and national requirements, and shall incorporate measures designed to ensure full use of both new and existing facilities.

Article VII: Measures, including legislation where appropriate, shall be introduced to ensure access to open country and water for the purposes of recreation.

Article VIII: In any programme of sports development, the need for qualified personnel at all levels of administrative and technical management, leadership and coaching shall be recognised.

3 POLITICAL IDEOLOGY, LEISURE AND THE STATE

Ideology

It is argued in chapter 2 that a concept of need, as a basis for public policy, cannot be adequately formulated without reference to some set of values. Values can be based on philosophical, religious or political systems of thought. While the philosophical and religious dimensions are not unimportant, they are beyond the scope of this text, but references to writings on those themes are given in the list of Further Reading at the end of the chapter. The aim here is to outline some major political ideologies and discuss their implications for public policy in relation to leisure and tourism in western capitalist societies. The nature of ideology is discussed first; this is followed by outlines of the basic ideas in six ideological positions.

The *Shorter Oxford English Dictionary* defines ideology as: 'A system of ideas concerning phenomena, especially those of social life; the manner of thinking of a class or an individual'. Generally, then, political ideology consists of sets of political ideas – ideas about how society should be run. People may agree with or support an ideology because of intellectual conviction or self-interest or a combination of both. Self-interest arises when individuals believe that the achievement of the sort of society envisaged by the ideology would be to their benefit. Since people in similar social or economic situations – classes – are likely to have similar views on which ideologies best serve their interests, ideologies are often class-based, as suggested in the definition.

The fact that ideology is concerned with how society should be run means that ideology is involved with the political process. People act in the political arena to attempt to ensure that society is run along the lines of *their* preferred ideology. Hence political parties are generally associated with particular ideologies. The party which gains power attempts to mould society to operate in accordance with its ideology.

There is a tendency to think that many of the elements of leisure – sport, recreation, the arts, tourism – are 'above politics' and that they are not a factor in competing ideologies and are not, or should not be, affected by party politics. This is far from true, as this chapter seeks to demonstrate.

In one short chapter it is not possible to provide a definitive analysis of even the leading political ideologies, but an attempt is made to outline key features of four major ideological positions: 1 conservatism, 2 liberalism, 3 democratic socialism and 4 Marxist socialism. Conservatism and liberalism are seen to be on the *right* of politics, while the two socialist doctrines are generally considered to be on the *left*. The left/right designation reflects where politicians sit in elected parliaments based on a tradition dating back to the French Revolution in the late eighteenth century. In most western democracies conservatism, liberalism and democratic socialism compete for power. Marxist socialism was of course the ideology which ruled Eastern Europe until the collapse of communism in the late 1980s; it still holds sway in a few countries, notably China, Cuba and Vietnam, and is still influential in some left-wing parties and labour movements in the west.

Other ideologies, such as fascism on the extreme right and anarchism on the extreme left, are not considered here because of lack of space (but see Leach, 1993, and Wilson, 1988, for detail on fascism and anarchism). In addition to the 'mainstream' ideologies, the chapter also considers two ideological movements which do not necessarily fit neatly into the 'left–right' spectrum of politics, namely: 5 feminism and 6 environmentalism.

1 Conservatism

Conservatism, as its name implies, is the ideology in which emphasis is placed on *conserving* what exists, that is, on *not* changing things, in contrast to all the other ideologies outlined below, which stand for social and economic change in one form or another. The roots of conservatism predate the period of industrial revolution in Europe, but it emerged as a political force in the eighteenth and nineteenth centuries in opposition to the rise of liberalism and socialism. At that time conservatives represented the landed classes, rural interests and 'old money'; they defended the right of the monarchy and the aristocracy to rule and resisted the democratic demands and the rising power of industrialists and professions and, later, the labour movement. While modern conservative parties maintain their traditional links with landed and rural interests, and sometimes with conservative religions, in contemporary political life they draw political support from conservative sentiment across a wide spectrum of society.

An important feature of conservatism, which distinguishes it from left-wing ideologies, is the defence of inequality; the belief that inequality is part of the natural order of things and that, for example, personal wealth is part of the reward system which maintains society as we know it. Generally, the conservative outlook favours elitism as a concept, but in the guise of such concepts as 'quality' and 'excellence'. As well as being conservative in economic and political matters, conservative doctrine also applies to social matters, such as defence of 'the family' and traditional religion, 'traditional values', and attitudes to defence and crime and punishment.

Conservatism is, however, nothing if not pragmatic, so that, over the years, the *status quo* which it has sought to defend has changed. For example, when they have regained power after a period of socialist rule, conservatives have not necessarily been in a hurry to dismantle the 'welfare state', to reduce personal taxation or to privatise government-owned industries. They have been in favour of stability and 'not rocking the boat'. They defend capitalism, but not with the ideological fervour of the liberals. Their attitude can often be viewed as paternalistic towards the working classes rather than confrontational – evoking the idea that 'we know best how to look after the country and will take care of you – trust us'.

In party terms, the Conservative Party in Britain was conservative in nature before the rise of the 'New Right'/liberal thinkers under Margaret Thatcher in the 1980s. The left wing of the Conservative Party – the 'wets' in Lady Thatcher's terms – remain the flag carriers for conservatism in Britain.

In terms of public policy, therefore, the conservative position is to continue to support those public services which have worked well in the past, and to strengthen services which uphold traditional values and elitism. On the other hand it would be reluctant to see the state take on new areas of public responsibility unless this is seen as necessary in relation to its traditional values such as defence, rural interests and so on.

In relation to leisure and the role of the state, therefore, the use of public funds to support elite activity and 'excellence' presents no problem. Indeed, the provision of high-profile, prestige facilities is consistent with the paternalistic approach to government. The gradual growth of public spending to provide community leisure facilities is also consistent with the paternalistic dimension of conservatism, but support for voluntary-sector activity would be favoured. Because conservatives do not adopt a hard ideological line on market economics, they would frequently find themselves supporting government aid to industry, such as rural industries and thence tourism. As far as environmental issues are concerned, however, conservatives are likely to be on the side of the exploiters of the environment rather than the conservationists.

2 Liberalism

The word liberalism shares the same Latin root as liberation and liberty: hence its basic tenet is the idea of freedom – of the individual. Its origins lie in the late eighteenth and the nineteenth centuries in Europe when the newly emerging capitalist and middle-class interests were trying to throw off the shackles of feudalism (the system under which monarchs ruled by divine right, hand in hand with the entrenched privileges of the aristocracy, the landed classes and the Church). Liberals, building on the ideas of philosophers such as Adam Smith, believed in the market system and so wanted all restraints on trade, investment and commerce removed: government control, linked as it then was to tradition and privilege, was to be dismantled and success was to be achieved by hard work and industry. The cry of the French Revolution was 'Liberty, Equality and Fraternity' – the liberals placed the emphasis on *liberty*. As with conservatives, inequality was seen as a positive force in society, providing incentives and rewards for effort.

In its modern guise liberalism has re-emerged in the form of the *New Right* of the British Conservative Party ('Thatcherism'). Rather than accepting, and even encouraging, the growth of the state, as previous Labour and Conservative governments had done, they want to reverse the tide of 'creeping socialism' and restore the free rein of the market. This involves reductions in personal and corporate taxation (tax is seen as a disincentive to work and an infringement of the freedom of individuals to spend their money as they see fit); reductions in industry protection, such as tariffs, to encourage competition and international competitiveness; privatisation of state assets (because it is believed that they would be more efficiently run by private enterprise); reduction of welfare spending (because of its cost and its encouragement of the 'handout' mentality); and reduction of government spending generally (to reduce taxes and free up resources for the private sector).

The analysis of the role of the state offered by mainstream economics, as outlined in chapter 3, is consistent with the liberal position – that is, even a liberal must accept that the market system is not perfect and cannot produce all of society's needs. But, whilst accepting the arguments for state involvement in specific instances, the liberal philosophy is suspicious of growth in the size of government *per se*. Therefore, even rational arguments for state intervention in the market may suffer from the perceived need to restrain the size of the government sector overall.

Generally, therefore, the liberal philosophy would espouse a private-enterprise solution to leisure services. Some of the mainstream economic arguments outlined in chapter 3 would be accepted, but would be very strictly interpreted. Even where it is accepted that government should be involved in leisure provision, for example in the case of urban parks, the liberal approach would be that such services, while being financed by government, should be managed where possible by private enterprise. The purist liberal would see no need for organisations which assist or usurp private-enterprise roles, such as government-funded tourism promotion agencies or government-owned airlines. In the interests of small government, liberals would also encourage involvement of the voluntary sector in leisure provision. As with the conservatives, the support of excellence and elitism – for instance in sport or the arts – is to be welcomed, but even here the preference would be for private-sector sponsorship. It might be argued from a liberal perspective that the very idea of leisure as freedom of choice is reflected in the free play of market forces, which seek to meet the expressed demands of the consumer.

Some liberal groups have advocated the legalisation of recreational drugs, a cause usually associated with the left, but on the grounds of upholding the individual's freedom of choice.

3 Democratic socialism

Democratic socialism or social democracy or, as Henry (1985) terms it, Utopian socialism, can trace its roots back to before the industrial revolution in Europe, in the form of various workers' and peasant protest and reform movements. However, it emerged as a reformist political movement under nineteenth century capitalism, reflecting the interests of the working classes as against those of the liberal industrialists and middle classes and the aristocratic conservatives.

The essential tenets of democratic socialism are an emphasis on equality and fraternity rather than liberty; defence of the interests of the working classes as against those of the middle and ruling classes; belief in the power of the state to control capitalism through state ownership and control of key industries; belief in the power of the state to create more equality and provide welfare for the community through progressive taxation and the establishment of a 'welfare state'; belief that change can be brought about by democratic means, via parliamentary methods; and a belief that capitalism can be 'tamed' and controlled and does not have to be overthrown. The major state organisations, such as the institutions of the welfare state, public health care systems, and state utilities and enterprises, have generally been established by democratic socialist governments.

Traditionally in Britain, the Labour Party, the political arm of the labour/trade union movement, has been a democratic socialist party, although, in its struggle to gain electoral support, it has faced a great deal of soul-searching over which of its long-standing socialist tenets to retain and which to abandon.

In the case of the democratic socialist, therefore, capitalism is tolerated and the state is embraced as the main vehicle for achievement of goals – which is the exact opposite of the liberal position, which is to tolerate the state and embrace the market. These beliefs translate into a very active role for the state in leisure provision in all its forms. Mainstream economics arguments about market failure are accepted and used to support and justify state activity where necessary, but concerns for equality and democracy are probably the stronger motivators. Thus democratic socialists would see a major role for governments to play in supporting sport, the arts and community and outdoor recreation. While excellence and elitism might be viewed with suspicion by some democratic socialists, for others it would be supported as a celebration of the success of state activity. However, at the same time, access, mass participation and democratisation of institutions would be stressed. At the local level, access to leisure facilities would be seen as a right and the provision of such services as a part of social welfare, a means by which the standard of living and quality of life of disadvantaged groups can be

improved. Even though tourism is a largely private-sector industry, democratic socialists would generally have no qualms about using government funds to promote tourism or to finance tourism enterprises – since
they believe in government involvement in economic development and
in the efficacy of state enterprise.

As with each of the political philosophies discussed in this chapter,
democratic socialism embraces a range of beliefs. The left wing are
happy to embrace much of Marxism, seeking fundamental change to
the capitalist system, but via democratic reforms. Right-wing democratic
socialists, however, would reject most of Marxism, would be happier to
call themselves 'social democrats' and may be indistinguishable from
some members on the left of conservatism.

4 Marxist socialism

Marxist socialism, or Marxism, might also be termed revolutionary socialism, 'scientific' socialism (Henry, 1984a) or communism. The ideology is based on the ideas of Karl Marx who, with his collaborator Friedrich
Engels, set out his ideas in a number of key works in the second half of
the nineteenth century, notably *The Communist Manifesto* and *Capital*.

Marx's thesis can be briefly summarised as follows. Capitalist society
is characterised by the irreconcilable clash of interests between the capitalists (or bourgeoisie), who own the 'means of production', and the
workers (or proletariat), who own nothing but their labour power. The
relationship between capitalists and workers is an exploitative one –
with capitalists minimising the wages they pay and retaining the profits
for themselves. The state in capitalist countries merely plays the role of
propping up the exploitative system by curbing the worst excesses of
capitalism and providing it with a 'human face'. Because opportunities
for further investment will eventually be exhausted and the maintenance
of profit levels will only be achievable by increased levels of exploitation
and 'immiseration' of the workers, capitalism will eventually collapse
under the stress of its own internal 'contradictions'. The workers should
hasten this process by combining to overthrow capitalism (revolution)
and transform society into a socialist state controlled by a working-class
party ('dictatorship of the proletariat'). In the final stage of transforma-
tion – the communist society – the state would no longer be required.

Later Marxist theorists – often referred to as 'neo-Marxists' – have
explained the continued existence of capitalism by a number of developments: for example, the institution of colonialism, or imperialism,
provided expanded, international, scope for investment and exploitation; 'neo-colonialism' (eg the 'Coca Cola-isation' of the world) has
achieved the effects of colonialism through economic means; and,
through the hegemony of the 'ruling class' and the engendering of 'false
consciousness' and 'false needs' via such means as advertising,
capitalist organisations have persuaded the workers that life under
capitalism is 'the norm' and that they need the products which
capitalism has to offer, and must work to obtain them.

Marxist socialism was in power in the form of the Communist Parties in the 'eastern bloc' or the 'second world' until recently and has influenced left-leaning trade unions and the left wings of democratic socialist parties. But, with few exceptions (eg Italy), it has had little direct impact on the political process in the western democracies and seems even less likely to do so in the near future. In particular, the threat of the 'dictatorship of the proletariat' (ie a one-party state) has often meant that the Communist Party has been a pariah in the western political system.

The relevance of Marxism to the study of leisure and leisure policy lies not so much in the proposals for leisure provision in a future communist society, but in the analysis of contemporary capitalist societies. The idea of 'false needs' is particularly pertinent to leisure, since many of the goods and services which people in western societies seek, once basic necessities have been acquired, are leisure goods and services, including such consumer goods and services as home entertainment equipment, leisure footwear and clothing, photographic and video equipment, swimming pools and boats, and such services as restaurant meals, concerts and holidays. Marxist analysis would suggest that it is the clever marketing activity of capitalism which keeps people on the materialist treadmill, working and striving to achieve these products of the market system, and thereby perpetuating the capitalist system. One view is that modern technology could release the masses from the burden of constant labour if capitalism were to be replaced by a socialist society (Gorz, 1980; Harrington, 1974). Leisure is also seen as a means of 'resistance' to the forces of capitalism: youth groups and sub-cultures, certain art and music forms, the historical struggle for reduced working hours, the phenomenon of 'dropping out', and institutions such as workers' clubs (Alt, 1979) are all means by which ordinary people are seen to attempt to 'do their own thing' rather than conform to the dictates of the capitalist system.

The Marxist critique also applies to the role of the state in leisure provision. In so far as the state provides those leisure services which the market is incapable of delivering – such as parks, sports facilities, children's play facilities, quality arts output, and conservation of the natural and historic heritage – it provides capitalism with a civilised face. Left to the market system, the leisure scene would be bleak indeed, and people might begin to question its efficacy. Not only does the state provide capitalism with a 'human face', but, the argument goes, it creams off the profitable by-products, by, for example, providing the sporting equipment and clothing of the sports enthusiast and ensuring that the profits from popular culture, such as popular music and film, goes into private pockets, rather than to support the arts generally. Additional Marxist analysis would point to the divisiveness, elitism and competitiveness of leisure institutions, particularly in sport, which perpetuate and reinforce the class divisions in society (see Clarke and Critcher, 1985: 147–50).

5 Feminism

While the struggle for women's rights dates back at least to the campaigns for women's voting rights in the early part of the twentieth century, modern feminism dates from the 1960s. Whether feminism can be described as a political ideology or a movement or pressure group is open to debate. A number of writers point out that feminism is not a single ideology, but comes in various forms, reflecting the mainstream ideologies discussed above – eg Marxist feminism. In party terms feminists have generally aligned themselves with the forces of the left; in general there have not been separate feminist political parties.

At the core of most feminist analyses of society is the idea of patriarchy – that is, that *men* organise and control society in their own interests, to the exclusion and disadvantage of women. Essentially, the argument is that men wield excessive power in society and that, historically, institutions and customs have developed to perpetuate this situation. Where various feminists disagree is over what should be done about it.

Reformist feminists believe that, through campaigns within the mainstream political process, reforms, such as equal pay, anti-discrimination legislation and improvements in child-care provision, can be instituted which will eventually achieve equality between men and women in society. Marxist, or radical, feminists, on the other hand, argue that patriarchy is as fundamental to capitalism as the struggle between the classes; the exploitation of women as a group is as endemic to the system as the exploitation of workers as a group. So the only solution is a socialist revolution. Under a socialist or communist society the conditions for the domination and exploitation of women would be removed.

There is a substantial literature relating feminist ideas and analysis to leisure (eg Deem, 1986; Henderson *et al.*, 1989; Wimbush and Talbot, 1988; Green, Hebron and Woodward, 1990). This literature points out that, because they continue to bear the bulk of child- and home-care responsibilities, women have much less leisure time than men, and their leisure is often subservient to the leisure of others, for example in entertaining at home, going out on a family picnic or a self-catering holiday, or in accompanying children or partners to *their* sporting or other leisure events. Social customs, frequently reinforced by commercial media and marketing, limit the range of activities considered to be 'suitable' for women. The *institutions* of leisure – especially sport – are dominated by men and orientated to men's needs and ways of doing things. Thus the whole pattern of leisure reinforces the patriarchal system of society. As with the Marxist critique, however, it has also been pointed out that such leisure as they enjoy can be used by women as a means to resist the patriarchal forces in society (Wearing, 1990).

In so far as state provision has supported the development of the current institutions (eg grants to men-only sports clubs), it has reinforced and perpetuated the inequality of women. The reformist feminist solution, as far as leisure provision is concerned, is to use the state to right the balance by, for example, greatly increasing child-care provision at leisure venues, providing more support for traditional women's activities, such as women's sports, and paying attention to such issues as transport access to leisure venues and safety.

6 Environmentalism

As with feminism, the status of the environmental, or 'green', movement as a political ideology alongside the mainstream ideologies discussed above is open to debate, given that, as with feminism, there is a variety of green perspectives, often reflecting the mainstream political ideologies. The green movement has been divided on whether it should campaign independently as a pressure group to bring about change, whether it should seek to infiltrate and change mainstream party policies or whether it should form 'green' parties to operate independently. All three solutions continue to be pursued.

The fundamental environmentalist argument is that, while the mainstream political ideologies differ on how society should be organised and which group should be in charge, in fact they all share the same, misguided aim, which is the pursuit of materialist economic growth. The greens argue that this should *not* be the goal of society because unlimited economic growth, of a conventional kind, is incompatible with the continued survival of 'planet earth'. Existing damage to the environment, in terms of pollution and excessive exploitation of natural resources such as forests demonstrates the long-term unsustainability of current practices (Porritt, 1984).

As with feminism, there are leftist and rightist sets of 'green' solutions. Greens of a right-wing or centrist tendency would argue that capitalism can and must be controlled and reformed to reduce pollution and environmentally exploitative practices through legislation and that private citizens' own efforts, encouraged by the state, in recycling, changing their consumption patterns and so on, can bring about change. More radical greens would argue that the inexorable search for profit by capitalism makes attempts at such reforms futile and therefore the only way to save the environment is to bring about a fundamental change through the overthrow of capitalism altogether. As André Gorz puts it:

> ... the ecological movement is not an end in itself, but a stage in the larger struggle ... what are we really after? A capitalism adapted to ecological constraints; or a social, economic, and cultural revolution that abolishes the constraints of capitalism and, in so doing, establishes a new relationship between the individual and society and between people and nature? Reform or revolution? (Gorz, 1980a: 4)

The environmental argument relates to leisure in two ways. Firstly, as in the neo-Marxist discussion of 'false needs', leisure can be seen as a major offender in the 'consumer society': in so far as people 'want more', it is often leisure goods and services which they want more of. Of course it could be argued that not all leisure depends on material props – much leisure activity involves the consumption of *services* or simple social interaction, which are relatively undemanding on material resources. Further, it could be argued that more leisure *time* means less work, which means less material production. Nevertheless it is clear that, in most capitalist societies, in practice, more leisure consumption entails more material consumption.

The second way in which the environmental debate relates to leisure is more direct, in that much leisure activity makes direct use of the natural environment. If the natural environment is not conserved then it will not be available for the recreational enjoyment of current and future generations. Conservation is generally achieved through the intervention of the state, either directly through such mechanisms as the designation of national parks and wilderness areas, or indirectly through planning and pollution controls. This relates to a subsidiary debate on the issue of 'eco-tourism', that is, whether tourism which seeks to bring people closer to nature is a good thing because of its educational value and possible economic spin-offs for host communities, or whether it is itself part of the problem – leading to the gradual destruction of the very resource which it exploits.

Ideologies compared

Ideologies can be characterised by their attitudes toward the question of social change: generally only the conservative ideology is *not* in favour of changing the *status quo*. This is, however, to some extent a reflection of the particular current situation in the western democracies. Where non-conservatives hold power for a long period of time, sufficient to bring about radical change, then what were previously conservative forces themselves become supporters of change and the previous radicals become conservative: hence the confusing terminology in the former communist states of Eastern Europe. But similar confusion could come about in western countries such as Britain, where the liberal right have held sway for some time: here the conservative 'wets' may in future be seen as the forces of change as they seek to return to a former, less market-dominated society.

The ideologies differ in their approach to social inequality. Liberals see inequality as the other side of the coin of incentive and freedom – the very mechanism that drives the successful market economy – whereas, at the other extreme, both forms of socialism see the inequalities of the capitalist system as its worst fault, and feminism focuses on the inequality between men and women.

Ideologies also differ in their attitudes towards the role of the state, with liberals being the most suspicious and Marxist and democratic socialists the most accepting.

Finally, the ideologies can be characterised by their attitudes towards economic growth and materialism. All the ideologies except environmentalism, and possibly feminism, favour economic growth and are basically materialist.

It cannot be said that leisure is the *focus* of any of the ideologies discussed above, but it can be shown that they each provide a distinctive perspective for viewing the role of leisure in contemporary society, and the role of the state in relation to leisure.

Further reading

Philosophical and religious aspects of leisure: Cooper, 1989; Dare, Welton and Coe, 1987; Fain, 1991; Pieper, 1965.

Political ideology generally: Bramham and Henry, 1985; Coalter, 1988; Henry, 1984, 1984a, 1985, 1993; Wilson, 1988; Maddox, 1985.

Feminism: Deem, 1986; Henderson *et al.*, 1989; Wimbush and Talbot, 1988; Green, Hebron and Woodward, 1990.

Environmentalism: Gorz, 1980a; Porritt, 1984; Papadakis, 1993; Spretnak and Capra, 1985.

4 MAINSTREAM ECONOMICS, THE STATE AND LEISURE

The market mechanism and mainstream economics

Since the collapse of the communist systems in Eastern Europe, most of the world now operates, or is attempting to operate, under a 'capitalist' or 'market' economic system. In this system the process of organising the production and distribution of goods and services is largely in the hands of private-enterprise companies, with governments playing a significant, but restricted, role. This idea, that the market mechanism is the 'norm' and government activity is permitted only in certain specified circumstances, is the basis of mainstream economics – which is taught in most western university economics courses. It is referred to here as 'mainstream' to distinguish it from Marxist socialist or radical economics, which, as the outline of Marxist ideology in chapter 3 indicates, rejects the market system on ideological grounds, and also from other critics, such as Galbraith (1973) and Hirsch (1977), who dispute the basis of mainstream economics on more technical grounds.

Mainstream economic analysis provides a useful framework for examining the roles of the state within the market system. When interpreted in its most extreme form this framework is referred to as 'dry' economics or 'economic rationalism'; it takes on ideological overtones associated with the liberal beliefs outlined in chapter 3. But aspects of the framework are also used by those of more left-leaning political persuasions to *justify* state activity in the economy. Taken as a whole, mainstream economics should perhaps be referred to as 'political economy', the area of academic thought which spans politics and economics.

The majority of people in 'western' societies, rightly or wrongly, appear to see capitalism as a basically acceptable system for running human economic affairs. Some want to see less state activity and some want to see more, but few wish to see the system changed fundamentally, to the extent that the society would no longer be basically 'capitalist'. This does not, of course, mean that the majority are correct and the minority are wrong: it merely indicates the apparent political *status quo.* It therefore seems reasonable, as part of our examination of the role of the state, to examine in more detail the analysis offered by mainstream economics of the situations in which the state might 'intervene' in a basically capitalist/market economy, but which are still consistent with the continuation of the capitalist/market system.

The economists Milton and Rose Friedman (1979) are examples of staunch advocates of the market system, arguing, as do most mainstream economists, that 'the market' is the most effective and efficient mechanism for meeting people's needs. The free, unregulated market mechanism should, according to mainstream economic theory, be the best means of organising the delivery of goods and services to meet people's needs. In the 'market place' people indicate their desires and preferences for goods and services by their willingness to pay; entrepreneurs note this and the willingness of people to pay enables them to pay for the labour and capital necessary to provide the service required. The entrepreneurs bid in the 'market place' to buy the labour and other resources, such as land, which are necessary to produce the goods and services which people want. No central body is needed to organise this – the market mechanism brings the resources, the supplier and the consumer together: the consumer pays and the consumer is believed to be 'sovereign'.

Therefore, it is argued, state activity should be kept to a minimum, because the state is *less* effective, efficient and responsive in meeting people's needs than the market, and because the state, through its coercive powers, such as regulation and taxation, is a potential threat to people's freedoms. Government activity, from this perspective, should therefore be permitted only where it is unavoidable and all efforts should be made to keep the activities of government to a minimum.

The Friedmans quote approvingly the eighteenth century political economist Adam Smith, who outlined three essential duties of government:

> ... first, the duty of protecting the society from the violence and invasion of other independent societies; secondly, the duty of protecting, as far as possible, every member of the society from the injustice or oppression of every other member of it, or the duty of establishing an exact administration of justice; and, thirdly, the duty of erecting and maintaining certain public works and certain public institutions, which it can never be for the interest of any individual, or small number of individuals, to erect and maintain; because the profit could never repay the expense to any individual or small number of individuals, though it may frequently do much more than repay it to a great society. (in Friedman and Friedman, 1979: 49)

The Friedmans add a fourth duty for government, namely 'the duty to protect members of the community who cannot be regarded as "responsible" individuals' (p. 53). These include children and the mentally ill or handicapped. The four functions of government approved of by the Friedmans are therefore: 1 national defence, 2 law and order, 3 public works and 4 humanitarian measures.

The Friedmans see the third of these duties as raising the 'most troublesome issue', because it can be 'interpreted to justify unlimited extensions of government power'. In fact all four categories could be seen as raising 'troublesome issues': defence expenditure can use up too much of a country's budget and often results in offensive rather than defensive activities; law and order issues can become highly controversial; and humanitarian and measures become politically controversial when they are widened to become 'welfare'.

Market failure

Much of the 'economics of the state' is aimed at analysing the Friedmans' third, 'troublesome', option – that is, attempting to analyse those situations where an activity is not profitable for the private sector to undertake, but is beneficial to society at large. There are some situations where the market mechanism does not work very well or at all – economists call these cases of 'market failure'. Other situations where the state becomes involved in markets are more social and political than economic. Cases of 'market failure' are outlined first and the social and political cases are outlined subsequently.

A number of different types of 'market failure' are considered in turn below. They are: a. public goods and services, b. externalities/neighbourhood effects, c. mixed goods, d. merit goods, e. option demand, f. infant industries, g. size of project and h. natural monopoly. The ideas are widely discussed in the economics literature, sometimes with slightly varying terminology. Only minimal reference is made to this literature in the following summaries, but references for further reading are given at the end of the chapter. While each criterion/phenomenon is discussed in turn, it should be noted that more than one criterion usually applies to a particular case of state provision.

a. Public goods and services

In economic jargon, *public* goods or services have two characteristics: they are *non-excludable* and *non-rival*. Non-excludable means that it is not technically possible to exclude anyone from enjoying the benefits of the good or service. Non-rival means that one person's enjoyment of the good or service does not preclude others from enjoying it also. The classic examples of public goods and services are national defence and the maintenance of law and order – two of Adam Smith's basic functions of government, as discussed above. Another example, which falls into Adam Smith's third category, is the provision of street lighting. These services are *non-excludable* because people in the areas affected cannot be excluded from benefiting from the service, and they are *non-rival* because the provision of the service to one person does not affect its provision to others.

In these circumstances the normal market mechanism – the consumer paying the provider for the service they individually receive – cannot function effectively. There is 'market failure'. The market system, left to its own devices, will not, in these circumstances, produce what people want. Government intervention to provide the service and recoup the costs via taxation is therefore seen as a solution.

Examples in the field of leisure include public broadcasting, public pride in the success of local or national athletes and public displays such as fireworks or street parades. In the case of public broadcasting, the product is 'free to air' and is therefore a public good. The fact that some governments choose to finance this public good by means of issuing a licence to operate a television set, and commercial organisations finance it by selling advertising space, does not alter its intrinsic 'public good' nature.

In some cases the public good dimension of a facility or service is directly enjoyed by the general public – as in a firework display or broadcasting. In other cases the enjoyment is more indirect – for example the general satisfaction and pride people might obtain from knowledge that the nation's, or even the world's, natural or cultural heritage is being preserved. People do not need to visit such places as the Tower of London, the Lake District, the Parthenon, or the Great Barrier Reef, to obtain some enjoyment from the knowledge that they exist. This enjoyment is worth something to the people who experience it. These non-users or non-visitors are sometimes referred to a 'vicarious' consumers, and their enjoyment is sometimes referred to as 'psychic' benefit, in contrast to financial or material benefit. Governments feel entitled to contribute to the upkeep and preservation of these phenomena on behalf of these vicarious consumers.

The maintenance of law and order and street lighting were mentioned as examples of 'classic' public services, but such services also have important implications for urban leisure and tourism which are rarely considered. If city streets are poorly lit and considered unsafe, then certain groups in the community are discriminated against in terms of their access to leisure at night; such groups include particularly the elderly, women and young people and those without access to private transport. In addition, such areas are not attractive to tourists. Law and order and street lighting are therefore important leisure-related public services.

In the case of the 'pure' public good it is technically impossible to charge the consumer for the service. In other cases it is possible to conceive of a charge being made, but the cost of collecting the charge would be likely to exceed the revenue. This situation is likely to apply in the case of many areas of public open space, especially when there are many access points. In this case the facility becomes, *de facto*, a public good.

It could be argued that individuals could contribute voluntarily for their enjoyment of public goods and services, but this would give rise to the problem of the 'free rider' – the person who enjoyed the good or service in question but did not pay. Contributions via the taxation system are seen as a fair and efficient means of collecting payment. While this may result in some people contributing who have not seen or did not enjoy the goods or services involved, in fact, taxation is levied on the basis of ability to pay, rather than services rendered.

b. Externalities/neighbourhood effects

In their discussions the Friedmans (1979) refer to the phenomenon of externalities as 'neighbourhood effects', and others have referred to it as 'third-party effects', but 'externalities' is the more widely accepted term. 'Externalities' arise when specific third parties are affected by transactions between providers and consumers or when society at large might be considered a third party. Externalities can be 'negative' or 'positive'.

The classic example of a negative externality is pollution: for example, smoke pollution from a factory or noise pollution from an airport. The factory or airport and its customers are the *first* and *second* parties involved in the transaction of producing and buying the products from the factory or airport; the members of the public adversely affected by pollution are the *third* party – they are affected by negative 'externalities'. There is 'market failure' here because the producers and consumers are not taking account of all the costs involved in producing the service in question. Either the producer should be required (by law) to install equipment to eliminate the pollution or the sufferers should be compensated (by the government making a levy on the factory or airport owners or by the sufferers suing the polluter in court). Either way, the costs of the factory or airport would rise (external costs would have been 'internalised'); the prices it would have to charge would rise; and so demand/output could fall.

In the extreme case costs would rise so much that the product would be priced out of the market and the factory or airport would be forced to close down. This would be accepted as right and proper by the economist. In the initial situation it would be said that the market is distorted because the factory or airport – and the buyers of their services – are not meeting all their costs, so that the product or service is artificially cheap. It would be said to be 'over-producing'.

This all sounds perfectly rational and reasonable. In practice, of course, such an issue could become very controversial and would focus on what minimal level of pollution is considered acceptable before the polluter is required to do something about it. It should be noted that the 'offender' in situations of externality is not always an organisation. It can be an individual. A classic example is road congestion. Every additional car which uses a road increases congestion and imposes a cost on other road users, in terms of delays and increased fuel consumption, not to mention the pollution costs imposed on the society at large.

In the leisure area, examples of negative externalities arise when leisure facilities impose noise or congestion costs on neighbouring properties.

Positive externalities work in the opposite direction. The third party can gain benefits which they do not pay for. In that situation the producer is receiving a lower income than is justified (that is, not obtaining income from the third-party beneficiaries); and it *under*-produces because the product or service is more expensive than it should be. In this case we talk of positive externalities.

An example might be the private golf course which preserves pleasant views for surrounding residents. The latter pay in terms of the higher cost of real estate, but not to the golf course owner. In fact, many 'resort'-style developments attempt to recoup this externality by building golf courses *and* the surrounding homes. When Walt Disney built Disneyland in California in the 1950s, the tourist-generated traffic provided enormous gains for landowners in the area, who sold to hoteliers to service the theme park. When Disney*world* was built in Florida in the 1970s the Disney organisation bought up much of the surrounding land – ensuring that it 'internalised' the externality.

In the case of tourism, the basic attraction of a destination area may be publicly owned, for example beaches, mountains, lakes or an historic town centre. The whole of the private-sector tourist industry may nevertheless be dependent on this resource. The resources are *de facto* public goods enjoyed by the public, but part of the benefit is gained by the tourist industry and might be termed externalities. Valuing these externalities may become an issue when questions arise as to the cost of maintaining the basic attractions and the contributions which the tourist industry is asked to make. This idea of the tourist industry being dependent on a common public attraction is known as the 'asset theory' of tourism (Gray, 1982).

A further example of positive externalities – or the prevention of negative externalities – is the question of provision of leisure facilities for youth. It is widely believed that young people in particular are liable to engage in anti-social activities in their leisure time – that is, activities which impose external cost on others. Such externalities may be short-term and immediate – for example vandalism and hooliganism – or long-term – for example becoming involved in criminal sub-cultures or harmful drugs. The private sector provides some facilities for young people; in fact it has been claimed that they can do a better job of 'keeping them off the street' than the state (Smith, 1975). But since the commercial sector cannot take account of the externalities (for example, reduction in vandalism and hooliganism) which accrue to the wider community, they will tend to 'under-provide'. State provision or subsidy of suitable leisure facilities for young people is therefore seen as justified. In the light of Smith's comments about the role of the commercial sector the most effective use of public funds in this area might well be to provide subsidies for commercial operators to provide the sorts of facilities that young people want. But other objectives, such as education, come into play, resulting in the provision of certain types of facility which are not always attractive to the most 'at risk' young people.

c. *Mixed goods*

The arts economists Baumol and Bowen (1976) coined the term 'mixed goods' to refer to those goods or services which combine 'public' and 'private' characteristics. For example, when a person attends an arts performance, it is argued, several things happen. Firstly, the person gains a personal benefit (the enjoyment of the performance), which he or she might be expected to pay for. Secondly, the person subsequently becomes a conveyor and supporter of culture – a contributor to a more civilised community. Thirdly, a society with viable cultural industries is believed to benefit in many ways – in terms of 'quality of life', in terms of 'creativity', in terms of spin-off in economic areas such as tourism, design and the attraction of industry and commerce, and in terms of maintaining a lively media sector. Finally, arts facilities can be a source of 'civic pride' even to those who do not use them. Therefore it is believed that the state should, in recognition of these wider social benefits, which are partly public goods and partly positive externalities, pay part of the cost of the public arts performance. This is then a justification for a *subsidised* theatre/opera/concert seat rather than either a totally free one or a fully economically priced one.

A similar argument could be applied to an urban park. The person entering the park obtains a certain amount of enjoyment, which he or she could be expected to pay for. The park also offers externality benefits to the owners of the buildings which overlook it. These benefits are reflected in the value of the land, which in turn is reflected in the rates levied on the properties, so some payment is made to the public provider of the park – the council – for the benefit received. A further group of beneficiaries of the park are those people who walk or drive past and benefit from viewing a green space rather than a built-up area. The benefit may be very small per person, but many thousands or even millions may enjoy this public good benefit in the course of the year. Finally, parks produce a public good benefit in cities by dispersing pollution and thus contributing to cleaner air. Thus a park produces a mixture of public and private benefits. In practice, as discussed above, few parks charge users for the 'private' element of the visit, because of the cost of collection.

Rural public open space, such as public forests, country parks and national parks are also mixed goods, in that they are enjoyed by the users directly (private good), in some cases by 'vicarious' users, as discussed above (public good), by property owners whose property overlooks the open space (externality), and by the general public who visit or live in the area and benefit from pleasant views (public good). This last phenomenon also occurs in relation to general planning powers exercised by councils to prevent unsightly development in rural or heritage areas: the resultant amenity which people enjoy in their leisure time can be seen as a public good.

Participation in sport or physical recreation can also be viewed as a mixed good. Individuals engaging in physical exercise gain some private benefit from the experience, in the form of increased fitness and/or enjoyment. However, if an individual who was previously inactive, with deteriorating health or poor health prospects, can be persuaded to take exercise resulting in improved health, other people benefit, including the person's family, his or her employer, and either taxpayers or other payers of health insurance, depending on how the costs of sickness would have been met. Thus, it is argued, the state, on behalf of these beneficiaries (family, employer, taxpayer or health insurance subscribers), would be justified in subsidising sport/exercise programmes and facilities or providing the individual with the means to buy such services.

It might be argued that the direct beneficiaries from the person's good health should pay rather than the community at large through the state. This is recognised by those employers who provide exercise facilities at the place of work; some who even require their employees to take exercise; and health insurance companies who also become involved in sport and fitness in various ways. However, because the benefits may be spread over a number of beneficiaries, including government organisations such as the health service, and because the state is involved in sport and fitness for other reasons, subsidisation and promotion of sport is accepted as an area of legitimate state involvement.

d. Merit goods

In some cases 'society' may decide that certain goods or services are highly desirable for the individual but that individuals require time, experience/exposure or even education in order to come to appreciate them; individuals are incapable of immediately appreciating their value. In this case, it is argued, the state is justified in intervening to provide that exposure to the good or service, by making direct provision or subsidising others to do so. The most common example of a merit good is education; however, as with many merit goods, it is difficult to disengage the 'merit good' argument from the 'public good' and 'externality' aspects.

The merit good argument can be criticised for being elitist or paternalistic. Who is to decide what is meritorious? The idea that the general public is incapable of appreciating the finer things of life unaided and that certain well-informed groups are capable of identifying these oversights and correcting for them can be a difficult proposition to defend. However, the process of deciding on what are and are not merit goods need not be elitist. In the same way that the smoker may agree that he or she should give up and may be happy to see public funds used to conduct anti-smoking campaigns, so many people might be willing to see public funds devoted to the support of the 'higher things of life', aware that they themselves might benefit in due course from such a move.

In the leisure area, examples of merit goods include environmentally based outdoor recreation resources, which may be deemed to require education and interpretation to develop public appreciation, and the more demanding art forms. Generally, the merit good argument can be used to justify educationally orientated programmes, for children or adults.

e. Option demand

Another idea put forward to support public-sector provision is the concept of 'option demand' – sometimes referred to as 'existence value'. This involves the proposition that there may be certain things which groups of individuals do not at present use and may have no specific plans to use, but may feel that these things should be maintained so that the option to use them is always there, for themselves or for their children or grandchildren. This applies particularly when the loss of the phenomenon in question would be irreversible. In this case people might wish the government to intervene to ensure that those things are maintained so that the option is preserved. The idea is similar to the 'vicarious' consumer in relation to public goods, but in this case the vicarious consumption is something which *may* happen in the future.

This argument could apply to virtually all leisure facilities and services which individuals do not currently use, but of whose existence they approve.

f. Infant industries

If a country, state or city sets out to establish a new industry where well-established outside competitors already exist, the industry may find that it is unable to become established because others already operating in the market place will be able to undercut the local product in terms of such things as price, quality, design and delivery. In these instances it is argued that governments may be justified in intervening for a period to protect the new, 'infant', industry from its competitors until it is well-established and can survive without help. Such intervention could include subsidies of various kinds, such as cash grants, tax breaks and low rents, or tariffs or controls placed on the competitors.

This idea, however, is not accepted by all mainstream economists because it involves governments trying to 'pick winners' – that is, deciding which new industries should be supported and which should not – and governments are thought by many to be very bad at this (although some point out that certain governments, such as Japan, appear to have been quite successful at it). It can also be seen as 'featherbedding' and preventing the new industry from becoming efficient in order to compete in the market place. It is argued that if the industry experiences a loss-making period while establishing itself, these losses should be borne by the investor as part of the set-up/investment costs, not by the taxpayer.

The infant industry approach applies particularly to tourism ventures, particularly in developing countries or less-developed areas of developed countries. The argument can also be seen to be applied in modified form in relation to cultural areas, such as film and the local content of television programmes. In these instances, the industry is generally seen as permanently 'infant', in relation to the size and power of the American industry in particular.

g. Size of project

It has been argued that certain investment projects are too large and have too long a time-scale to be taken on by the private sector and can only be handled by government. This argument, however, has now become somewhat outmoded as we see such projects as Euro-Disney, the Alaska oil pipeline, and the Channel Tunnel being privately financed (although sometimes not without substantial government involvement).

h. Natural monopoly

The mainstream economic scenario of the market system producing the optimum range of goods and services depends on the market being perfectly competitive – that is, no single or small group of firms being able to dominate a market situation. Once the number of firms becomes small (oligopoly), or even singular (monopoly), excess profits are made and the consumer loses out. Governments in capitalist economies therefore generally have powers to regulate, and even break up, monopolies.

In leisure and tourism, however, there are often 'natural' monopolies. For example, there is only one Tower of London, only one Grand Canyon and only one Great Barrier Reef. Some natural monopolies are social or economic in nature – for example, major transport infrastructure or sewerage systems – where it makes sense to have only one operator. In these instances, the argument goes, government is justified in intervening to prevent private operators exploiting monopolistic advantage, particularly by charging extortionate prices. Such government intervention may take the form of intervention – for example the regulation of air fares – or complete public ownership and/or control, as is the case with the national heritage.

Market failure in summary

Each of the above arguments is fairly technical in approach. They attempt to establish that there are things which people want *and would probably be prepared to pay for* but, for technical reasons, the potential consumers and potential producers are unable to communicate effectively through the normal market mechanisms. Government is therefore seen as the main means of overcoming the problem, by levying taxes and paying for the goods or services to be produced, or subsidising their production so that the price is reduced and more are consumed.

The question of how governments assess the *extent* of the various forms of demand, and how they determine the scale of public funds to devote to the public provision of leisure services, is addressed in chapter 8.

Social/Political arguments

While the following arguments for government involvement might, in some circumstances, find favour with mainstream economists, they are in fact less 'technical' in nature and so have been treated separately here. They are: i. equity, j. economic management and development, k. tradition and l. incidental enterprise.

i. Equity

Equity means fairness. It impinges on leisure and tourism because of the belief that certain goods and services – a certain quality of life – should be available to all regardless of their ability to pay, and that some leisure goods and services are among the minimal package required for a satisfactory quality of life. This is in contrast to all the arguments considered so far, which apply to *everyone* regardless of their ability to pay.

The equity argument is the most appealing of arguments because it is not technical in nature; it appeals to people's sense of fairness and everyone likes to think of themselves as fair (Cushman and Hamilton-Smith, 1980). It is at the heart of the difference between the left and the right in politics, since the right believes that a considerable degree of *inequality* is *equitable*, because it reflects the rewards given for effort and risk taking, whereas the left thinks that the level of inequality we generally see in western societies is *inequitable* and therefore unacceptable. The question is very complex, involving consideration of such issues as the distribution of income, payments in cash or in kind, and universal versus targeted benefits.

There is nothing in mainstream economics which suggests that everyone, in a market economy, will be able to earn a 'living wage', since not everyone has skills which command a living wage in the labour market place. However, in most societies it is accepted that there is a basic minimum subsistence below which no one should be allowed to fall – hence most western societies have introduced 'welfare' payments such as unemployment pay, age and disability pensions and child allowances. There is also 'progressive' taxation, which means that the well-off contribute a greater proportion of their income towards government costs by way of taxes. In short, there is a 'redistribution of income' from rich to poor.

This process, while widely accepted as necessary or desirable, is nevertheless controversial in application. Some argue that taxation of the well-off or rich is too high, resulting in 'disincentives' to work or invest, and that unemployment and pension payments are too high, producing disincentives to seek work. Others argue exactly the opposite. Despite the controversy, the idea of the 'welfare' state is that everyone should have a sufficient minimum income to buy the necessities of life.

If everyone is deemed to have been provided with a minimum income sufficient to provide for the necessities of life, then why are certain additional 'necessities' provided 'in kind' by the state? Why are people not able, with the incomes provided, to pay for their own housing, education, health services – and leisure services?

Suppose that one of the services considered to be a necessity is access to a swimming pool or some similar form of physical recreation. Suppose that the full cost of entry to a public pool would be £2 and that the average user might be expected to visit once a week. If swimming is considered a necessity of life then welfare payments, such as pensions and unemployment benefit, should include £2 per week so that everybody could afford to attend. Instead, it would appear that we have the situation where, say, £1 is included in the pension for such purposes, but the visit to the pool is subsidised by £1. There are many of these sorts of concessions and subsidies. To gain full benefit from them a pensioner must go swimming, live in public housing, be ill periodically, attend an adult education course, and so on. Suppose the average pensioner benefits to the extent of £25 a week from such subsidies. Would it not be easier to increase the pension – or other forms of benefit – by £25 a week and let the pensioner or other beneficiary decide how to spend the money?

One fear might be that the recipients of such a payment might not spend the money on leisure but might choose to spend it on 'basics', such as food or clothing. This would imply that the pension or other benefit is not adequate to meet basic needs, and therefore the provision of certain leisure facilities or services is not a priority. Another possibility is that benefit recipients might not spend the money on approved leisure *or* on food or clothing but might 'fritter' it away on 'undesirable' items such as gambling or alcohol. In this case, the argument might go, surely we are entitled to subsidise the swimming pool – to provide benefits 'in kind' – because we cannot trust poor people to spend money wisely. This, of course, is a paternalistic attitude which flies in the face of the values held by proponents of the market system, who believe that individuals are the best judges of their own needs, and is at variance with the values of critics of the market who would advocate self-determination and freedom from bureaucratic regulation.

Thus we can see that the equity-driven 'poor cannot afford to pay' argument can also be seen as an argument which says 'pay them in kind because you cannot trust them to do the right thing with the money'. Some have advocated a 'voucher' system for leisure along the lines of the American welfare food stamps (Sears, 1975), but this again implies that people cannot be trusted with money. A substantial proportion of the support for public provision and subsidy of leisure services is probably based on the 'poor cannot afford to pay' argument, but few appear to see that such an argument can also be seen as a form of paternalism reflecting nineteenth-century attitudes towards the 'undeserving' poor.

One of the reasons for the widespread use of the equity approach is that 'payment in kind' is the only means open for some levels of government to make a contribution to the needs of the less well-off sections of the community. Thus a local council cannot give cash handouts to its pensioners – and may be legally constrained over how it levies rates – but it can give concessions at its various facilities. Further, it could be argued that the *marginal* cost of this sort of assistance is small, so that the 'in kind' payment is a cheaper option for the public sector than the cash payment option.

If it is accepted that equity is to be pursued through the provision of benefits 'in kind', then the question arises as to how this should be done. In the example discussed above, the pensioner was subsidised by means of a concessionary charge. But some argue that such a 'targeted' approach carries a 'stigma' and that the free or reduced charge should be available for everybody – a 'universal' approach. Subsidising everybody for the sake of a small number of poor users is, however, extremely costly and could be seen as a wasteful and irresponsible use of public funds. In fact, pensioners could be disadvantaged if the subsidised facilities are crowded out with non-pensioners and the facilities are inadequate because of lack of funds from charges.

This does not mean that public leisure facilities should not be subsidised for the general user for *market failure* reasons as discussed above. But if the aim is to give *particular* benefits to the poor, then some means of targeting that group should ideally be found.

Children and young people merit a special mention under the heading of 'equity'. It might be argued that children and young people who are still dependent on their parents are the responsibility of their parents and that their parents should therefore provide them with leisure resources. In practice, however, there is a feeling that children and young people should be treated more generously than adults and that children's opportunities should not be entirely dependent on their parents' means. This is shown, for example, in attempts to provide equal educational opportunity, but also extends to leisure – and in some cases to tourism. Here, in the 'cash vs kind' argument, paternalistic attitudes (ie not trusting the kids with the money) are probably more justified and there is no problem about stigma in offering concessions to young people. However, the problem still arises that some young people have well-off parents, so targeting is not very precise.

j. Economic management/development

It is widely accepted that governments have a role in overall economic management of market economies – although 'New Right' and 'monetarist' theorists claim that the ability of government to manage the economy is exaggerated and that they often do more harm than good and should do less rather than more in this field. Nevertheless, most governments feel responsible for trying to ensure high levels of material prosperity, high levels of employment, a favourable balance of payments and so on. To achieve this they often feel justified in intervening directly to assist industries which can provide jobs or income. Such concerns can be felt at national, state or local level, although the lower levels of government have less power in this area.

Tourism is often seen as a suitable industry for such attention, but local leisure industries are also seen to be an increasingly important part of the economic infrastructure. One way in which leisure facilities become involved in this area is when certain facilities – for example golf courses or theatres – are seen as key elements in the local 'quality of life' necessary to attract general industrial and commercial investors to an area. Governments at all levels therefore feel justified in providing or subsidising such facilities for economic development reasons.

k. Tradition

It is clear that many publicly provided services are maintained because of tradition; there may have been a 'rational' basis for their provision originally, but not at present. They are maintained, or free or subsidised entry is continued, because it is politically difficult to introduce changes.

The reason why it may be politically difficult to change such situations is that there is often a 'lobby' or 'interest group' which would be offended by the change. The enjoyment which the members of such groups gain from the continued existence of the public service/facility in question may well be a 'public good' or a 'mixed good', but, as with all such provisions, there is still the question of balancing the cost of provision with the value of the benefits being received by the users; and over time the benefits may have been eroded, for example by falling population or use levels, while the costs may have risen. Nevertheless, the service is continued because of political expediency.

l. Incidental enterprise

Often governments find themselves involved in certain areas of service provision accidentally, because the provision is incidental to some other activity. For example, government bodies which own theatres also find themselves running bars and restaurants which happen to be part of the theatre complex. Museums often include restaurants and gift shops. Public broadcasting bodies become publishers of books, records and videos.

The difference between this and other sorts of public service is that there is no reason why they should be run any differently from commercial enterprises: they generally seek to make a profit. In fact, if the government body is competent at running them, they can be used to generate income to 'cross-subsidise' the 'public' activities of the organisation.

Sometimes a public body, such as a large council or state government, finds itself running a number of such outlets and sets up an organisation – such as a catering section – to run them. In other situations the operation is let out to private operators (see Compulsory Competitive Tendering on page 52).

Mainstream economics and ideology

In this chapter and chapter 3 we have reviewed a variety of political ideologies and their implications for leisure policy and also the basic tenets of mainstream economics as they apply to the role of the state and the implications for leisure. While a significant amount of leisure provision is probably made on the basis of pragmatism, tradition and political expediency, it can nevertheless generally be analysed using one or more of the above frameworks. The various perspectives have implications for later sections of the book. For example, political ideologies must inevitably influence the overall objectives set by public bodies, as discussed in chapter 5, while the mainstream economics arguments provide a structure for the discussion of cost-benefit analysis in chapter 8.

Before leaving this discussion of the underlying philosophy of public leisure provision, a number of further issues are discussed below; they are the question of profit-making versus loss-making, and the question of government size and 'government failure'.

Profit-making or loss-making?

Various combinations of the above arguments give rise to a wide range of public-sector leisure and tourism activity. It is clear that most of the arguments show that the costs of making the provision should be borne by the community at large through taxation, rather than by the immediate consumer of the service. This means that such public provision must, by definition be *loss-making*, in commercial terms. If this were not the case then there would be no reason for government to be involved in the first place: if a profit could be made from the service provided at the level required, then a private company could provide it – there would be no 'market failure'. It could therefore be argued that a profit-making public enterprise is a contradiction in terms. Thus criticisms of public services for 'making a loss' are entirely misplaced.

This is not to say that public services cannot often be criticised for being *inefficient*. It is often possible to run things more cheaply or to obtain a better service from the resources employed. But if a service can be run *profitably* and still achieve the social objectives required, then in general there is no need for the state to become involved. The state only becomes involved when a level of service deemed to be necessary cannot be provided by the market – that is, it *cannot* be provided at a profit.

This does not mean that if profits can be made from a service there is no need for *any* government intervention. For example, if there were no public provision of swimming pools, some commercial swimming pool operations would be profitable, but probably only in certain central locations where a sufficient market exists. If it was considered by the appropriate government body – for whichever of the above reasons – that more swimming pools should be provided so that more people could swim more often, then those additional pools would almost inevitably be loss-making; if they could have been provided profitably then they would have been provided by the commercial sector. Thus a decision to intervene on the part of the state inevitably costs money.

It should be noted that, in this context, 'profitability' means not just covering running costs but also providing a return on *capital investment* comparable to expectations in the commercial sector – that is, a rate of return sufficient to attract investment funds, given the level of perceived risk.

Government failure/Government size

Many of the arguments advanced above are in the realm of 'market failure' – that is, they recognise the imperfections or failure of the market mechanism and the need to correct this with government intervention.

However, as discussed in the opening paragraphs of this book, the demands on government are seemingly endless, and all lobby groups can no doubt quote one or more of the above arguments in support of their own particular pet project. This then raises the question of the size of government.

Liberals would argue that the size of government should be limited for two reasons. Firstly, government organisations are generally seen as less efficient than private organisations, so the larger the government sector the less efficient the economy is overall (this notion of generalised inefficiency of the public sector is sometimes referred to as 'X-inefficiency'). Secondly, it is believed that the taxation required to finance government distorts the market, reduces incentives, such as the incentive to work, and reduces personal freedom, particularly people's freedom to spend their income as they wish.

The 'New Right' in particular believe that government has become too big under post-Second World War Labour and Conservative governments. Others dispute such a view and argue that state organisations are not necessarily less efficient than private organisations and that a large government is necessary to provide vital services and to preserve a humane and civilised society.

Further reading

For discussion of mainstream economics and its analysis of the role of the state in general see Musgrave and Musgrave, 1980; as applied to leisure, see Gratton and Taylor, 1985, 1991; Vickerman, 1983, 1989; to tourism: Bull, 1991.

5 LEISURE PLANS AND STRATEGIC PLANNING

Introduction

While the first four chapters of the book are concerned with theoretical ideas and the context of public policy, the next five chapters are concerned with decision-making techniques and their use. One way in which decisions come about is purely political, particularly involving the play of pressure groups and party politics. However, political processes are underpinned to a greater or lesser extent by a technical, analytical process administered by public servants, including planning and evaluation. The results of such analyses may often appear to be ignored or manipulated by politicians and other actors in the political process, but they are also often fundamental to the decision-making process. It should not, of course, be assumed that these more technical processes are completely divorced from, or 'above', political values, interests or processes: for example, most decision-making processes require initial goals to be established and these are invariably political in nature.

In an increasingly complex world, the question of just how organisations should make decisions to best fulfil their commitments and meet their objectives has been the subject of much debate among practitioners and theorists. At one level decision-making procedures are clear: in the political arena democratic procedures are used – the majority rules. But not all decisions are made in the political arena, and political decision-makers frequently look to non-political decision-making procedures for assistance. Leisure is a case in point. Leisure policy is rarely the subject of political debate, although *aspects* of leisure arise from time to time, for instance in relation to competitive sport, the funding of the arts, or conservation issues. Much of leisure policy is therefore developed by public servants and ratified by politicians. Further, in some instances, the broad thrust of policy is determined politically, but the detail must be worked out technically. For example, politicians may decide that they want the country to win more Olympic medals, but they look for technical advice on what policies should be developed to achieve this.

In the public sector the activity of *planning* – the process of establishing a programme of action for the medium to long term – has a long and varied history. The plans of government bodies often provide not only programmes for the government organisations' own operations but also the framework within which others must operate. This can be because of the statutory nature of the plan, as in town and country planning, or because of the strategic importance of the government's activities, for example in provision of transport infrastructure. The activity of *planning* is therefore a key function of government bodies, with the *plan* often being seen as an end in itself. In fact, leisure management within the public sector has often suffered from a lack of careful planning because day-to-day management has been the dominant concern. Those with expertise in and responsibility for planning, for example in the planning departments of local government, have tended to devote comparatively little effort to understanding the phenomenon of leisure because they have been preoccupied with what are widely seen as more important issues, such as transport or housing. And yet the need for firmly based planning in the area of leisure is as great, if not greater, than in many other areas of public policy. Leisure plans not only have to present decision-makers with proposals concerning the desirable quantity, types and distribution of facilities and services; they also very often have to present the case for any provision at all.

In the private sector the terms *strategic planning* and *strategic management* have been used to distinguish the approach to planning and management which seeks to ensure that medium- to long-term goals are given prominence, and day-to-day management is harnessed to the achievement of those goals rather than displacing them with *ad hoc*, short-term objectives. Recently this terminology has also been adopted in the public sector. Thus public bodies have been required to behave more like private corporations, preparing strategic plans which are 'rolled forward' annually and which integrate forward planning with budgeting, implementation strategies and performance appraisal. The terms *strategic planning* and *strategic management* are used interchangeably by some, but strategic *planning* can be seen as the initial process of preparing a strategy for the organisation, whereas strategic *management* can be seen as those aspects of management which are concerned with ensuring that the *strategy* is implemented and that the organisation does not lose sight of its strategy because of day-to-day concerns.

We all make decisions, as individuals and as part of social groupings, such as a household or a group of friends. Some of the decisions are short-term or day-to-day in nature, such as what brand of instant coffee to buy; others are more significant, often with a number of long-lasting consequences, for example buying a house, embarking on an educational course or getting married. These more significant decisions might be called *strategic* – they imply a *strategy* for the future with a range of factors, and further decisions, being dependent on them. A lot more time and care is generally taken over these strategic decisions than over day-to-day decisions; often they involve complete appraisals of our lives, our values and our relationships. Leisure and tourism organisations similarly make day-to-day decisions and *strategic* decisions. Examples of ranges of decision-making, from the minor day-to-day level to the *strategic* level, in leisure organisations, are given in Table 5.1.

Table 5.1 Levels of decision-making

Level	Leisure Centre	Tourist Commission	National Park
Day-to-day	Choose brand of floor cleaner	Decide what information to send to an inquirer	Close park due to flooding
	Decide annual price increases	Commission a market research project	Appoint one ranger
	Employ new manager	Choose marketing themes	Adopt user pays principle
	Reorganise staff structure	Adopt user pays principle	Designate new National Park
Strategic	Build extension to centre	Cease international advertising	Allow mining in National Parks

While personal strategic decision-making may be complicated enough, it usually involves relatively few people, but when an organisation makes strategic decisions many people may need to be involved and many may be affected by the decisions made. The more strategic the decision the more people are likely to be involved or affected. For example, if a large manufacturing company makes a strategic decision – such as to build a plant to produce a new product or to close down a plant and cease producing a particular product – hundreds or even thousands of staff and their families, local communities and possibly millions of customers may be affected. When an organisation makes strategic decisions therefore, considerable care must be taken both in the *process* of making the decisions and in considering their *effects*.

Although most commentators on strategic management emphasise the importance of the *process* rather than 'end products', nevertheless the results of the process must be recorded and communicated and this is usually done in the form of a document, referred to variously as the *strategic plan* or the *corporate plan*. When the process is carried out thoroughly and realistically, and with the full commitment of management, the resultant document can be an essential management tool and a valuable guide for all parts of the organisation and for associated organisations. However, if it is not carried out with care, the process can be seen as a waste of time and effort, producing a document which no-one in the organisation is committed to and which simply gathers dust on shelves.

The term 'document' is used deliberately. It has become something of a cliché in recent years to insist that planning is a *process* and not a *document*; that the production of a document should not be seen as the end of the process, only the beginning; and so on. This cannot be denied, but it is nevertheless the case that the planning process *is* usually focused on a document or documents; such documents embody the results of the planning process and form the agreed basis for the implementation of the plan. It is the requirement to produce a document, usually by a specified date, which drives the process along. Later, it is the need to revise the document which provides the focus for updating the plan. Focusing on the production of a document is therefore no bad thing, as long as it is borne in mind that the document is, ultimately, a means to an end: the provision of leisure services.

In this chapter the overall process of producing a plan is examined, while the question of specific techniques is addressed in chapter 6. The intention here is to consider leisure plans in a generic sense, rather than the requirements for any particular legal or institutional context. Plans produced in differing contexts and for differing purposes, such as an 'in-house' document designed to meet the needs of one organisation, or an exercise forming part of some wider statutory planning process, have certain principles in common, and it is these principles which are addressed below. Nevertheless, the contents of this chapter are addressed primarily to the local government sector, since local government is the level of government which has a comprehensive range of powers and responsibilities with regard to leisure services.

This chapter is structured around a model of the strategic planning process as presented in Figure 5.1. The nine steps involved are discussed in turn below.

Step 1: Establish terms of reference

Any task must have clear terms of reference, and producing a comprehensive or strategic leisure plan is no exception. Typically, the terms of reference for a team about to embark on such a task might be:

> To determine the leisure requirements of the community over the next 15 years and prepare a feasible strategy to address those requirements.

The other steps in the process are focused on determining leisure requirements and developing a feasible strategy. Two aspects of these terms of reference, however, need initial consideration; they are time-scale and scope.

Figure 5.1 Strategic planning process

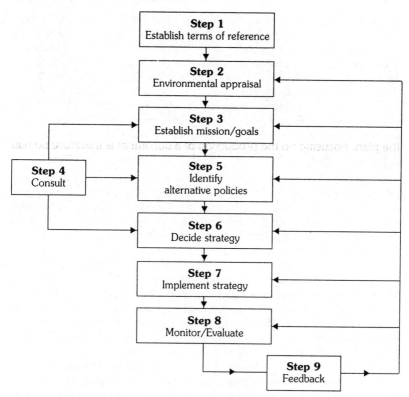

Time-scale

The time-scale for the strategy could be longer or shorter than 15 years, depending on the rate of change within the community and, perhaps, the political horizons of the elected authority. In fact, different aspects of the strategy will relate to different time-scales. For example, in step 3, the question of mission, goals and objectives is discussed. The *mission* of an organisation does not generally have a time-scale, unless the organisation has a specific task, such as holding a one-off event. *Goals* tend to be long-term, but may become obsolete or need modification: for example, the goal 'to provide a comprehensive range of leisure facilities in all neighbourhoods' could, once it was judged to have been achieved, be changed to: 'to maintain a comprehensive range of leisure facilities in all neighbourhoods'. *Objectives* tend to have specific times attached to them, and may be staged. For example, an objective might be to 'double the level of sports participation in the community over a 15-year period'. Each year during the 15 years of the plan, a specific participation target would be set.

Scope

It is particularly important to clarify the *scope* of the plan, particularly the scope and meaning of the word *leisure*. Local government is in the unique position of being able to take a comprehensive view of leisure in the community. In practice, however, this opportunity is rarely grasped. Since, for a variety of reasons, local government is itself involved in direct provision or funding of only a limited range of leisure facilities and services, leisure plans which they produce often deal only with that particular range. Frequently, planning documents begin by considering leisure – or recreation – in its entirety, but then proceed to ignore major aspects of leisure, simply because the local council is not directly involved in their provision.

Examples of major aspects of leisure which are usually excluded from local authority plans are: home-based leisure, entertainment, pubs and restaurants and holidays. Such aspects are ignored presumably because local authorities feel that, since they are not direct providers, they have no powers or rights to engage in planning in these areas. The commercial and the private sectors are deemed to be 'out of bounds'. This logic, however, is not applied in areas such as retailing and industrial and office space, where detailed planning activity is undertaken, despite the fact that these are primarily commercial activities. In the past the leisure facilities which were 'in' and those which were 'out' of the planning process at least corresponded to broad sectors, but, increasingly, with privatisation and the effects of Compulsory Competitive Tendering, this will no longer be the case: almost all forms of leisure will be served by a mixture of public- and private-sector organisations. The fact that the local authority identifies a need and puts forward a plan to meet the need does not necessarily imply that it will be the agency which will be responsible for meeting that need.

Because the inclusion of these particular areas of leisure in the public planning process is so rare, it is perhaps worth considering briefly just how they might be incorporated into plans and what relationship the plan and the local authority might have with them.

Home-based leisure

It is known from leisure surveys that the home is the most important site for leisure for virtually everybody. It is sometimes noted in plans that people living in flats are likely to be in need of more out-of-home leisure provision because of lack of access to gardens, but such observations are rarely followed through into policies. In mainland Europe, allotments often take the form of 'leisure gardens', rather than areas for growing food, but this has not generally happened in Britain. This may be because of differing cultural traditions, but it may also be because local authorities have not considered the question of home-based leisure in their planning, so the provision of leisure gardens has not arisen. It might also be suspected that the somewhat untidy collective appearance of leisure gardens, with their summer houses and sheds, and varying standards of upkeep, would not conform to the architect-planners' vision of the ideal urban landscape.

Electronic forms of entertainment are generally accepted as being the most significant of the home-based leisure activities. One way in which the public sector has been involved for many years with this area is the facility to borrow recorded music through libraries. However, in considering the quality of *leisure* in a community, local councils could adopt a position on, for example, local broadcasting or, in contrast, on the need to encourage alternatives to television for young people.

Entertainment, pubs, restaurants

This area of what might be termed 'social leisure' could be said to be a major contributor to the quality of life of a community. The contribution which the quantity, quality and distribution of such facilities make to the character of an urban environment is often considered in plans – although not very systematically – in the context of visitors to an area, but rarely in relation to the needs of local residents. There is clearly a difference between a successful 'leisure precinct' in a town centre, whether it has been deliberately planned or not, and an unsuccessful one. In the successful precinct, transport systems, cinemas, bingo halls, theatres, pubs, restaurants, gardens, walking areas and associated retail activity all complement one another, and there is an appropriate 'ambience', so that the whole is greater than the sum of the parts, business booms, and more investment in facilities is attracted. Such a scenario can be facilitated or hindered by planning (Jansen-Verbeke, 1985; Stansfield and Rickert, 1970). Little work has been done on standards of provision for such facilities, but the 'hierarchies' approach discussed in chapter 6 is one way in which levels of provision might be addressed.

Holidays

While local authorities commonly produce plans or marketing strategies to attract tourists *to* their areas, they tend not to consider the holiday needs of their own residents. And yet a holiday is, arguably, one of the most important forms of leisure. In the same way that variable access to sporting facilities is examined in leisure plans, there is no reason why variable access to holidays should not also be examined. National tourism organisations tend not to collect data on who *does not* go on holiday – they concentrate on those who do. The idea of 'social tourism' – assisting deprived groups, such as people with disabilities or carers, to take a holiday – is not a new idea (Finch, 1975). In this case social services organisations would be more likely to be involved.

If it is accepted that strategic plans should indeed be comprehensive in their coverage of leisure, then an appropriately comprehensive definition of leisure should be appended to the terms of reference, and some indication that the local authority will not be the only organisation involved in implementing the plan.

Step 2: Environmental appraisal

Environmental appraisal involves bringing together all the available information relevant to the terms of reference. This sounds simple enough, but can be extremely complex and demanding of resources, especially when being undertaken for the first time, and especially in the public sector. For example, one item of information which might be expected be available for such an appraisal would be trends in output or 'sales'. In the private sector the output of the organisation is sold in the market and paid for, so sales figures are always available; but in the public sector, information on 'sales' – for example the number of users of a local authority's parks – is not readily available and must be gathered by means of research projects.

The environmental appraisal might be expected to include a number of different types of information, as set out in Table 5.2. A complete appraisal of this kind could involve an enormous data-collection exercise, which could take an inordinate amount of time and resources; and the results could be somewhat indigestible. Initially, therefore, judgements need to be made about the balance between the need for information and the time and cost of collecting it. But as experience with the strategic planning process develops, so the data base is likely to develop, in terms of its content and its presentation.

Table 5.2 Information for an environmental appraisal

Type	Information items	Source
a. Political	Commitments of ruling group	• Party manifesto, speeches, etc.
b. Existing policies	Policy statements	• Policy documents
c. Legal	Legal obligations	• Legislation
d. Existing facilities/ services	Inventory Use levels Coverage – areas of unmet need Performance measures Age/state of repair etc. Private/voluntary sector provision – actual and planned	• Files • Ticket sales/counts • Financial records/ research etc. • User surveys • Facility appraisal • Private-sector survey
e. Other organisations	Activities/plans of clubs and firms	• Surveys of clubs and firms
f. Neighbouring areas/ Regional dimension	Major provision – actual and planned Local use of regional facilities	• Consultation with neighbouring authorities, special studies
g. Population trends	Increases/decreases in population Changing age structure	• Planning Department
h. Demands/Social trends	Activity demand forecasts Trends in tastes, social values, etc.	• Literature, special studies • Social surveys
i. Visitors	Numbers, origins, activities	• Visitor surveys

The third column in Table 5.2 suggests the need for a well-developed Management Information System (MIS) – that is, procedures which routinely produce information necessary for strategic planning and management. Thus a public leisure provision agency should, ideally, have available:

- an accurate, detailed and up-to-date inventory of facilities;
- regular reports on usage levels from ticket sales and, where ticket sales are not available, from special counts;
- regular public/customer feedback from user and community surveys;
- regular financial reports on sections/facilities.

It has often been the case in the past that planning exercises have been overwhelmed by the data-collection process and, as a result, the analysis of the data has been neglected, so that both planning and data collection have acquired a bad reputation in some circles, due to the poor return on the time and effort invested. It is likely that this situation may now have improved as better management information systems have developed. In addition, modern computer-based technology, and increasing familiarity with it, has made data collection and analysis simpler and cheaper. Thus most public bodies now have a good inventory of their own facilities (although not necessarily of others') – this was not always the case. Similarly, computerised ticketing provides good usage data for many facilities, and user and community surveys are no longer the rarity they once were.

The nine types of data listed in Table 5.2 are discussed in turn below.

a. Political

Political commitments are generally of more significance at national level than at local level. Commitments made by politicians in manifestos, and in speeches and public statements, are usually 'sacrosanct', despite public cynicism about politicians' broken promises. Such commitments, which are deemed to have been sanctioned by the democratic process, must therefore inevitably be included as part of any plan.

b. Existing policies

It makes sense to gather together existing policies of the organisation and its management units, whether they result from earlier comprehensive planning exercises or have developed in an *ad hoc* manner. Part of the input to the plan will be an evaluation and review of such policies. If monitoring and evaluation procedures have been built into the policies in the past, then this may not be a large task.

A key aspect of existing policies relates to the general planning framework of the organisation. The leisure plan may be part of a wider planning exercise, but even if it is not, there are likely to be advantages in seeking to complement other planning activity. Complementarity may involve using the same time horizons, so that use can be made of such things as existing population projections. It may also involve utilising existing planning zones or precincts, which divide the local authority area into neighbourhoods. Of course the choice of such zones will also be influenced by the existence of zones for management purposes, or by research which may reveal that spatial patterns of leisure suggest suitable zones for planning purposes. All aspects of data collection and subsequent analysis and policy formulation will relate to the zones chosen.

This information might initially be assembled as a 'library' of documents, but in due course summaries for analysis and for inclusion in the plan document will have to be prepared.

c. Legal obligations

Local government in Britain generally possesses *powers* in relation to leisure provision, but not duties or obligations. National organisations, on the other hand, often have their duties enshrined in legislation or charters and these are often the starting point for any planning activity.

d. Existing facilities/services

As discussed above, most local authorities now have comprehensive inventories of their own facilities and services, including detailed descriptions, such as the areas of open space and the facilities they contain. Ideally they should be available in map form. Information is generally less complete with regard to facilities and services owned or managed by other organisations. Often information is available on voluntary organisations because authorities often work closely with such organisations, offering grant aid, the use of facilities and compiling documents such as sports directories. It is in the commercial and 'social leisure' area where information is often lacking. Ideally such gaps in the information available should be remedied, via 'Yellow Pages', land-use maps and directories, so that a *comprehensive* picture of leisure provision is available. Table 5.3 provides an indicative list of the facilities and services which might be included in an inventory.

In addition to an inventory of facilities, information should be collated on current levels of utilisation. Levels of utilisation and catchment-area information can indicate patterns of under-supply and over-supply of facilities and services. The question of measuring use levels and capacity is discussed in relation to the 'organic' approach to planning discussed in chapter 6.

Table 5.3 Facility/Service inventory content

• Public open space
  – playing pitches/courts
  – parkland
• Other open space, playgrounds
• Sport/leisure centres
• Gyms/fitness/squash centres
• Swimming pools
• Adult education centres
• Education facilities
• Sporting clubs
• Hobby clubs
	• Public halls
	• Private halls
	• Clubs
	• Pubs
	• Restaurants
	• Amusement arcades
	• Libraries
	• Bookshops
	• Theatres
	• Cinemas
	• Bingo halls

Ideally, identical information should be collected for both private- and public-sector facilities and services, but in practice, where facilities and services are run by organisations other than the local authority, it may be difficult or even impossible to gather information directly, although it may be collected via community and visitor surveys as discussed in the section on Demand/Social trends below.

e. Other organisations

Information on policies of significant other organisations, such as voluntary sports and social organisations, neighbouring authorities, central government instrumentalities and major commercial organisations, should be collated, in so far as they are readily available in written form. If they are not readily available then the requisite information might be more suitably collected by special surveys or in the consultation phase.

f. Neighbouring areas/Regional dimension

Planning should take account of the facilities, services and resources available and planned in neighbouring areas and/or the region. This information may be gathered by routine examination of the written plans of neighbouring authorities, by special surveys and by reference to plans produced by organisations such as Regional Councils of Sport and Recreation.

g. Population trends

Establishing the socio-demographic characteristics of a community is a relatively simple task making use of the Census of Population. Problems do arise, however, in areas where significant population change is taking place and the Census is out of date. Usually in these situations the local planning department is in a position to provide population estimates.

For the local authority area as a whole and for each of the selected planning zones, the following data should be collated:

• resident population by: age/sex, occupation, car ownership, housing type;

- workforce members.

Planning departments are also generally the source of population forecasts. While the population is static or growing very slowly in most areas in Britain, the *ageing* of the population continues to be a significant phenomenon.

h. Demand/Social trends

A community survey is the only practical way of obtaining comprehensive information on current patterns of leisure participation in an area. Such a survey can obtain information on:

- levels of participation in a range of leisure activities;
- use of a range of leisure facilities and services;
- resident opinions.

Information on participation is essential if policy is to focus on participation rather than purely on facilities and programmes. There is a reluctance among many authorities to commit themselves to policies related to participation, since this appears to be 'telling people what to do'. The preferred approach is, very often, to express policies in terms of 'providing opportunity'. But it would seem illogical to be concerned with providing opportunity but not with whether or not those opportunities are taken up. At the facility or programme management level maximisation of participation – or attendances – is the norm. Success is at least partly measured in terms of visits. It is sometimes argued that it is *quality* that matters rather than *quantity*, although the two are not really alternatives but are complementary: since leisure is voluntarily undertaken, maximising participation must usually be achieved by offering a high-quality product.

A well-designed community leisure participation survey can form the focus of much of the planning exercise. As discussed in earlier chapters, certain activities, such as sport and the arts, are widely supported by the public sector because of the social benefits which they bring. It makes sense for public policy to seek to maximise those social benefits, which will be achieved by maximising participation levels. It therefore makes sense for the aim of the plan to be to maximise participation and for the *success* of the plan to be measured in terms of participation levels achieved. The starting point and subsequent progress can best be measured by some sort of community survey.

Focusing on levels of participation as measured by a community survey has the potential to involve a wide range of organisations in the implementation of the plan, since the local authority is only one provider of facilities and services. Further, it provides the local authority with criteria by which to judge its own activities and requests by other organisations for assistance: namely, to what extent will the activity contribute to increased participation?

The Sports Council led the way in this approach when, in 1982, in its national plan, it set targets for increasing indoor and outdoor sports participation by men and women (Sports Council, 1982). Their starting point was survey evidence on national levels of sports participation in Britain in the late 1970s, as shown by the General Household Survey; progress towards the targets was measured by reference to subsequent General Household Surveys.

It is not proposed to explore the methodology of a community leisure participation survey here; such matters are dealt with in more special-ised texts (eg Veal, 1992). Suffice it to say that, if the survey is to be the basis for assessing the overall success of the plan, it must be well de-signed and conducted and must involve a sufficiently large sample to enable comparisons to be made from one survey period to the next. Typically, at least 1000 interviews would be required and, especially if the sample is to be divided into zones, preferably more.

In addition to gathering information on participation, a community-wide survey can also be used to gather information on levels of use of specific facilities and services, as discussed under 'Existing facilities/ services' above. Further, it can be used to gather opinions on existing facilities and services, perceived deficiencies and requirements, and on proposals. The survey can therefore be seen as part of the 'consulta-tion' process discussed below.

Social surveys can generally only be conducted among adults, typi-cally from around 14 years old. Information on leisure activities of chil-dren can either be collected from parents, or a special survey can be conducted via schools.

i. Visitors

Gathering information on visitors is clearly important in tourist areas, but visitors can be of significance, even in areas which are not thought of as tourist attractions. Many urban centres attract visitors from be-yond the local authority boundary, for shopping and similar purposes and the viability of some town centre amenities, such as pubs, restau-rants and entertainment facilities, may be affected by such visitors. Visi-tors to tourist areas are often treated separately in a 'tourism strategy' rather than a leisure plan. There are, however, good reasons for treat-ing them all in the one plan, or at least ensuring that data collected for the tourism strategy is useable, and used, in the leisure plan. Many of the facilities used by tourists, such as parks, museums, theatres, pubs and restaurants, are in fact community leisure facilities: more often than not, even in recognised tourist areas, locals form the majority of the patrons of such facilities. This is, of course, highly desirable from the tourists' point of view, since most would prefer to 'mix with the locals' rather than visit a tourist 'ghetto'. Generally, the locals also benefit from a higher level of provision and greater variety than would be possible without the visitors. Planning for the leisure of tourists and for the lei-sure of residents should therefore be complementary.

Again, some sort of periodic survey is the most effective means of gathering the required data, involving random sampling and interview-ing of visitors in areas which they frequent. The aim would be to dis-cover just how many visitors there are, and what facilities they use.

Some forecasting of future visitor numbers would also be required (see chapter 7).

Step 3: Establish mission/goals

Mission vs purpose vs goals vs objectives

Before considering this step in detail it is worth giving some attention to the question of the difference between 'mission', 'purpose', 'goals' and 'objectives'. The *mission* of an organisation is its overall *raison d'etre*, which is generally, if possible, summarised in a succinct phrase or two. In this book *purpose* will be considered as meaning the same as 'mission', so a 'statement of purpose' could substitute for a 'mission statement'. *Goals* are simply more detailed statements of the mission. *Objectives* are more specific, and generally include a time dimension and quantification. Using the examples of the three types of facility used in Table 5.1, possible missions, goals and objectives are set out in Table 5.4. In effect there is a mission/goals/objectives hierarchy. The mission is the starting point. Goals may emerge simply as a result of further elaboration of the mission statement or may emerge from the strategic planning process. Objectives emerge from the strategic planning process discussed below.

Table 5.4 Missions – Goals – Objectives

	Leisure Centre	**Tourist Commission**	**National Park**
Mission	To provide members of the local community with fulfilling recreational experiences	To maximise the nation's benefits from tourism while minimising costs	To conserve the flora, fauna and ecological integrity of the park area while providing fulfilling recreational experiences for visitors
Goals	• To attract as wide a cross section of the community as possible • To maximise the use of the Centre • To maximise net income	• To extend the tourist season • To encourage tourists to visit areas outside the capital city • To improve the standard of service offered to tourists	• To preserve endangered species • To reduce the effects of erosion • To improve educattional services for visitors
Objectives	• To double the number of elderly people using the Centre over the coming year • To increase utilisation of the squash courts from 70% to 80% over two years • To reach an income of £1m by 1997	• To increase off-season tourist trips by 10% over two years • To increase non-metropolitan tourist trips from 20% to 30% of all tourist trips by 1998 • To increase 'customer-service' training programmes by 50% over two years	• To restore species A, B, C, etc. to viability over a five-year period • To double the programme of rehabilitation of eroded areas over the coming year • To build one new visitor interpretation centre each year over the next three years

Mission/Goals statements

Drucker, in discussing the importance of getting it right, refers to the mission statements of a number of organisations, including the Girl Scouts of the USA: '... to help girls grow into proud, self-confident, and self-respecting young women'; and a hospital emergency room: '... to give assurance to the afflicted' (1990: 3).

A feature of many public-sector leisure agencies is their multi-purpose nature. Hatry and Dunn suggest the following combination of goals and mission statement for a local authority recreation service.

> Recreation services should provide for all citizens, to the extent practicable, a variety of adequate, year-round leisure opportunities which are accessible, safe, physically attractive, and provide enjoyable experiences. They should, to the maximum extent, contribute to the mental and physical health of the community, to its economic and social well-being and permit outlets that will help decrease incidents of antisocial behaviour such as crime and delinquency.
> (Hatry and Dunn, 1971: 13)

In chapter 9 the implications of such a comprehensive statement for the on-going management of a leisure service are explored. This statement is an attempt to provide an 'all-purpose' statement to which any local authority might subscribe. However, the discussion in the opening chapters of this book suggests that different people and political groups hold different values and have differing views on the role of the state, in relation to leisure as much as in relation to other areas such as education or defence. It might be expected, therefore, that differing values and philosophies would lead to differing mission or goals statements. Table 5.5 summarises the main philosophical positions outlined in chapters 2 to 4 and offers suggestions as to what effect such positions might have on the mission/goals of a public leisure agency.

While mission/goals statements might be expected to reflect such value positions, it is possible that statements could be devised which are sufficiently general in nature that it would be acceptable to most shades of opinion – the *differences* emerging only at later stages in the planning process. For example, a statement to the effect that an authority aimed to enhance health by promotion of participation in sport might have wide acceptance, but one group might wish to do this by making public sports facilities freely available to all, while another group might wish to facilitate a private enterprise approach.

In addition to complications arising from value differences arising from political and interest groups, most public bodies are faced with differences of outlook within their own organisation, both horizontally (across a range of services) and vertically (from top management via line management to the operational level). In practice, the multi-purpose organisation is likely to have a hierarchy of mission/goals statements relating to different levels and sections of the organisation. The strategic planning process described in this chapter proceeds to ask 'how might this mission and these goals be best pursued?' The result is a set of policies, programmes and facilities, with an organisational and management

Table 5.5 Values/Ideologies and goals

Source	Goal/Objective
Leisure rights and needs (Ch. 2)	
Leisure as a right	Access to facilities for chosen leisure activities for all
Leisure as a need	Provision for need for all
Ideological perspectives (Ch. 3)	
Conservative values	Maintenance of traditional provision and promotion excellence
Liberal values	Minimisation of state involvement
Democratic socialist values	Equality of opportunity; democratisation; maximum state provision
Marxist socialist values	Facilities and opportunities which counter commercial exploitation
Feminist values	Radical: facilities and opportunities which counter patriarchy Reformist: access to facilities for women; child-care provision
Environmentalist values	Promotion of environmentally friendly activities; protection of the natural environment
Economic factors (Ch 4)	
Public goods Externalities Mixed goods Merit goods Option demand Natural monopolies	Provide facilities and services which correct market failures, where enhanced community benefit can be shown
Infant industries Large projects Economic development Incidental enterprise	Public sector as entrepreneur and economic manager
Equity	Counter market inequalities and inequities through leisure provision
Tradition	Maintain existing services

structure to go with it. Each of the sections of the organisation would then be expected to subscribe to the mission of the whole organisation, and would be given their overall goals and targets. But each section will engage in its own strategic management process – considering alternative ways of achieving the goals which it has been given.

For example, if a local authority has as one of its goals the enhancement of the health of the community, as discussed above, it might decide, as a result of its planning activity, to pursue that goal by means of the provision of a public swimming pool and the organisation of an annual marathon. The pool manager is given the goal of maximising health benefits through swimming participation, while the officer responsible for organising the marathon is given the goal of maximising health benefits through marathon participation. Each of these managers now has a 'mini-strategic plan' to prepare; each has a range of possible courses of action which might be pursued. Thus the sorts of facility-based mission/goals/objectives arise as seen in Table 5.4.

Of particular note in the public sector, and leisure in particular, is the often very diverse nature of organisational goals. In the private sector the main goal is usually to make the maximum possible profit. In practice it is more complicated than that, with short-term versus long-term considerations to take into account, which leads to consideration of growth, assets, liquidity, etc., as well as profit. But all the goals and indicators of success tend to be quantitative and can be relatively easily compared between different companies (Gratton and Taylor, 1988: 150). In the public sector goals are not only diverse, but often difficult to quantify in any meaningful way – for example goals related to excellence in the arts or related to conservation of the environment or heritage. Further, goals can often be conflicting, for example conservation versus recreational access in natural areas and some conceptions of excellence versus popularity in the arts.

The mission statement and related statement of goals can perform a number of functions. Firstly, they are the lynch-pin of the rest of the strategic planning process – all proposals should be orientated towards the fulfilment of the mission statement and pursuit of the goals. Secondly, if well formulated, they can provide a common focus of attention for all members of an organisation, including elected and staff members, whether or not they are directly engaged in the strategic planning process, and others with an interest in the activities of the organisation, particularly the public, as both electors and consumers of its services – the 'stake-holders'. Thirdly, in appropriate format, they can also assist in establishing the 'corporate identity' of the organisation.

Quality

At this point it is appropriate to refer to the notion of quality and in particular *Total Quality Management*. This particular approach to management has become fashionable in recent years following its apparent success in Japanese industry (Logothetis, 1992). The approach suggests that the guiding principle in any organisation's planning and management should be the idea of *quality*. Quality is something which every person in an organisation can strive to achieve in their own area of responsibility and it can provide common goals towards which organisations and parts of organisations can strive collectively. In the commercial sector, for example, while profit maximisation may be the overall goal, few members of the organisation can relate to that goal directly –

they are not able to see their own particular contribution to profit. But they *can* see their own contribution to quality and, it is argued, if the product or service is of sufficient quality, profits will follow. The idea readily translates to public-sector service organisations, since everyone in the organisation can understand the idea of a high-quality recreational experience. Further, the quality idea focuses attention on customer or client needs, since, ultimately, the customer is the arbiter as far as quality is concerned. While this is broadly true for most areas of the leisure services, problems can arise in certain areas of the arts and environmental conservation where professionals, politicians, pressure groups and the general public can differ over what is an appropriate, 'quality' product, programme or practice.

Thus, in 'Total Quality Management' parlance, the mission/goals statement suggested by Hatry and Dunn above would be simplified into a statement of the kind:

To provide high-quality recreation experiences for the community.

The statements about accessibility, safety and so on would then be elaborations of the basic idea of quality.

The idea of quality in management has been promulgated by the publication of British Standard 5750, which provides guidelines and principles for the establishment of a total quality management system within an organisation. It has been welcomed as a useful tool for the leisure manager (Mills, 1992).

Step 4: Consultation

Consultation with the public, other organisations and members of the local authority itself is a vital component in the planning process. In chapter 6, the 'community development' approach to planning is put forward as a means by which public involvement and participation becomes the basis of the whole exercise. In most statutory planning activities public consultation is a legal requirement.

As with data collection, consultation can be a time-consuming process which can be mishandled. If not undertaken competently, far from broadening the inputs to the planning process, it can have a narrowing effect, if sectional interests are permitted to 'hi-jack' the process.

As Arnstein (1969) pointed out, public participation can take many forms, from 'tokenism' to total citizen control. The steps in Arnstein's 'ladder' of citizen participation are:

1 Manipulation
2 Therapy
3 Informing
4 Consultation
5 Placation
6 Partnership
7 Delegated power
8 Citizen control

Consultation can vary in its purpose, in the range and types of people and organisations involved, in its form, and in its timing. These issues are discussed in turn below.

Purposes

Consultation may be undertaken as a means of gathering information, for example to generate ideas, to obtain information on the issues of concern to particular groups, or to obtain feedback on the feasibility of particular proposals; or it may be seen as integral to the decision-making process, involving opinions and attitudes of different groups concerning issues and proposals. Since leisure is not an issue which is thoroughly discussed on the political hustings, and since it is such a wide-ranging phenomenon involving everyone in the community, the information-gathering and decision-making aspects of consultation are both highly relevant.

Involvement

Consultation usually involves the public at large, organisations and their representatives, and the staff of the public organisation doing the planning. Of particular importance in the area of leisure, which is not a statutory service in the public sector, is to produce a plan which is *implemented*. It is generally believed that this will only be achieved if those who are expected to be involved in implementing the plan are also involved in preparing it: many individuals and organisations must feel that they 'own' the plan. Table 5.6 provides an indicative list of the range of individuals and organisations which might be involved in the consultation process for a leisure plan.

Table 5.6 Individuals and organisations involved in consultation

• Public at large	• Sports/arts/environmental/special
• Particular age/gender/ethnic/disability	interest clubs
groups	• Chambers of Commerce
• Staff of the Leisure Department	• Owners/managers of private-sector
• Elected members of Council	facilities
• Other departments of Council	• Facility/service users

Form

Consultation can take a variety of forms, including the following:

- one-on-one meetings/interviews
- media notices
- competitions
- letters inviting comment – to residents and/or organisations
- public exhibitions (static or mobile) with opportunity for comment
- public meetings
- production/distribution of printed and/or video material
- focus groups

- attendance at group meetings (eg clubs)
- establishment of working parties with outside membership
- postal questionnaire survey of organisations
- community surveys
- user surveys

Each of the techniques has its merits and drawbacks. For example, while involvement of the media can produce good publicity, it can result in an unrepresentative response. While a community survey ensures wide representation, it may not elicit the detailed information which can be obtained from focus groups.

Timing

In Figure 5.1 consultation is shown as 'step 4', but in fact it can take place at many stages in the whole process. If the purpose is to generate ideas, consultation might take place at the beginning of the process; if it is to obtain reactions to proposals, it would take place later in the process. If the idea of consultation is fully embraced and its political role is recognised, then it is likely to take place in various forms throughout the process.

Step 5: Identify alternative policies

While research and an MIS are necessary elements of an environmental appraisal, total reliance on these sources could be inflexible, missing key information which does not 'fit' the procedures, and failing to use the knowledge and experience of managers. An approach which is often used to complement the more formal approach is a 'SWOT' analysis, standing for Strengths, Weaknesses, Opportunities, Threats.

A SWOT analysis is usually carried out as a sort of 'brainstorming' exercise involving senior management staff. A group of managers 'brainstorms' the organisation's strengths, weaknesses, opportunities and threats, based on their own knowledge of the organisation and/or on information assembled as described above. Possible plans of action begin to emerge which:

- build on and reinforce strengths
- avoid or seek to overcome weaknesses
- seek to exploit opportunities
- take account of or attempt to neutralise threats

The end result of the SWOT analysis, public consultation and collated information on political and policy commitments and legal obligations should be a 'shopping list' of actual and potential policies and actions, ideally related to the mission and goals of the organisation, as illustrated in Figure 5.2. For example, if the goal was to increase attendance at the performing arts, the alternatives which might be evaluated could include:

- subsidising ticket prices
- giving people 'vouchers' to attend the arts
- building more performing arts venues
- offering larger grants to existing arts companies
- establishing new performing arts companies
- launching a publicity campaign, via various media
- providing more education programmes concerning the arts
- developing mobile arts facilities and companies
- offering more training for performing artists
- offering more training for arts managers, eg in marketing

Figure 5.2 Identification of alternative policies

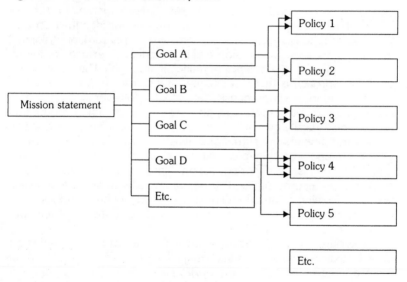

Step 6: Decide strategy

Theories of decision-making

There are various theories about how decisions are or should be made in the public sector. Since it is widely accepted that decisions should be made on a rational basis, taking account of as many possibilities and options as possible, the 'base case' approach is known as 'rational–comprehensive' decision-making. Goals are set and all conceivable alternative ways of pursuing the goals are identified and evaluated, to see which is best. The best course of action is then adopted as the plan and then implemented.

In the rational–comprehensive approach, alternative policies are examined in detail and their costs and outcomes estimated. In the arts example given above, the chosen policy would be the one that is expected to achieve the highest increase in performing arts attendances, taking account of costs. Exploring and evaluating all these alternatives in equal detail would, of course, be an enormous undertaking. Leisure service organisations in particular rarely have available the resources for research and data gathering which are available to other public service sectors, such as health or transport.

It is generally believed that the rational–comprehensive approach, while it remains a model of perfection, is in fact impractical, and is rarely implemented. In the 1950s, Lindblom (1959) argued that organisations, in practice, did not use the rational–comprehensive approach; they considered only a few alternatives, and, rather than beginning 'from scratch' with the goals of the organisation, they started with consideration of where they were now – current policies, commitments and practices. This view of decision-making suggests that only *incremental* change is considered; alternative courses of action are not identified on a rational–comprehensive basis, but in a somewhat haphazard, or 'disjointed' manner. This style of decision-making Lindblom termed 'disjointed incrementalism' or the 'science of muddling through'. The advantage of such an approach is that it is cheaper and quicker to implement than the ideal 'rational–comprehensive' approach. However, while disjointed incrementalism may reflect what goes on in most organisations in practice, it could hardly be recommended as an ideal way to proceed; in particular, it favours the *status quo*, whether or not that is the best set of policies, and, in failing to consider all alternative courses of action, it is in danger of missing important opportunities for change. Etzioni (1967) proposed, as a compromise, the idea of 'mixed scanning', a two-stage process involving a 'broad brush' review of all possible courses of action, followed by more detailed evaluation of just a few, selected alternatives.

The leisure area is particularly afflicted by a further alternative approach to decision-making, which might be termed 'hallmark' decision-making. The name seems appropriate because it generally arises in relation to what have come to be called 'hallmark' events or projects (Syme *et al.*, 1989). Such phenomena include major events such as the holding of the Olympic Games, and major building and planning projects, such as the building of a national theatre or developments such as the London Docklands. Because of their high profile such projects usually involve politicians directly, there is a great deal of media attention, and normal planning, decision-making, budgeting and evaluation procedures are often by-passed, for example by means of special legislation. Cost over-runs and controversy tend to be the norm. The decision-making process involved appears to consist of making the decision to go ahead with the project *first*, then seeking ways of justifying it. While all areas of the public sector are affected by hallmark decision-making, leisure seems to suffer particularly because so many non-experts either consider themselves to be expert in the area, or assume that no particular expertise is necessary. The work of Hall (1980) on *Great Planning Disasters* and Syme *et al.* (1989) on sporting events represent the beginnings of a literature on this phenomenon.

Decision-making techniques

The question of evaluation – choosing the best options – raises some difficult issues for the public sector, especially given the diverse, sometimes conflicting, and often unquantifiable nature of the goals as discussed above. Various approaches to evaluation are available.

Mixed scanning

This technique comes closest to describing the approach to decision-making which is implicit in the 'strategic management' procedures discussed here, in that SWOT analyses, political considerations and public consultation often provide the initial 'broad brush' evaluation of policy options. It is also similar to the 'issues approach' discussed in chapter 6.

Economic evaluation techniques

Techniques such as cost-benefit analysis and economic impact analysis, are dealt with in chapter 8. While such techniques are used in policy areas such as transport to evaluate programmes and projects in advance, in leisure they have generally been used to evaluate projects *after* they have been implemented.

The performance–importance technique

Originally developed in relation to individual consumer choice (Martilla and James, 1977), this technique can also be utilised in organisational decision-making, as indicated in work by Harper and Balmer (1989) on perceived benefits of public leisure services; it is also related to the idea of 'conjoint analysis', as outlined, for example, by Claxton (1994). The performance–importance approach involves listing the various performance criteria considered to be important in relation to the project or programme under consideration. The relative importance of each criterion to the individual decision-maker or group of decision-makers is then scored (say 1 to 10). The criteria and their weights might arise from political philosophy or from community consultation. Each proposal is then given a score (say 1 to 10) for its level of performance in relation to each criterion. The product of the two scores provides the overall preference score for the proposal. Table 5.7 illustrates the method in relation to three hypothetical proposals before a local authority; on the basis of the scores in the table, project C would be favoured.

Table 5.7   Performance–importance decision-making – a hypothetical example

Criteria	Importance to Council (a)*	Project A	Project B	Project C
		Performance score (b)**		
Benefit to residents	10	5	10	9
Benefit to tourism	6	10	5	2
Low net running costs	8	8	6	10
Political popularity	5	7	7	10
Total score (Σ a × b)		209	213	232

- Project A: upgrading the seafront park and promenade, or
- Project B: indoor swimming pool and leisure centre, or
- Project C: community centre for a range of health and community organisations

* 1=low importance, 10=high importance   ** 1=poor performance, 10=high performance

Constraints

It will generally not be possible to implement all the projects and programmes identified as desirable, because of resource constraints; projects and programmes have to be ranked and only the best, and those that can be financed, are implemented. Constraints may be of an organisational or economic kind. Organisational constraints refer simply to the practical problems of managing growth. Judgements have to be made about just how fast an organisation can develop without losing managerial control.

In fact, *financial* constraints tend to be the important limiting factor. The resources available to public bodies are always limited. The limitations may be political in nature – when governments find it politically unacceptable to raise taxes. Or they may be economic – when borrowing limits are imposed as a result of macro-economic policy. The former tends to relate to on-going running costs and the latter to capital expenditure.

The question arises as to how a strategy should take account of economic constraints. There are two approaches. One is to outline all the community's needs/demands and the programme which would be required to meet them in the medium to long term, regardless of resource constraints, and deal with the resource questions on a shorter-term basis. Thus the plan might be costed at £50 million, but the short-term plan, over the next two years say, might commit the organisation to expenditure of, perhaps, £5 million only. This is the approach adopted by the Sports Council in its various national plans (1972, 1982, 1988). The second approach is to determine the resources likely to be available

over the period of plan and put forward only those projects and programmes which can be funded.

In practice, some sort of compromise between the two approaches is
usually achieved. There may be little point in publishing a plan which is
so ambitious that it is not treated seriously. On the other hand, a plan
which contains 'ambit claims', and which sets out the full extent of community needs/demands, may inspire politicians and the community to
find the necessary funds. Whether the 'ambit claim' part of the exercise
is conducted publicly via a published plan, or behind closed doors, resulting in the publication of a 'realistic' plan, varies in practice.

The strategy

The selected programmes and projects which emerge from the evaluation and decision-making process provide the basis for the strategic
plan. Each programme or project will have been chosen because of its
potential to achieve certain of the goals of the organisation. Each programme or project will therefore have a set of goals. Specific objectives
may be partially laid down in the strategic plan, but may also be worked
out at the facility/programme or project level.

A typical strategy document will involve:

1 Mission statement
2 Goals statement
3 Summary of environmental appraisal
4 Summary of alternatives considered and evaluation process
5 Selected policies/projects/programmes
6 Goals of individual projects/programmes and objectives/targets for
   the strategy period
7 Performance measures for objectives/targets
8 Indication of persons/departments responsible for implementation

In some cases items 6–8 are presented in a separate document. Typically, a strategy will relate to a specific period, usually three or five
years. Objectives/targets include dates: for some the time period for
their achievement is the whole strategy period, for others a year or two
years; in other cases the objective/target is to be achieved in specified
stages throughout the strategy period.

Step 7: Implementation

The detail of implementation of strategic plans is the subject of management books and is not dealt with here. Clearly, the *preparation* of a
strategic plan is the easy part. Implementation can, however, be aided
by the way in which the strategy is prepared in the first place. Among
the approaches which may help are: involvement of all sections of an
organisation in strategy preparation; wide dissemination of the mission
statement, goals and strategy outline in a readable form; inclusion of
features in the strategy to which all members of the organisation can
relate (such as the idea of 'quality' discussed above); incorporation of a

reward system for achievement of targets (very difficult, but not impossible in the public sector); and leadership from the top to ensure that the strategy is taken seriously.

Steps 8/9: Monitoring, evaluation and feedback

Monitoring progress towards achievement of strategy objectives and evaluating performance generally are discussed in chapter 9. Again this process can be made easy or difficult depending on the design of the strategy itself. If the strategy is vague and lacks specificity, then performance will be difficult to assess.

Feedback means that, as the organisation moves into the strategy period, information produced by the monitoring and evaluation process should be used to keep the organisation on track. Some feedback processes are day-to-day in nature, for example ensuring that staff are adhering to various codes of behaviour or noting income and sales figures. However, as discussed above, there is always the problem of day-to-day concerns blocking out consideration of the longer-term concerns of the strategy, so reporting mechanisms must be put in place at various levels to ensure that strategic matters get dealt with.

Up-dating of the strategy can take two forms. One approach is for an annual programme report to be produced in each year of the strategy period. This reports on progress in the previous year and re-sets the following year's targets as necessary, while the overall strategy stays in place. The alternative is to 'roll forward' the whole strategy each year, so that there is always a three-year or five-year horizon. The first approach is generally favoured in the public leisure service area, since the environment is less volatile than in some areas of the private sector.

Further reading

Strategic planning/management: Certo and Peter, 1991; Wheelen and Hunger, 1989; Wortman, 1979.

Decision-making: Burton, 1989; Ham and Hill, 1984; Lindblom, 1959.

Public participation: Arnstein, 1969; Ministry of Housing and Local Government, 1969.

Quality: Logothetis, 1992; Mills, 1992.

Leisure planning: Burton, 1989; Dower *et al.* 1981; Gold, 1973, 1980; Hall, 1980; Henry and Spink, 1990; Sports Council, 1968, 1975, 1978; Hertfordshire Association of Leisure Officers, 1978; Garrett and Spedding, 1977; Ministry of Culture and Recreation, n.d., 1976; Marriott, 1990.

6 PLANNING FOR LEISURE: TECHNIQUES AND APPROACHES

Introduction

In chapter 5 a general approach to leisure plans and strategies was considered. In this chapter more detailed consideration is given to techniques and approaches which might be used within the planning and strategy preparation process. It might be argued that elaborate methodologies for planning for leisure are impractical because the responsible agencies – particularly local authorities – are simply not prepared to devote substantial resources to this relatively low-status activity. However, it is not necessarily the case that substantial resources are required to implement more advanced methodologies: several of the approaches suggested here make use of readily available data and can be implemented virtually on a 'back of an envelope' basis. In fact, considerable resources *have* been devoted to planning for leisure in the past, but they have often been devoted to data collection rather than analysis: only a marginal increase in resources would have been required to make better use of the data assembled.

Planning for leisure in Britain can be said to have passed through three phases since the 1960s (Veal, 1993). The period 1960–72 can be designated the *demand phase*, when planners were concerned with responding to rapidly increasing population numbers, rising real incomes and rising car-ownership. From 1973 to 1985 – the *need phase* – attention was focused less on general demand and more on the needs of particular groups in the community, such as deprived inner city residents. From the mid-1980s to the present – the *enterprise phase* – leisure planning has reflected the dominant government view that leisure is ideally a private-sector function. Each era has spawned planning methods to meet the policy challenges presented. However, successive techniques and approaches have not necessarily replaced one another but have complemented each other. Thus a range of techniques now exists which enable the leisure planner to assess present and future demand, to focus on different groups in varying states of need, to incorporate community concerns and to consider the potential of public- and private-sector provision. This chapter draws together information on available techniques.

Ten approaches are considered in turn in this chapter. They are: 1 the use of standards; 2 the gross demand approach; 3 spatial approaches; 4 hierarchies of facilities; 5 priority social area analysis; 6 the Recreation Opportunity Spectrum; 7 the grid or matrix approach; 8 the organic approach; 9 community development; 10 the issues approach.

1 The traditional approach: the use of standards

Leisure planners and local councils love standards. This a great paradox: when government ministers try to tell local authorities how to organise their affairs they complain of threats to local democracy. And yet in the area of leisure provision, the one area where local authorities are relatively free from government interference, they frequently look nervously over their shoulders to ensure that *they* are sanctioning their activities, by providing standards. *They* are not necessarily the government as such, but some national or regional body whose pronouncements at least *sound* authoritative.

A standard in planning for leisure can be defined as a prescribed level of provision of facilities or services related to some criterion such as the level of population. Such standards can be developed at local level to provide guidance for the production of local plans; however, a feature of leisure planning is that such standards have been developed by a number of organisations at national level. So there is a tendency for local planners to use such nationally promulgated standards rather than develop their own at local level. In a number of cases in the past, standards developed for use at local level, particularly in the development of new towns, have been adopted by others as if they had been developed for national use: examples are the Greater London Council open space hierarchy, discussed later in this chapter (GLC Planning Department, 1968) and, in Australia, the standards developed for the capital, Canberra (National Capital Development Commission, 1981). Examples of nationally promulgated standards used in Britain are summarised in Table 6.1. Standards have a number of advantages and disadvantages. These are discussed in turn below.

Advantages

Simplicity
Standards are generally easy to understand. This can be particularly important when communicating with non-experts such as officers from other professions, or politicians.

Efficiency
Standards avoid duplication of effort. Every local authority or agency does not have to undertake the detailed research necessary to arrive at a standard or other assessment of requirements; the research and consultation, which can be costly and time-consuming, is done once only, by the central organisation.

Table 6.1   Leisure facility/service provision standards

Facility/Service	Standard of provision	Body responsible
1 Playing fields	6 acres per 1000 population	NPFA
2 Allotments	$^1/_2$ acre per 1000 population	Thorpe Committee
3 District indoor sports centres	1 per 40,000–90,000 population plus 1 for each additional 50,000 ($17m^2$ per 1000 population)	Sports Council
4 Local indoor sports centres	$23m^2$ per 1000 population (approx.)	Sports Council
5 Indoor swimming pools	$5m^2$ per 1000 population (approx.)	Sports Council
6 Golf courses	1 9-hole unit per 18,000 population	Sports Council
7 Libraries	1 branch library per 15,000 population. Maximum distance to nearest library in urban areas: 1 mile. Book purchases: 250 p.a. per 1000 population	DES
8 Children's play	$1^1/_2$ acres per 1000 population	NPFA

Sources: 1 NPFA, 1971; 2 Thorpe Committee, 1969; 3 Sports Council, 1972, 1975, 1977; 4 Sports Council, 1977; 5 Sports Council, 1972, 1977, 1978; 6 Sports Council, 1972; 7 Ministry of Education, n.d.; 8 NPFA, 1971

Equity
If implemented everywhere, standards would ensure that, regardless of where they lived, people could expect to find a level of provision based on the same criteria of need or demand. The idea might be related to the idea of 'leisure rights' as discussed in chapter 2; it is an accepted goal in social services such as education, but is an unfamiliar idea in the area of leisure. It can be particularly important to national governments or agencies when making direct provision or giving grants to local providers: such national bodies would wish to appear even-handed in their treatment of different areas of the country.

Authority
In making a case within an organisation for provision of services it can be useful to be able to quote from an external, authoritative source in support of the case. Fellow professionals and elected members of councils may be reassured that the expenditure of resources is justified if some external agency is, in effect, sanctioning it.

Measurability
Progress towards the achievement of standards is relatively easy to assess, partly because of their simplicity, but also because of the way they are expressed, which is usually in quantitative terms. Policies based on standards can therefore be effectively monitored.

Disadvantages

Validity
The ways in which standards have been derived are often open to question. It may be that those who draw them up use the best available methods and it may be that the documents setting out the standards make their limitations very clear. But such qualifications are frequently ignored by users of standards. As a result the standards are often invested with greater authority than is justified and are used with insufficient care.

Locality
Documents setting out standards usually indicate that they should not be rigidly applied and, particularly, that local conditions are likely to vary. But rarely is any guidance given on how standards should be varied to accommodate these local variations in conditions. Even when such advice is available it is often ignored by those applying the standards. Variations in local conditions could suggest that provision be above or below the standard. For example, an area with a higher than average elderly population might require fewer squash courts but more golf courses than the standards specify. But standards tend to be treated as the fixed, required level of provision in all circumstances.

Priority
Standards are isolated pieces of advice. In themselves they take no account of the real world in which all the desirable facilities and services cannot always be provided. Decisions on priorities have to be made within the leisure service area and also between leisure services and other areas of public expenditure.

Quality and capacity
Most standards in leisure provision fail to take account of the quality of provision and, in many cases, its capacity. Good quality provision could, in some circumstances, compensate for a low level of provision. In addition, apparently similar facilities can vary a great deal in their capacity to accommodate recreational visits – either as a result of design or management features – for example, a well-drained sports pitch can accommodate more games than a poorly drained one.

Substitutability

Very little is known about substitutability between leisure activities. If there are no squash courts in an area will people play badminton? If there is no theatre will they attend the cinema more? It is possible that concentration on a few good facilities and a limited range of activities could produce more beneficial results – however assessed – than an attempt to provide facilities across the board. As an example, in an area where land costs are high, good indoor sports facilities may represent better value for money than a vain attempt to increase the area of open space to bring it up to 'the standard'.

Spatial specificity

Standards usually present some gross assessment of requirements and do not of themselves provide guidance on the appropriate spatial distribution of the facilities prescribed. Spatial aspects are discussed in detail later in this chapter.

Sufficient advantages of standards have been set out for it to be clear that, in this book, it is not being suggested that standards be abandoned entirely. The suggestions for alternative planning methods made later in this chapter are intended to be means by which a more local perspective can be injected into the planning process. The proposals could go some way to overcoming some of the disadvantages of standards. The most serious criticism of standards is the first one, that their validity is sometimes suspect. This issue is explored in relation to the most commonly used standard: the open space standard of the National Playing Fields Association (NPFA).

The NPFA standard for open space dates from 1925, when it was observed that, for every 1000 population, 500 were below the age of 40; of these it was assumed that 150 would either not want to play sport or would be unable to because of infirmity. A further 150 would use school facilities. Thus 200 people in every 1000 would need to be catered for. Given the size of sports teams and frequency of play, it was estimated that the needs of these 200 people could be accommodated on:

- 1 senior football pitch
- 1 junior football pitch
- 1 cricket pitch
- 1 three-rink bowling green
- 2 tennis courts
- 1 children's playground of $1/_2$ an acre
- 1 pavilion

The facilities would occupy six acres, hence the standard of six acres of open space per 1000 population (NPFA, 1971). The standard *excluded* school playing fields, HM Forces' sports grounds, verges, woodlands, commons, gardens and parks, golf courses, large areas of water and indoor facilities.

In 1971 the NPFA reviewed the standard and concluded that the effects of rising living standards (which would have increased the standard), and changing age structure (which, because of the growth in the numbers of elderly, would have reduced the standard) cancelled each other out and left the standard at six acres.

What, then, is wrong with such a standard? A number of criticisms can be levelled at it. Being based on participation rates which are themselves partly dependent upon the level of supply of facilities, the standard is somewhat tautological. Age structures vary from area to area, but the standard assumes one common age structure. Tastes vary from area to area. People in one area may prefer, or have a tradition of, for example, swimming or (as in Scotland) playing golf, rather than playing team sports, but neither of these activities is included in the standard. Successful management and/or promotion could result in participation rates well in excess of those suggested by the NPFA. The environment varies from area to area: where land is expensive and housing needs pressing, as in inner city areas, the standard of six acres may be unrealistic, and areas with access to the sea or the countryside may have fewer needs for formal provision. Hard porous, other artificial surfaces or floodlighting affect the capacity of sports pitches. Such devices can reduce the overall demand for land. The effect of joint provision or dual use is not clear in the standard, nor does it provide guidance on the spatial distribution of open space. The standard implicitly assumes that all demand should be met. This rarely happens in other areas of social provision. While it may provide a set of ultimate goals it does not provide a plan of action in the usual conditions of limited resources.

As already indicated, the NPFA was aware of many of these problems and suggested that the standard should be applied taking local conditions into account. But a methodology to indicate just how local conditions should be taken into account, how local conditions should be assessed, and how they would affect the application of the standard was not proposed.

The NPFA standard and its derivatives have a long history, with numerous studies and reports having been produced over the years to attempt to wean planners off it (eg Willis, 1968; Sports Council, 1968; Greater London and South East Sports Council, 1977; Sports Council, 1993), but its longevity, despite its limitations, is evidence of the importance of the advantages of standards as discussed earlier.

2 Gross demand approach

The 'gross demand' approach to planning for leisure overcomes certain of the disadvantages of the normal 'standards' approach, but not all. Its advantages and disadvantages are discussed below, after the general approach has been described. The approach is basically the one put forward in *Planning for Sport* in 1968 (Sports Council, 1968).

The gross demand technique can be implemented with varying degrees of complexity or sophistication. The initial, simplified, version takes an overall level of participation for a particular activity as derived from a national or regional participation survey and applies it to the

local community. A number of such surveys exist which might be utilised. For example the 1987 General Household Survey (GHS) indicated that 2.6 per cent of the population aged 16 and over played
squash at least once per month. An 'average' community with a population aged 16 and over of 100,000 would therefore be expected to
contain approximately 2600 squash players.

The *Planning for Sport* approach was slightly more sophisticated
than this in that it suggested dividing the population into age groups
and applying age-specific participation rates to each group. Thus, in
the case of squash, the participation rate among the 20–24 age group
was, in 1987, 6 per cent whereas the rate among the 30–44 age group
was 4 per cent. Therefore a community with a higher than average
proportion of its population aged 20-24 would, other things being equal,
have a higher overall rate of participation than the national average of
2.6 per cent and consequently a higher than average requirement for
squash courts.

The age-structure of the population makes a difference to demand
for most activities, but so do other factors, such as the occupational
or socio-economic composition of the community or its level of car-
ownership. Any divergence from the national average in these factors is
likely to change the level of demand from the average. Combining all of
these factors into a single measure, using multiple regression techniques,
is a theoretical possibility but not generally a very practical one (see
Cross-sectional analysis in chapter 7). But a number of separate demand estimates based on these various social factors could be prepared
and an average used for planning purposes. Thus if the age structure of
the population was likely to push demand above the average but the
socio-economic composition seemed likely to pull it down then it might
be concluded that these factors cancelled each other out and that use of
the national average participation rate would be appropriate.

Having determined a level of demand, planning requires the transla-
tion of this into facility requirements. Such a method can be applied to
a wide range of leisure activities where facility capacity can measured in
terms of number of users or visits. Table 6.2 lists examples of such
facilities and possible measures of capacity. In the case of the squash
example, the average community with 2600 squash players, each wishing to play once a week, could be accommodated on between 10 and
11 squash courts if the courts could be used to full capacity; but, assuming that they were used at, say, 75 per cent capacity, the requirement
would be for 14 courts.

Table 6.2 Facility capacities

Facility	Visits/week
Indoor sports hall (2 ct.)	1500
Community hall (1 ct.)	450
Grass playing pitch	220
Outdoor hard-court	140
Squash court	250
Weights room	330
25 metre indoor pool (year round)	3500
50 metre indoor pool (year round)	7000
25 metre outdoor pool (summer)	3500
50 metre outdoor pool (summer)	7000
Athletics track	500
Golf course (18-hole)	800
Bowling green	270
Informal park	235/ha
Theatre (400 seat)	2000

Source: See Appendix 6.1

The less formal the activity the less appropriate the gross demand method is. Thus while it may be interesting to have an estimate of the number of people who visit facilities such as parks or museums it is difficult to translate that number into a specific facility requirement. For activities such as countryside recreation, or major spectator attractions such as motor racing or horse race meetings, where the pattern of travel transcends local boundaries, the method would need to be applied at a regional rather than a local level.

What advantages does the gross demand approach have over the standards approach? Even in its simplified form it has the advantage of presenting estimated *numbers of participants* in various activities in a local area, which could be a useful innovation, even for informal activities where the figure cannot be directly translated into facility requirements. To know that there are potentially 2600 squash players in the community helps to put squash playing into perspective. Such a figure is meaningful to the non-expert such as the elected representative or the ratepayer. Further, the relative popularity of different leisure activities can be illustrated. Bearing in mind that the GHS refers only to people aged 16 and over, the sort of picture which might be presented for a typical community of 100,000 is as set out in Table 6.3.

Table 6.3 Gross demand for typical community of 100,000 adult population

Activity	No. of participants
Cycling	8,400
Golf	3,900
Riding	900
Football	4,800
Rugby	400
Cricket	1,200
Tennis	1,800
Bowls	1,700
Badminton	3,400
Squash	2,600
Swimming (indoor)	10,500
Table tennis	2,400
Keep fit/yoga	8,600
Visits to parks	7,000
Visits to museums/galleries	8,000
Visits to cinema	11,000

Source: Based on 1987 General Household Survey

Another advantage of the approach is its relative flexibility. It allows local authorities to adjust their targets according to trends. Thus if the level of participation in squash rose, according to the GHS, from 2.6 per cent in 1987 to, say, 2.9 per cent in 1995, then the number of squash players and the required number of squash courts could be expected to rise by some 10 per cent. Assessments of requirements can be constantly adjusted in the light of new information.

Despite the advantages of the gross demand approach, it is still subject to many of the limitations of the standards approach as discussed above. In particular, the tautological element remains, in that prescribed levels of provision are based on participation rates which are themselves partly dependent on current levels of provision. Because the gross demand approach uses national or regional survey data, the participation rates used are not constrained by local supply conditions, but the widespread use of the method would tend towards a very uniform level of demand and provision. The lack of guidance on spatial aspects of demand is also a limitation. Other approaches discussed below attempt to overcome these limitations.

3 Spatial approaches

The catchment area idea

A great deal of information has now been accumulated on the spatial aspects of leisure facility use. The potential of this information has, however, not generally been fully exploited in the leisure planning process. The basic fact upon which spatial approaches are built is that leisure facilities have *catchment areas* – that is, there are generally identifiable areas from which most users travel to visit a facility. The size of such catchment areas varies depending on the type of facility. Thus theatres generally have larger catchment areas than swimming pools; and, among swimming pools, larger, newer pools generally have larger catchment areas than smaller, older pools.

Catchment areas can be an important basis for planning. Figure 6.1 illustrates the catchment area idea, using two hypothetical facilities. The shaded areas are the areas from which the majority, say 75 per cent, of the users of the two facilities A and B are drawn. It can therefore be seen that the facilities serve the populations living in the shaded areas but do not serve the populations living in the unshaded areas. There is a tendency for providers of leisure facilities to believe that, once they have provided a certain type of facility, their job is done – the community is served. But information of the type presented in Figure 6.1 enables the *extent* to which the community is being served to be assessed.

The unshaded areas in Figure 6.1 therefore become areas for further investigation. Provided there are people actually living in these areas, and assuming that the policy of the authority is to make the service available to all, the findings point to the need for additional provision to serve these areas. This is couched in 'public service' terms, but could equally well be expressed in 'market' terms: an organisation wishing to maximise usage and income would also be well advised to investigate the market potential of the unshaded areas in Figure 6.1.

Figure 6.1 Hypothetical facility catchment areas

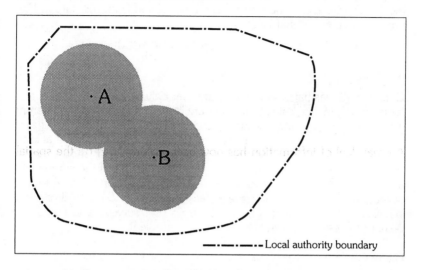

—·—·—·-Local authority boundary

Measuring catchment areas

It is possible to establish the catchment area of a facility by means of a user or visitor survey – interviewing users of existing facilities to discover where they have travelled from. Although a user survey is desirable it is not always necessary, at least for initial appraisals: it is possible to *infer* catchment areas from user surveys carried out at similar facilities elsewhere. Thus, for instance, it has been found that about 75 per cent of users of swimming pools travel from within one mile of a pool (Veal, 1979). Therefore an approximate assessment of requirements using one-mile radius circles is a possibility.

In cases where membership schemes exist, membership records can be used as the basis for estimating catchment areas: this has traditionally been done in the case of libraries, for example. The problem with membership records is that the spatial distribution of *membership* may not reflect the distribution of *regular users* – for example, people who live close to a facility may use it more frequently than people who live far away. This information would be captured in situations where records are kept of actual attendances of members rather than simply records of membership. It should also be noted that some people travel from their place of work or school to use leisure facilities rather than from their home address, so the spatial distribution of *home addresses* may not provide an accurate picture of the catchment area.

Visit rates
Ideally, the question of catchment areas should be examined in terms of *visit rates* – that is, in terms of the visits to the facilities per 1000 population per week from different areas. Figures 6.2 to 6.4 show how

such visit rates can be established in the case of swimming pools in a local authority area. The visit rates are calculated from the data in Figures 6.2 and 6.3 – that is, for each area:

Visit rate = Visits per week ÷ (Population ÷ 1000)

Social groups

Catchment areas have been discussed so far only in terms of 'people' and 'population'. In fact, catchment areas are likely to be different for different groups in the population. Thus car-owners are likely to be able to travel greater distances than non-car-owners and adults are likely to be able to travel greater distances than young children. Research has shown that in this respect the more deprived and less mobile groups of the community are less well served by facilities than the rest of the population – simply because they are not able to travel to facilities (BERG, 1978a; Hillman and Whalley, 1977). Findings of this sort from user surveys would lead the planner to designate even larger areas as 'unserved'.

Figure 6.2 Swimming pool catchment areas – visits per week (hypothetical)

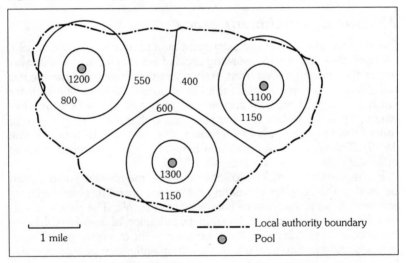

Source: User surveys

In developing policy on this basis, it is necessary not only to identify unserved areas, but also to quantify the level of unmet demand in such areas. The swimming example is used to illustrate this approach, as shown in Figure 6.5. Demand for a hypothetical new pool is estimated using an average of the visit rates for the three existing pools applied to the population in the area (Visits per week = Visit rate x Population ÷ 1000). Total visits to the hypothetical new pool are estimated at 2900 per week. It should be noted that the new pool also affects the catchment area and level of use of the existing facilities, but the effect is minimal because the hypothetical new facility impinges only on the fringes of the existing catchment areas, where visit rates are low.

Figure 6.3 Swimming pool catchment areas – population levels (hypothetical)

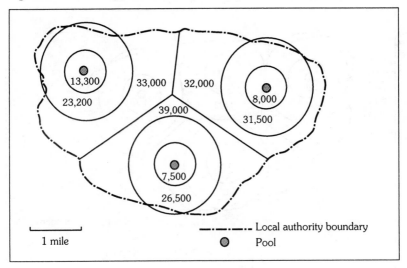

Source: Census

Figure 6.4 Swimming pools – visit rates (per 1,000 population per week)

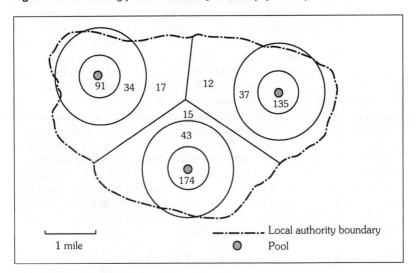

Source: Figures 6.2 and 6.3

The example in Figure 6.5 produced a 'viable' result – that is, the estimated level of demand in the unserved areas was sufficient to justify a new facility. But what if this were not the case? It is clear that, in the example in Figure 6.5, even with the new facility, there would remain areas which would still be poorly served, but chances are they would not generate enough demand to justify the provision of large facilities such as a swimming pool.

Figure 6.5 Estimating demand for a new facility (visits per week)

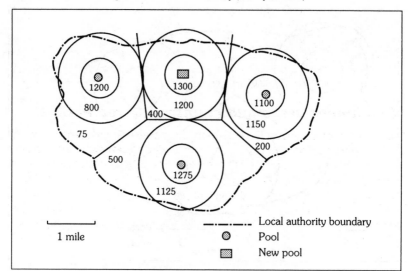

⊕	Pool	
▦	New pool	

Local authority boundary

1 mile

    The idea of 'viability' is a potentially contentious one. In a commer-
cial context it is relatively unproblematical: if there are not enough customers to support a minimum-sized facility in a particular area, then
such a facility will not be provided. Planners in companies such as Marks
and Spencer, MacDonalds Restaurants and cinema chains are fully aware
of the minimum size of population necessary to support one of their
facilities. In the public sector, however, things are not so simple: questions of equity have to be addressed. Thus, while the commercial organisation could ignore the remaining unserved areas in the example
shown in Figure 6.5, public bodies must give them some consideration.
Solutions could lie in the development of small-scale facilities which,
while they may be costly to run in relative terms (eg in subsidy per
head), may be acceptable in absolute terms (Veal, 1979a). In addition to
simply reducing the size of the facilities provided to match the scale of
local demand, the form of the provision could be changed, involving,
for example, dual use of education facilities, possibly at primary school
level (Murphy and Veal, 1979), the development of multi-purpose facilities and the provision of mobile facilities.

Catchment areas in a rural setting

So far it has been assumed that the setting for the spatial analysis is
urban, with facilities located within substantial residential areas. In rural
areas the situation is different, with 'points' of population located in
small settlements within a 'green fields' setting. Catchment areas still
apply, although rural residents generally travel further for their recreation than urban residents (because they have to!).
    Knowledge of the catchment areas of existing facilities can be just as

useful in rural settings as in urban settings, but the approach to planning and provision is different, because of problems of access. In fact, the 'hierarchies of facilities' approach discussed on pages 88–9 would be more appropriate than some of the methods described here. In addition, because of the rural tradition of community self-help, the 'community development' approach discussed on pages 103–105 would also be more appropriate.

Catchment areas and countryside recreation

In the case of countryside recreation the pattern is different again. In this case recreation sites are dotted around the countryside and the bulk of the visitors come from urban centres. If the urban centres are beyond day-trip distance the activity becomes 'tourism' rather than 'recreation'. In fact, this is one of those areas where the difference between tourism and non-tourism becomes difficult to sustain. For example, a daytripper from London to the Cotswolds would have the same *recreation* demands as someone from Wolverhampton who may be staying overnight, and is thus classified as a tourist.

In the case of countryside recreation, planning must be examined at the regional rather than the local level. Catchment area analysis, showing which parts of the countryside are utilised by residents of which urban centres, becomes vital. While the analysis could conceivably be achieved by means of a series of user surveys at recreation sites throughout the region, it is probably best done by means of a household survey throughout the region. Knowledge of spatial patterns of recreation demand can be used as the basis for planning countryside recreation provision. Population growth is not currently a common feature of British urban areas, but it is still a factor in other countries and could become so again in Britain. Catchment area analysis makes it possible to identify those areas of the countryside which would come under increased demand pressure from population growth in particular urban areas. The use of visit rates would enable the growth to be quantified.

Modelling

The descriptions of catchment areas and resultant planning approaches have been presented here in conceptual rather than highly quantified terms. However, the quantitative nature of the basic data lends itself to quantitative modelling – that is, using the catchment area data to simulate the spatial process mathematically. Thus it might be found that the visit rate could be related to distance from a facility, in the form of a 'gravity model' equation of the type:

$$V = a + bD^{-c}$$

Where V is the visit rate, D is distance travelled or travel cost, and a, b and c would be found by regression analysis. Such an exercise would use data similar to that shown in Figures 8.4 and 8.5 and Table 8.4, on page 151.

4 Hierarchies of facilities

The idea of hierarchies

The idea of hierarchies of facilities is a spatial one, but is sufficiently distinct to be discussed separately from other spatial approaches. Nevertheless, it is founded on the idea that different sizes and types of facility have different catchment areas. A further principle is also invoked, that different sizes and types of facility require different numbers of 'customers' to be viable, as discussed above, and therefore are suited to the needs of different sizes and types of community.

The GLC parks hierarchy

Perhaps the most well-known example of the hierarchy approach is that developed for parks by the then Greater London Council (GLC), in the late 1960s. Surveys conducted by the GLC had established that people travelled different distances to visit different types of park with different functions. For example, people travelled relatively short distances to small parks to exercise the dog or to use children's play facilities, whereas they tended to travel longer distances to larger parks for family picnics or formal sporting activities. The GLC planners used this information to establish a 'parks hierarchy' (see Table 6.4), which became the basis for strategic parks planning by many of the London Boroughs and by the GLC until its abolition in 1986.

Comprehensive hierarchies

Hierarchies come into their own in the comprehensive planning of new communities – an activity which has been rare in Britain in recent years, because of the lack of growth in the population. In the 1960s and 1970s, however, numerous new towns were developed, including such places as Harlow, Stevenage, Telford and Milton Keynes. It was necessary to specify the whole range of facilities required in such communities. The new towns were themselves usually developed on a hierarchical basis, with neighbourhoods at the lowest level, a cluster of neighbourhoods forming some sort of district and finally a town or city level. Services of all kinds, including leisure, were planned within this framework, with education facilities often being the key organising factor.

Three examples of such hierarchies developed for different new town situations are summarised in Table 6.5. The size and nomenclature of the various levels of community varies, as does the range of facilities prescribed. The hierarchies nevertheless offer a comprehensive picture of leisure provision and ways in which leisure facilities relate to other social and commercial provision and to the idea of 'community'. While it is recognised that 'new community building' is no longer undertaken in Britain, it is perhaps surprising that, while local councils in London were prepared to take on board and utilise a parks hierarchy as a framework for planning within existing settled areas, councils have not taken up these more comprehensive hierarchical frameworks as a basis for comprehensive planning.

Table 6.4 Greater London Council hierarchy of parks

Park type	Main function	Size (approx. minimum ha.)	Max. dist. from place of residence (miles)	Characteristics
Metropolitan	Weekend and occasional visits by car or public transport	61	2	Either (i) areas of attractive landscape (heathland, down-land, commons, woodlands, etc.), or (ii) formal parks containing both pleasant surroundings and a variety of facilities for both active and passive recreation
District	Weekend and occasional visits – mainly pedestrian	20	0.75	Open space containing both pleasant surroundings and general facilities for active recreation
Local	Short duration pedestrian visits (including from workplaces)	2	0.25	Small spaces containing facilities for court games and children's play, and old people's sitting-out areas, all set in a pleasant landscaped environment
Small local	Shorter pedestrian visits by less mobile members of the population and workers	Under 2	Below 0.25	Small gardens, sitting-out areas, children's playgrounds

Source: Greater London Council Planning Department, 1968

5 Priority social area analysis

In existing developed areas, while the hierarchy idea might provide a useful framework for an overall planning strategy, a short- to medium-term strategy might well be based on social priorities: that is, it could be decided that public leisure provision should be directed towards those areas with the greatest social or recreational need. Early experiments using this approach were conducted by the Greater London Council (Nicholls, 1975) and by the Tourism and Recreation Research Unit (TRRU) (1982) in Scotland.

The GLC study was based on a supply/need matrix. Wards across the whole GLC area were given a recreational *supply index score* and a *need index score* based on the scoring systems shown in Table 6.6. They were then grouped according to their two scores, as shown in Table 6.7. The results of this analysis were then presented in map form, as shown in Figure 6.6. The pattern shown was one of deprivation in the inner areas of London, as might be expected, but also showed a number of pockets of relative deprivation throughout the metropolitan area.

Table 6.5 Hierarchies of social facilities

'Needs of New Communities' Report	Telford Master Plan	Washington New Town Master Plan

'Others' level
 	
Facilities which might be singly located in areas of housing:
  Church
  Public house
  Meeting rooms
  Local shops
  Children's playgrounds
	'Dwelling Group' (100 people)
	Immediate contact
	Toddlers' play area
		'Group' (75–100 people)
		Community open space
		Parking
		
		'Place' (1500 people)
		Nursery school
		Community kickabout
		Minor walkways
		Vending machines
		Telephone booths
		Post boxes

'Local' level (4–5000 people) Primary school with play centre and pre-school playgroup Meeting rooms Maternity & child welfare clinic Local shops Children's playground	**'Intermediate Community Unit' (4000 people)** Equipped play areas Nursery schools, Primary schools Local shops Neighbourhood police Public house Petrol filling station	**'Village' (4500–5000 people)** Youth club Village common room Primary school School playing field Organised play area and park Inter-village walkway Shop cluster Filling station Public house
'Local Centre' Maternity & child welfare School health clinic Library Primary school Secondary school with multiple-use recreation facilities	**'Community Unit' (8000 people)** Middle school Supervised playground Small supermarket Sub-post office Community centre Mini-clinic Old persons' club Religious facilities	**'Local Centre' (18–20,000 people)** Working men's club Youth centre Community centre Secondary school Indoor sports hall Playing fields Inter-village walkway Local health centre, Shop cluster, Sub-post office, Private offices Filling station/garage/used car sales, Public house

'District Centre' (50,000 people)
New Town Corporation district office
Social services (various)
District Recreation Centre, including:
  Sports hall
  Swimming pools
  Library
  Meeting rooms
  Hall
  Catering
	'District Unit' (24–30,000 people)
	Secondary school with adult social centre
	Senior school with adult social centre
	RC Primary school
	Adventure park
	District shopping
	Health centre
	Group practice
	Old persons' home
	Youth club
		'Town' (80,000 people)
		
		Entertainment centre
		Arts centre
		Private playing fields
		Main library
		School for physically handicapped
		RC Comprehensive school
		Indoor & outdoor sports centre
		Riverside recreation parks
		Town playing fields

'District Centre' cont'd		'Town' cont'd
Extensive shopping Nursery schools Old people's homes		Golf course Town park-garden Major health centre Hospital
City-wide/regional City hall/Local government offices Main shopping centre Restaurants and clubs Theatres Cinemas Dance halls Art gallery Museum Central library Churches Sports stadium Central clinic Centre for youth organisation	**City (250,000 people)** Retailing Banks Government offices Other offices Hotels Pubs, restaurants Hairdressers, betting shops, cleaners, etc. Filling station & car sales Cinemas Halls Library, art gallery, etc. GPO sorting office Wholesaling Manufacturing	Old people's home Ambulance station Adult retraining centre Mentally handicapped training centres Town shopping centre Central post office Central fire station Town police HQ Professional services Bus station Hotel, motel Public houses County administration offices Local authority offices Crown buildings Magistrates' courts Civil defence

Source: Veal, 1975

Table 6.6 GLC Recreation Priority Areas: scoring system

Supply index		Need index
Facility	**Score**	**Factor**
Swimming pool	6	% in shared dwellings
Local sports hall	5	% living at high density
Pitches	3	% with no car
Netball court	1.5	% manual workers
Bowling green	1.5	
Tennis court – hard – grass	1.5 1	

Source: Nicholls, 1975

The prerequisites for such analyses are small-area census data, which are now readily available to all local authorities, and a spatially identified facilities inventory. Modern computer technology makes the latter also relatively easy to assemble. Such census-inventory analysis was pioneered in Scotland by TRRU in their study for Lothian Regional Council. By basing their analysis on kilometre grid squares rather than wards, they were able to measure not just facilities located within local areas but the distance to the nearest available facilities. The analysis was carried out for particular social groups – eg youth and the elderly – in relation to a range of facilities (TRRU, 1982).

Table 6.7 Grouping of wards on supply/need indices

		Score letter for supply					
	Worst	**a**	**b**	**c**	**d**	**e**	
Score letter for social need	**a**	aa	ab	ac	ad	ae	
	b	ba	bb	bc	bd	be	
		A	B	C	D	E	
	c	ca	cb	cc	cd	ce	
	d	da	db	dc	dd	de	
	e	ea	eb	ec	ed	ee	
							Best

Source: Nicholls, 1975

Recent variations on this approach are the various 'geo-demographic' analysis packages, the most well-known of which in the UK is ACORN (A Classification Of Residential Neighbourhoods). Data on the population characteristics of residential areas are subject to multi-variate analysis to produce residential area 'types'. While these tend to reflect the housing, socio-economic and demographic data upon which they are based, it is also believed that residents of the various area types will have distinctive leisure and consumption patterns – or lifestyles.

Based on analysis of some 40 census variables, covering age structure, mobility, socio-economic factors and housing, the ACORN analysis results in some eleven 'area types:

A   Areas of modern family housing for manual workers
B   Areas of modern family housing for white-collar workers
C   Areas of better terraces and mixed housing
D   Poor-quality older terraced neighbourhoods
E   Rural areas
F   Areas of urban local authority housing
G   Severely deprived tenement areas and council estates
H   Low status multi-occupied and immigrant areas
I   High status non-family areas
J   High status suburbs
K   Resort and retirement areas

Any ward or census enumeration district can be classified according to one of the above types. The commercial company which produces ACORN can provide printouts and maps for any specified geographical area. Shaw (1984) demonstrated that there is a relationship between leisure participation and the ACORN type area in which people live. Commercial and public-sector organisations can therefore use ACORN to target neighbourhoods in which their priority client groups are concentrated – whether this be for the purposes of marketing or provision of services to alleviate deprivation. The potential of ACORN has been explored in a number of studies (Bickmore *et al.*, 1980; Jenkins, *et al.*, 1989; Williams *et al.*, 1988; Nevill and Jenkins, 1986), but whether the 'lifestyle' variable is superior to more traditional variables, such as social class or life-cycle, as a basis for market and leisure analysis, has been questioned (O'Brien and Ford, 1988; Veal, 1991).

6 The Recreation Opportunity Spectrum

An idea related to the idea of hierarchies is the Recreation Opportunity Spectrum (ROS) – a framework developed in America by Clark and Stankey (1979) for classifying open space. The ROS classifies areas in which outdoor recreation might be sought along a continuum from the totally undeveloped, such as pristine wilderness ('primitive'), to the highly developed, such as a fully serviced camping site and recreation area ('modern'). Against this are set the sorts of activity which the management and other users of these areas might engage in to maintain the appropriate 'ambience' of the site and compatibility with visitor expectations. These ideas are summarised in Table 6.8.

Table 6.8 The Recreation Opportunity Spectrum

Management/on-site activities	Spectrum of settings			
	Modern	**Semi-modern**	**Semi-primitive**	**Primitive**
1 Access (roads etc.)	Easy	Moderately difficult	Difficult	Very difficult
2 Non-recreation resource uses (eg forestry)	Compatible on large scale	Depends on circumstances	Depends on circumstances	Not compatible
3 Management site modification	Very extensive	Moderately extensive	Minimal	None
4 Social interaction (contact with other users)	Frequent	Moderately frequent	Infrequent	None
5 Visitor impact	High	Moderate	Minimal	None
6 Regimentation (overt visitor control)	Strict	Moderate	Minimal	None

Sources: Clark and Stankey, 1979; Pigram, 1983: 27

While the spectrum is designed primarily as a management tool, it can also be used for planning purposes in the same way as hierarchies are used – that is, to provide guidelines for ensuring that a full range of recreational provision is available to the user. Conflicts arise when one group of users attempts to use an area for a purpose which is incompatible with the use of the space by other user groups – for example trail bike riders attempting to use an area which is being used for picnicking.

Figure 6.6 GLC priority areas
Source: Nicholls, 1975

The ROS reminds the planner and policy maker that outdoor recreation is a multi-faceted phenomenon requiring a variety of types of provision and management. While it has been developed primarily in the context of resource-based outdoor recreation, the ROS is also adaptable, in modified form, to the urban setting (Jackson, 1986).

7 The grid or matrix approach

A goal of local councils, which is often expressed but rarely very fully addressed, is the desire to meet the requirements of 'all sections of the community'. However, while councils may express such goals and may seek to provide a 'wide range of opportunities' to achieve them, it is rare that any evaluation is carried out to assess the extent to which it is being achieved. In fact, in the case of public leisure policy, this is extremely difficult, because of the wide range of groups and interests which must be served.

The grid or matrix approach to planning accepts this complexity from the beginning. It recognises that it may be impossible to serve all groups equally; indeed, the policy may be to favour certain groups, but that policy should be based on *information* about the patterns of provision among different groups. Essentially, the grid approach is a methodology for studying the current situation with regard to leisure provision in general in any community. It is a means of examining the impact of currently available facilities and services – the interaction between facilities and people.

The grid in question has two dimensions: the first refers to the range of groups comprising the community and the second refers to the range of facilities and services available to the community. The body of the grid contains an analysis of the extent to which each group is served by each facility or service. Table 6.9 shows a grid in simplified form. The development of the grid approach can be considered under three headings: the groups, the facilities/services and the analysis.

Table 6.9 Planning grid in simplified form

Facilities/ Services	Groups in the community					
	A	B	C	D	E	etc.
I	●	○	.	●	.	
II	•	•	.	●	.	
III	.	●	•	•	.	
IV	●	•	○	●	●	
etc.						

Key: ● Very well served • Well served . Poorly served ○ Not served at all

The groups

There are a number of possible criteria which could be used to define groups which make up the community and which might have distinct leisure demands. Among these are:

- age/life-cycle
- gender
- economic status/socio-economic group
- ethnicity
- degree of mobility (ie primarily: with car/without car)
- health/disability
- housing type
- geographical areas/neighbourhoods
- residents/businesses/workers

The choices of grouping for the grid would depend on council corporate policies and priorities and on data availability. One of the requirements of a fully developed grid system is information on the numbers of individuals in each group defined; in general this would come from the Census, but in some cases data would need to be gathered from other sources, for example health or social service authorities.

Facilities/Services

The range of facilities and services available for leisure, from the public, voluntary and private sectors, is enormous. Ordering information on this range of provision therefore presents a considerable challenge. While councils have, over the years, developed inventories of their own facilities, they have been slow to consider the range of facilities and services provided by the voluntary and commercial sectors. With privatisation, Compulsory Competitive Tendering and increasing emphasis on 'user pays', the sharp dividing line between public and private sectors is fading. In considering the requirements of the 'whole community', therefore, councils might be expected to make greater efforts to inventory all facilities available within their communities. The idea of examining *all* of the leisure facilities available to a particular group is at the heart of the grid approach, since it could be found that a group which is poorly serviced by the public sector is in fact being adequately served by the private sector.

Facilities and services might be classified on two or three levels. Level one would be types of provision, for example children's play, sports facilities, arts facilities. Level two would sub-divide these groups, as suggested in Table 6.10, while level three would involved named facilities. It would be possible to carry out a grid analysis at any one or all three of the levels.

Table 6.10 Facility/Service inventory for grid analysis

Level 1	Level 2	Level 3
Children's play	• Adventure playgrounds • Conventional playgrounds – supervised • Unsupervised playgrounds • Play centres	• Named facilities
Youth facilities	• Youth centres • Electronic games parlours	• Named facilities
Sports facilities	• Outdoor pitches • Outdoor courts • Bowling greens • Indoor halls • Gyms • Squash courts • Outdoor pools • Indoor pools • Ice rinks • Spectator sports • Cycle tracks	• Named facilities
Parks/Open space	• Gardens • Small parks • Major parks • Country parks	• Named facilities
Social facilities	• Community centres • Day centres • Pubs • Clubs	• Named facilities
Arts/Entertainment	• Theatres • Galleries • Museums • Arts centres • Cinemas • Exhibitions • Libraries • Disco/clubs • Restaurants	• Named facilities

Analysis

The cells of the grid should indicate the extent to which a particular item of provision serves the particular social group or area. Information for this process could come from a variety of sources, including:

- common sense (for example, children's play facilities should be serving children)
- informal observation (for example, a particular pub is known to cater for young people)
- published research (for example, national or regional surveys which indicate which social groups engage in particular activities)

- special research (for example, a survey of sports centre users which indicates the socio-economic characteristics of users and where they live)

An initial assessment can be made on the basis of incomplete local data and indicate the need for specific local research. While surveys at individual facilities would provide the most detailed information, a household survey, if it could be conducted on a large enough scale to provide acceptable samples for target social groups and areas, would be more effective in providing information across the whole range of provision.

Using a grid/matrix for planning

The gaps and inequities which arise from the grid analysis can provide the basis for developing leisure policy in an area. Table 6.11 provides an example of how the process might work. The data relate to a hypothetical local authority area with a population of 100,000. The data on total visits per week are derived from ticket sales or counts. The distribution of these visits among the demographic groups and neighbourhoods is based on site or household survey data. Row A of the table shows the total visits of the particular group to the range of facilities represented. The ratio of visits to population in row C gives a broad indicator of the level of use of services made by each group. This hypothetical example shows that the older age groups are the least well served of the age-groups, that females are less well-served than males and that neighbourhood D is the least well served geographical area. It would be possible to use separate 'sub-ratios', for example for sports or the arts, or for local authority services only. In addition, the analysis could be replicated using number of users as well as number of visits (see page 118).

8 The organic or incremental approach

The use of the organic or incremental approach can be seen as an adjunct to the grid approach. It would relate to a specific row of the grid, particularly when the concern is with spatial inequalities in provision. In that sense it also relates very much to the spatial analysis discussed earlier. The organic approach is concerned with how to justify and go about planning the development of a particular type of leisure facility.

The approach is predicated on one main principle: that the case for additional provision should be based on analysis of levels and patterns of use of existing facilities. It is therefore ideally suited to areas and facility types where a facility or facilities already exist – for example, a local authority area with two existing swimming pools looking for a means for developing future policy for swimming pool provision.

The process is summarised in Figure 6.7. Various decision-making points are numbered in the diagram, 1 to 11, while research tasks are lettered A to E. The approach consists of two decision-making processes; one related to existing facilities and the areas they serve (steps 2–7) and one related to those areas not served by existing facilities (steps 8 and 9). Both processes come together in the plan preparation and implementation stage (steps 10 and 11).

Table 6.11 Detailed grid/matrix analysis

Facilities	Visits per week	Age groups					Sex		Neighbourhoods			
		Under 15	15–24	25–39	40–59	60+	Male	Female	W	X	Y	Z
Swimming pool I	4000	2500	750	630	100	20	2600	1400	2100	1300	500	100
Swimming pool II	2500	1500	500	430	50	20	1400	1100	300	1700	300	200
Sports centre	3000	300	1500	800	350	50	2000	1000	400	500	700	1400
Tennis courts	2800	250	1200	950	350	50	1500	1300	700	950	350	800
Football pitches	2000	400	1350	200	50	0	1980	20	600	700	500	200
Library 1	5500	800	1250	1000	950	1500	2000	3500	3000	1500	750	250
Library 2	3000	650	850	750	350	400	1100	1900	500	1800	600	100
Library 3	6000	1100	850	1700	1050	1300	2500	3500	500	800	3500	1200
Community centre 1	550	50	350	75	25	50	200	350	50	50	100	350
Community centre 2	800	50	200	250	150	150	250	550	100	200	400	100
Community centre 3	1100	200	350	250	100	200	300	800	750	250	100	0
Parks	9000	1200	1950	1750	2300	1800	4400	4600	3100	2400	1700	1800
Cinema	2200	350	1100	400	200	150	1200	1000	800	500	650	250
Pubs	10,000	0	4700	2800	1450	1050	6850	3150	4100	2200	2100	1600
A Total visits	52,450	9,350	16,900	11,985	7475	6740	28,280	24,170	17,000	14,480	12,250	8350
B Population '000s	100	22	15	20	23	20	48	52	30	24	25	21
C Ratio (A/B)	525	425	1127	599	325	337	589	464	566	619	490	397

Figure 6.7 An organic or incremental approach to planning

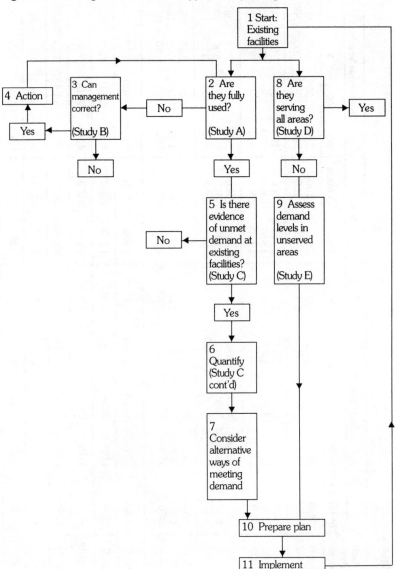

Step 1: Start: Existing facilities

The basis of the method is to begin by examining existing facilities of a particular type, for example swimming pools or community centres. In situations where there are no existing facilities, other planning methods are more appropriate.

Step 2: Use levels of existing facilities
This seems an obvious starting point in any planning, but rarely seems to be part of the formal planning process. If existing facilities are under-used then the case for additional provision will need to be considered very carefully. Conversely, evidence of heavily used – and even over-used – facilities can provide support for further provision.

Study A: Capacity and use

In order to discover whether facilities are being fully used it is necessary to determine (a) the capacity of the facilities and (b) their level of use. This is more or less demanding, depending on the type of facility. Thus, for example, in the case of a theatre, capacity is related to the number of seats and use levels are measured by the number of tickets sold: assessments of level of use are therefore routine. Similarly, in the case of squash courts the number of booking slots available and the number of those slots 'sold' is clear. In the case of a swimming pool the process is a little more difficult in that the level of use is usually carefully monitored through ticket sales, but the *capacity* of a pool is more difficult to assess because, while safety determines the number of people who are permitted in the pool at any one time, such factors as the length of sessions and use for special events can affect overall capacity considerably. At the other extreme, in the case of parks, both usage levels and capacity present problems. In all cases overall management practices, such as opening times, affect the capacity of a facility. Table 6.2 presents the results of an exercise to estimate facility capacities in general terms, but every facility is unique, so these figures can be taken only as a guide. The basis of the capacity assessments is presented in Appendix 6.1, while Appendix 6.2 provides an overview of the measures necessary to assess usage levels.

Step 3: Management correction
If it is decided that facilities are under-used, then, before considering the planning of new facilities, the question must first be asked as to whether this situation can be corrected. As a result of study B, it may be found that remedial measures can be taken (progress to step 4) or it might be decided that nothing can be done, that the situation must be 'lived with' (progress to step 8).

Study B: Management study

More detailed studies of under-used facilities will be required. Under-use may be due to poor management, poor design, poor maintenance, or wrong decisions made in the past on scale, type and location of the facility.

Step 4: Action
This step involves implementation of the measures investigated in Step 3. It would be hoped that the measures result in full use of the facilities so that, on repeating step 2, the answer is 'Yes'.

Step 5: Unmet demand

It is possible that existing facilities are over-used and not adequately serving their local areas, due to changing tastes, increasing population or changing population characteristics, because the facilities provided had been inadequate from the start, or because of the success of management in stimulating demand. Discovering the extent of any unmet demand would require a monitoring study (study C). If there is unmet demand, the process moves to step 6. If there is no unmet demand the process, as far as existing facilities is concerned, comes to an end and attention turns to step 8.

Study C: Monitoring

The managers of existing facilities are in possession of useful information on latent demand in the local community, but it is not usually systematically recorded. This is information on demand that they are *unable* to meet, which is evidenced by requests for bookings which they are unable to meet, over-use of facilities, and the results of any market research conducted within their catchment areas. A monitoring study could be instituted to ensure that, over a specified period of time, this information is recorded. Such data may then be supplemented by other survey data and 'gross demand' estimates of potential demand in the area. Quantifying the demand would be difficult, involving judgement about just how 'real' the expressed demand is.

Step 6: Quantify unmet demand

As indicated under study C, quantifying unmet demand is difficult, but must be done if provision is to be made to meet it.

Step 7: Consider alternatives

If the unmet demand is substantial, considerable additions to facilities may be contemplated on existing sites or on additional sites within the area. However, if the unmet demand is not great it might be possible to accommodate it in existing facilities by, for example, extending opening hours, changing programmes, increasing staff, adopting off-site programmes, or by minor alterations to physical plant. The conclusions of this step are then fed into the plan preparation stage, step 10.

Step 8: Areas served and unserved

This step and step 9 refer to the spatial approach to planning already discussed. Facilities have catchment areas and so the corollary is that, in most cases, there are areas which are *not* being served by the facilities provided, because they lie outside the catchment areas. It is these unserved areas which are the focus for planning in this part of the process. Of course, if study D indicates that all areas of the local authority *are* being served, then no further action is required in this part of the process.

roach

planning has been designed to eliminate t
netimes wasted research and preparatory wo
ny of the more traditional approaches to pla
pproach in British leisure planning lies in t
nment (1977) Circular containing guidelin
of Sport and Recreation on the preparatic
Strategies, which suggested that the initial r
aration process should be an *issues repor*
ontain a brief statement of principles, a bac
of sport and recreation in the region and a
initial assessment of priorities. The final stra
ies of reports on each of the issues identifie
to planning the plan emerges only after
sive examination of the field. In chapter 5 th
mprehensive' planning and decision-makin
approach is in effect another name for th
discussed there; and it is related to the Nom
ned by Ritchie (1994).
m the guidelines for Regional Recreationa
'issues' are supposed to emerge. The impli
ved in the preparation of the strategies woulc
h the problems of sport and recreation for
the key issues facing the region without the
ch. Further, they would be able to produce
uld be 'manageable' and would avoid the
ming research and data collection of other
that the Regional Councils of Sport and
of substantial committees, representative of
sport and recreation interests in a region, it
hey did indeed have little difficulty in
lists' of issues. These were reduced to more
often ten or so issues – by a process of
with the membership and amalgamation of

e Greater London and South East Regional
eation (GLSECSR, 1977) was typical in iden-
lows:

ts of way

ing
ities
rticipation in sport
sources

neral workings

Study D: Catchment area study

This study follows the approach suggested in the discussion of spatial approaches above. Membership records where available, or user surveys, are used to identify the catchment areas of existing facilities and those unserved areas outside the catchment areas. This might be done for all potential users or for separate socio-economic groups.

Step 9: Demand assessment

In order to determine what provision should be made in the unserved areas, it is necessary to assess the level of demand for the activity/facility involved in those areas. This is done by study E.

Study E: Demand assessment

As discussed in the spatial analysis section of this chapter, the catchment area studies of existing facilities provide one means of assessing likely levels of demand for facilities in currently unserved areas (see Figure 6.1 and discussion). In addition, gross demand methods could also be used.

Steps 10 and 11: Prepare plan and implement

The analysis contained in steps 1 to 9 and resulting from studies A to E, provide data and proposals for input to a plan or strategy, which might be for leisure as a whole in the community, or just for the one specific type of facility studied. Plan preparation and implementation are discussed in chapter 5.

9 The community development approach

The essence of the community development approach to planning is public involvement and planning at the neighbourhood level. Activities such as community development, *animation* and public participation are all relevant to this process, but have generally been peripheral to recreation planning and management. Community development has been developed by 'community workers' under the auspices of education authorities in Britain, and so, except for some specific experiments, has not featured greatly in the 'tool kit' of the leisure professional. The related idea of 'animation' has been developed in France and elsewhere in Europe and by the arts community in Britain, so again has not been central to the more hard-nosed management approach of the British leisure professional. Public participation has been most fully developed by the planning profession, largely because of statutory requirements, but has had some impact on leisure (Limb, 1986).

There are two main elements in these processes. The first is the concern to increase the level of public involvement in decision-making, particularly at the neighbourhood level. The second is a concern with the communal and human aspects of leisure as opposed to the facility-orientated and individual aspects. Each of these aspects is discussed below.

Public involvement and consultation is discussed in the context of plan-making in chapter 5. Direct public involvement in the planning process generally has had a chequered history since the publication of the *Skeffington Report* on public participation in 1969 (Ministry of Housing and Local Government, 1969). Public response to meetings and questionnaire surveys on broad planning policies have often been minimal. Formal public enquiries are seen as inflexible and too expensive for all but the most powerful pressure groups to become involved in. At the local level more success can be claimed: people can more readily understand and relate to problems and issues concerning their own neighbourhoods.

An early plea for more involvement of people in decision-making on leisure planning came from Gold (1973), who argued that such involvement should be routine rather than a feature of special schemes. The *Quality of Life* experiments (DoE/DES, 1977) suggested that if resources were allocated and decisions on how to use the resources were left to community groups, then useful and original schemes would emerge and could operate successfully, and public involvement was certainly a feature of the 'new culture of leisure provision' recommended in *Leisure Provision and People's Needs* (Dower et al., 1981).

The other aspect of the community development approach is more concerned with community organisation and communal leisure than with participation in the formal planning process. A number of traditions can be identified in this area, including community and social development, animation and community arts, youth work and sports and play leadership.

Community and social development and the animation and community arts movements reflect a concern with a perceived decline in 'community'. The view is that, with people no longer living and working in the same geographical area, with increased mobility and the advent of television, there has been a decline in the more collective forms of leisure. Privatisation of leisure has led to a sharp reduction in social interaction and mutual support at the neighbourhood level, leading to loneliness for some and alienation for others. Community development workers and *animateurs* therefore attempt to reverse this 'collapse of community' by encouraging and supporting community groups of all kinds, from tenants' associations to children's play groups, old people's bingo clubs and soccer teams. Some would see these activities as ends in themselves, while others take a more political view – that communities need to learn to act collectively in the political arena in order to improve their living conditions generally, or even to bring about fundamental change in society.

The French words *animateur* and *animation* are more closely associated with arts-based community initiatives which take the form of the 'community arts movement' in Britain (see Kingsbury, 1976; Simpson, 1976; Kelly, 1984) and elsewhere (Hawkins, 1993). As Baldry put it:

Communi
by their a
Their prin
to it: by as
of their si
facilities t
deepen th
enrich its
whether
1976: 2.

Thus, up ar
in the 197(
aided by th
the area of
with painti
with suspic
perceived
and someti
1984). Fur
the 1980s

Mention
ers: youth
clubs and
priate skills
not so muc
and workir
leader has
munity dev
young peo
sport (Glyr

Do thes
ment have
are more
the longer
would, hov
process. Ir
out plans
may requi
having pec
tified and
provided t
given expr

10 The issues app

The *issues* approach to
lengthy, expensive and so
which is necessary for ma
ning. The origin of the a
Department of the Envirc
for the Regional Councils
of Regional Recreational
port in the strategy prep
The issues report would c
ground review of the state
identification of issues and
egy was envisaged as a se
In traditional approaches
thorough and comprehen
alternatives to 'rational–c
were discussed: the issue
'mixed scanning' approac
nal Group Technique outl

What was not clear fr
Strategies was just how th
cation was that those invo
be sufficiently familiar wi
them to be able to identify
need for extensive resear
a list of issues which wc
expensive and time-consu
planning exercises. Giver
Recreation are composed
all local government and
is not surprising that
producing initial 'shoppin
manageable dimensions
discussion and consultatio
similar groups of issues.

The *Issues Report* of t
Council for Sport and Rec
tifying eleven issues, as fo

- Marinas and moorings
- Walking, riding and rig
- Recreational cycling
- Camping and caravann
- Community sports faci
- Encouraging greater pa
- Making better use of re
- Canals and minor river
- The after use of wet m

- Raising standards of performance
- Recreation in the inner city

Such a list illustrates the main problem with the approach, namely that, because of the quasi-democratic way in which they are identified, there is a tendency for the issues to cover more or less all the areas of responsibility of the organisation, rather than identifying priorities. Wide consultation increases this tendency, since all interested parties wish to see their particular pressing issue included in the list.

The final strategy report of the GLSECSR, without explaining how, in fact reduced the main issues to four:

- Greater participation
- Recreation in the inner city
- Making better use of resources
- Community sports facilities

The approach is not confined to British regional recreation planning. The United States' *Third Nationwide Outdoor Recreation Strategy* (Heritage, Conservation and Recreation Service, 1979) started with a consultation process in which over 5000 organisations were approached. Some 3000 organisations and individuals responded, identifying between them over 1000 separate recreation issues. The report indicated that these 1000 issues were classified into 30 groups and reduced to 21 issues of 'national significance', through discussion, analysis by Departmental staff and consultation and meetings with interested organisations. However, it did not state what the original 1000 issues were, what the 30 groups were, what the 21 issues selected were, nor what were the criteria for selecting them. The 21 were submitted to the Secretary of the Interior who selected 16 'priority issues' – but again how or why was not reported. The 16 issues identified were:

- Appropriate roles of government and profit and non-profit organisations
- Federal land acquisition programme
- Methods to protect significant open space and recreation resources
- Methods to protect coastal resources
- Evaluation of National Wild and Scenic Rivers, and National Trails Systems
- Federal water programmes and recreation
- Recreation needs of special populations
- Contribution of recreation to physical and mental health
- Federal role in urban recreation
- Federal agency research
- Outdoor recreation and energy conservation and environmental education

As with 'mixed scanning', the danger with the issues approach is that key issues will be overlooked and that issues will be identified on the basis of the lobbying skills of various interest groups or the 'flavour of the month' rather than by any objective evaluation. Against this, however, must be posed the various defects of rational–comprehensive planning, as discussed in chapter 5.

Conclusion

This review of ten alternative planning approaches is intended to offer the leisure planner a range of tools commensurate with the diversity of the phenomenon of leisure and of the various organisations responsible for planning for it. Two issues should be addressed before leaving this topic: firstly the question of goals and objectives and secondly the question of feasibility.

Goals and objectives

In chapter 5 it was seen that the mission and goals of an organisation are the starting point for all planning activity and that, as a result of policies, projects and programmes adopted, the strategic management process results in a set of more detailed objectives which the various parts of the organisation seek to achieve. Table 6.12 summarises the goals which are implicit or explicit in the planning techniques discussed in this chapter. These and the goals discussed in chapter 5 are taken up again in chapter 9, which deals with performance evaluation.

Table 6.12 Planning approaches and goals/objectives

Approach	Goal/Objective
Standards	Meet standards (various)
Gross demand	Raise demand at least to the average Maximise participation
Spatial analysis	Serve all areas
Hierarchies	Ensure full range of facilities at all community levels
Priority Area Analysis	Meet needs of target groups in specified areas
Recreation Opportunity Spectrum	Provide full range of experiences
Grid/matrix	Appropriate provision for all groups and areas
Organic	Maximise utilisation of facilities Provide service to all areas
Community development	Meet community/group wishes
Issues	Meet concerns of community groups/professionals/politicians

Feasibility

The greatest difficulty in implementing any of the planning approaches discussed in this chapter is not their intrinsic complexity but the availability of resources. The question of resources for planning for leisure is a fraught one. As suggested at the beginning of the chapter, the leisure profession itself is management-orientated rather than planning-orientated: leisure professionals are 'action' people! They have also learned, over the years, to be opportunistic – to exploit the fact that the whim of a powerful politician can achieve more in a few months than the most carefully researched plans and strategies, which may have been gathering dust on shelves for years. However, every anecdote of such whims producing positive outcomes can be matched by stories of disasters, of 'white elephants', wasted resources and real needs neglected.

The ideal approach is surely a combination of research-based planning and opportunism – what might be called 'informed opportunism'. This means that, when a politician has a 'whim', a pressure group arises, or a disaster, crisis or other media event focuses the public's attention, the professionals are ready with information and ideas rather than 'off the top of the head' solutions. This may appear to be 'Yes Minister' style manipulation but in fact it is not. The role of the professional in the public service *is* to offer professional expertise in the decision-making processes. Such expertise must be based on sound information and analysis.

Further reading

For general approaches to planning, see the Further Reading list in chapter 5.

See also, Kelsey and Gray, 1985; Gratton and Taylor, 1988; Hillman and Whalley, 1977; Lieber and Fesenmaier, 1983; Ravenscroft, 1992; Howard and Crompton, 1980; Torkildsen, 1986.

The Recreation Opportunity Spectrum: Clarke and Stankey, 1979.

Spatial methods: Coppock and Duffield, 1975.

Modelling: Burton, 1971: 307–44; Field and MacGregor, 1987; Smith, 1989.

Appendix 6.1: Estimation of facility capacities

The estimates in this appendix are not meant to be definitive, but indicative. They are intended to illustrate an approach. Capacities may vary from community to community, depending on local conditions, including the design of facilities and management practices.

Grass playing pitches

It is assumed that one match or practice session involves 30 participants – players, referees, coaches, reserves, etc. It is assumed that a pitch accommodates four practice sessions (typically during the week) and four matches (typically at the weekend) per week.

8 sessions **x** 30 participants = 240

In winter time weekday evening practice is not possible without floodlights. However, it is assumed that such pitches are used for lunchtime practice and for schools. During daylight-saving periods non-floodlit pitches can be fully used by non-school users. It is assumed therefore that, on average, the non-school use of pitches without floodlights is 200 participants per week.

Average the floodlit and non-floodlit pitches gives 220 users per week.

Hard courts, outdoor

Tennis

A court can be used for singles or doubles. Assuming one-hour bookings and an equal number of singles and doubles bookings, it can be assumed that a court will accommodate three users per hour on average. In summer a court is useable for some 80 hours a week, but 100 per cent bookings would be most unusual, because of weather factors, 'unpopular' hours, etc. Assuming 60 per cent usage, gives a capacity of 144, say 150, users per week. In winter a floodlit court would have a similar capacity, but a non-floodlit court would have a capacity of 100 users per week, giving an annual average of 125. Averaging floodlit and non-floodlit courts gives about 140 users per week per court.

Netball/Basketball

One match can be assumed to involve 16 participants, referees, coaches and reserves. Courts are available for the same number of hours as tennis courts, but because of the team nature of the sports, usage by non-school groups is likely to be similar to that of grass pitches – that is, a certain number of evening practice sessions and weekend games. Assuming nine two-hour sessions per week, this gives 144 users per week, which is similar to that for tennis.

Study D: Catchment area study

This study follows the approach suggested in the discussion of spatial approaches above. Membership records where available, or user surveys, are used to identify the catchment areas of existing facilities and those unserved areas outside the catchment areas. This might be done for all potential users or for separate socio-economic groups.

Step 9: Demand assessment

In order to determine what provision should be made in the unserved areas, it is necessary to assess the level of demand for the activity/ facility involved in those areas. This is done by study E.

Study E: Demand assessment

As discussed in the spatial analysis section of this chapter, the catchment area studies of existing facilities provide one means of assessing likely levels of demand for facilities in currently unserved areas (see Figure 6.1 and discussion). In addition, gross demand methods could also be used.

Steps 10 and 11: Prepare plan and implement

The analysis contained in steps 1 to 9 and resulting from studies A to E, provide data and proposals for input to a plan or strategy, which might be for leisure as a whole in the community, or just for the one specific type of facility studied. Plan preparation and implementation are discussed in chapter 5.

9 The community development approach

The essence of the community development approach to planning is public involvement and planning at the neighbourhood level. Activities such as community development, *animation* and public participation are all relevant to this process, but have generally been peripheral to recreation planning and management. Community development has been developed by 'community workers' under the auspices of education authorities in Britain, and so, except for some specific experiments, has not featured greatly in the 'tool kit' of the leisure professional. The related idea of 'animation' has been developed in France and elsewhere in Europe and by the arts community in Britain, so again has not been central to the more hard-nosed management approach of the British leisure professional. Public participation has been most fully developed by the planning profession, largely because of statutory requirements, but has had some impact on leisure (Limb, 1986).

There are two main elements in these processes. The first is the concern to increase the level of public involvement in decision-making, particularly at the neighbourhood level. The second is a concern with the communal and human aspects of leisure as opposed to the facility-orientated and individual aspects. Each of these aspects is discussed below.

Public involvement and consultation is discussed in the context of plan-making in chapter 5. Direct public involvement in the planning process generally has had a chequered history since the publication of the *Skeffington Report* on public participation in 1969 (Ministry of Housing and Local Government, 1969). Public response to meetings and questionnaire surveys on broad planning policies have often been minimal. Formal public enquiries are seen as inflexible and too expensive for all but the most powerful pressure groups to become involved in. At the local level more success can be claimed: people can more readily understand and relate to problems and issues concerning their own neighbourhoods.

An early plea for more involvement of people in decision-making on leisure planning came from Gold (1973), who argued that such involvement should be routine rather than a feature of special schemes. The *Quality of Life* experiments (DoE/DES, 1977) suggested that if resources were allocated and decisions on how to use the resources were left to community groups, then useful and original schemes would emerge and could operate successfully, and public involvement was certainly a feature of the 'new culture of leisure provision' recommended in *Leisure Provision and People's Needs* (Dower et al., 1981).

The other aspect of the community development approach is more concerned with community organisation and communal leisure than with participation in the formal planning process. A number of traditions can be identified in this area, including community and social development, animation and community arts, youth work and sports and play leadership.

Community and social development and the animation and community arts movements reflect a concern with a perceived decline in 'community'. The view is that, with people no longer living and working in the same geographical area, with increased mobility and the advent of television, there has been a decline in the more collective forms of leisure. Privatisation of leisure has led to a sharp reduction in social interaction and mutual support at the neighbourhood level, leading to loneliness for some and alienation for others. Community development workers and *animateurs* therefore attempt to reverse this 'collapse of community' by encouraging and supporting community groups of all kinds, from tenants' associations to children's play groups, old people's bingo clubs and soccer teams. Some would see these activities as ends in themselves, while others take a more political view – that communities need to learn to act collectively in the political arena in order to improve their living conditions generally, or even to bring about fundamental change in society.

The French words *animateur* and *animation* are more closely associated with arts-based community initiatives which take the form of the 'community arts movement' in Britain (see Kingsbury, 1976; Simpson, 1976; Kelly, 1984) and elsewhere (Hawkins, 1993). As Baldry put it:

Community artists are distinguishable not by the techniques they use ... but by their attitude towards the place of their activities in the life of society. Their primary concern is their impact on a community and their relationship to it: by assisting those with whom they make contact to become more aware of their situation and of their creative powers, and providing them with the facilities they need to make use of their abilities, they hope to widen and deepen the sensitivities of the community in which they work and so to enrich its existence. To a varying degree they see this as a means of change, whether psychological, social or political, within the community. (Baldry, 1976: 2.2)

Thus, up and down the country, numerous groups and individuals arose in the 1970s, some based in arts centres, some peripatetic, some grant-aided by the Arts Council, some by local authorities. Some worked in the area of drama, others, such as 'artists-in-residence' (Braden, 1979), with painting, sculpture or literature. Such activity was often viewed with suspicion by traditional authorities, sometimes because of their perceived political motivation, sometimes their controversial activities and sometimes their ability to 'cause trouble' in the community (Kelly, 1984). Funding for such activities has been substantially eroded during the 1980s and 1990s.

Mention should also be made of more established community work-ers: youth workers and leaders and play leaders. It is accepted that youth clubs and play centres need to be staffed with professionals with appro-priate skills for working with their respective clients. Their emphasis is not so much on planning or managing facilities, but more on relating to and working directly with their client groups. More recently the sports leader has emerged, with a combination of sports coaching and com-munity development skills, whose job is to be a catalyst in engaging young people in particular, and often groups of unemployed people, in sport (Glyptis, 1983).

Do these various forms of community worker and community involve-ment have a place in planning for leisure? It might be argued that they are more part of the day-to-day management of leisure resources than the longer-term planning process. A comprehensive view of planning would, however, see a need for these skills and concerns in the planning process. In seeking to provide for leisure, it is not always possible to set out plans in the conventional sense. Neighbourhoods vary, and each may require different solutions to their problems: it may be only by having people working at the grass roots that these needs can be iden-tified and communicated. Even when a network of facilities has been provided there may be unmet needs: those needs may be identified, given expression or even met through a catalyst, *animateur* or leader.

10 The issues approach

The *issues* approach to planning has been designed to eliminate the lengthy, expensive and sometimes wasted research and preparatory work which is necessary for many of the more traditional approaches to planning. The origin of the approach in British leisure planning lies in the Department of the Environment (1977) Circular containing guidelines for the Regional Councils of Sport and Recreation on the preparation of Regional Recreational Strategies, which suggested that the initial report in the strategy preparation process should be an *issues report*. The issues report would contain a brief statement of principles, a background review of the state of sport and recreation in the region and an identification of issues and initial assessment of priorities. The final strategy was envisaged as a series of reports on each of the issues identified. In traditional approaches to planning the plan emerges only after a thorough and comprehensive examination of the field. In chapter 5 the alternatives to 'rational–comprehensive' planning and decision-making were discussed: the issues approach is in effect another name for the 'mixed scanning' approach discussed there; and it is related to the Nominal Group Technique outlined by Ritchie (1994).

What was not clear from the guidelines for Regional Recreational Strategies was just how the 'issues' are supposed to emerge. The implication was that those involved in the preparation of the strategies would be sufficiently familiar with the problems of sport and recreation for them to be able to identify the key issues facing the region without the need for extensive research. Further, they would be able to produce a list of issues which would be 'manageable' and would avoid the expensive and time-consuming research and data collection of other planning exercises. Given that the Regional Councils of Sport and Recreation are composed of substantial committees, representative of all local government and sport and recreation interests in a region, it is not surprising that they did indeed have little difficulty in producing initial 'shopping lists' of issues. These were reduced to more manageable dimensions – often ten or so issues – by a process of discussion and consultation with the membership and amalgamation of similar groups of issues.

The *Issues Report* of the Greater London and South East Regional Council for Sport and Recreation (GLSECSR, 1977) was typical in identifying eleven issues, as follows:

- Marinas and moorings
- Walking, riding and rights of way
- Recreational cycling
- Camping and caravanning
- Community sports facilities
- Encouraging greater participation in sport
- Making better use of resources
- Canals and minor rivers
- The after use of wet mineral workings

- Raising standards of performance
- Recreation in the inner city

Such a list illustrates the main problem with the approach, namely that, because of the quasi-democratic way in which they are identified, there is a tendency for the issues to cover more or less all the areas of responsibility of the organisation, rather than identifying priorities. Wide consultation increases this tendency, since all interested parties wish to see their particular pressing issue included in the list.

The final strategy report of the GLSECSR, without explaining how, in fact reduced the main issues to four:

- Greater participation
- Recreation in the inner city
- Making better use of resources
- Community sports facilities

The approach is not confined to British regional recreation planning. The United States' *Third Nationwide Outdoor Recreation Strategy* (Heritage, Conservation and Recreation Service, 1979) started with a consultation process in which over 5000 organisations were approached. Some 3000 organisations and individuals responded, identifying between them over 1000 separate recreation issues. The report indicated that these 1000 issues were classified into 30 groups and reduced to 21 issues of 'national significance', through discussion, analysis by Departmental staff and consultation and meetings with interested organisations. However, it did not state what the original 1000 issues were, what the 30 groups were, what the 21 issues selected were, nor what were the criteria for selecting them. The 21 were submitted to the Secretary of the Interior who selected 16 'priority issues' – but again how or why was not reported. The 16 issues identified were:

- Appropriate roles of government and profit and non-profit organisations
- Federal land acquisition programme
- Methods to protect significant open space and recreation resources
- Methods to protect coastal resources
- Evaluation of National Wild and Scenic Rivers, and National Trails Systems
- Federal water programmes and recreation
- Recreation needs of special populations
- Contribution of recreation to physical and mental health
- Federal role in urban recreation
- Federal agency research
- Outdoor recreation and energy conservation and environmental education

As with 'mixed scanning', the danger with the issues approach is that key issues will be overlooked and that issues will be identified on the basis of the lobbying skills of various interest groups or the 'flavour of the month' rather than by any objective evaluation. Against this, however, must be posed the various defects of rational–comprehensive planning, as discussed in chapter 5.

Conclusion

This review of ten alternative planning approaches is intended to offer the leisure planner a range of tools commensurate with the diversity of the phenomenon of leisure and of the various organisations responsible for planning for it. Two issues should be addressed before leaving this topic: firstly the question of goals and objectives and secondly the question of feasibility.

Goals and objectives

In chapter 5 it was seen that the mission and goals of an organisation are the starting point for all planning activity and that, as a result of policies, projects and programmes adopted, the strategic management process results in a set of more detailed objectives which the various parts of the organisation seek to achieve. Table 6.12 summarises the goals which are implicit or explicit in the planning techniques discussed in this chapter. These and the goals discussed in chapter 5 are taken up again in chapter 9, which deals with performance evaluation.

Table 6.12 Planning approaches and goals/objectives

Approach	Goal/Objective
Standards	Meet standards (various)
Gross demand	Raise demand at least to the average Maximise participation
Spatial analysis	Serve all areas
Hierarchies	Ensure full range of facilities at all community levels
Priority Area Analysis	Meet needs of target groups in specified areas
Recreation Opportunity Spectrum	Provide full range of experiences
Grid/matrix	Appropriate provision for all groups and areas
Organic	Maximise utilisation of facilities Provide service to all areas
Community development	Meet community/group wishes
Issues	Meet concerns of community groups/professionals/politicians

Feasibility

The greatest difficulty in implementing any of the planning approaches discussed in this chapter is not their intrinsic complexity but the avail-ability of resources. The question of resources for planning for leisure is a fraught one. As suggested at the beginning of the chapter, the leisure profession itself is management-orientated rather than planning-orien-tated: leisure professionals are 'action' people! They have also learned, over the years, to be opportunistic – to exploit the fact that the whim of a powerful politician can achieve more in a few months than the most carefully researched plans and strategies, which may have been gather-ing dust on shelves for years. However, every anecdote of such whims producing positive outcomes can be matched by stories of disasters, of 'white elephants', wasted resources and real needs neglected.

The ideal approach is surely a combination of research-based plan-ning and opportunism – what might be called 'informed opportunism'. This means that, when a politician has a 'whim', a pressure group arises, or a disaster, crisis or other media event focuses the public's attention, the professionals are ready with information and ideas rather than 'off the top of the head' solutions. This may appear to be 'Yes Minister' style manipulation but in fact it is not. The role of the professional in the public service *is* to offer professional expertise in the decision-making processes. Such expertise must be based on sound information and analysis.

Further reading

For general approaches to planning, see the Further Reading list in chapter 5.

See also, Kelsey and Gray, 1985; Gratton and Taylor, 1988; Hillman and Whalley, 1977; Lieber and Fesenmaier, 1983; Ravenscroft, 1992; Howard and Crompton, 1980; Torkildsen, 1986.

The Recreation Opportunity Spectrum: Clarke and Stankey, 1979.

Spatial methods: Coppock and Duffield, 1975.

Modelling: Burton, 1971: 307–44; Field and MacGregor, 1987; Smith, 1989.

Appendix 6.1: Estimation of facility capacities

The estimates in this appendix are not meant to be definitive, but indicative. They are intended to illustrate an approach. Capacities may
vary from community to community, depending on local conditions,
including the design of facilities and management practices.

Grass playing pitches

It is assumed that one match or practice session involves 30 participants – players, referees, coaches, reserves, etc. It is assumed that a
pitch accommodates four practice sessions (typically during the week)
and four matches (typically at the weekend) per week.

   8 sessions x 30 participants = 240

In winter time weekday evening practice is not possible without floodlights. However, it is assumed that such pitches are used for lunchtime
practice and for schools. During daylight-saving periods non-floodlit
pitches can be fully used by non-school users. It is assumed therefore
that, on average, the non-school use of pitches without floodlights is
200 participants per week.

Average the floodlit and non-floodlit pitches gives 220 users per week.

Hard courts, outdoor

Tennis

A court can be used for singles or doubles. Assuming one-hour bookings and an equal number of singles and doubles bookings, it can be
assumed that a court will accommodate three users per hour on average. In summer a court is useable for some 80 hours a week, but 100
per cent bookings would be most unusual, because of weather factors,
'unpopular' hours, etc. Assuming 60 per cent usage, gives a capacity of
144, say 150, users per week. In winter a floodlit court would have a
similar capacity, but a non-floodlit court would have a capacity of 100
users per week, giving an annual average of 125. Averaging floodlit and
non-floodlit courts gives about 140 users per week per court.

Netball/Basketball

One match can be assumed to involve 16 participants, referees, coaches
and reserves. Courts are available for the same number of hours as
tennis courts, but because of the team nature of the sports, usage by
non-school groups is likely to be similar to that of grass pitches – that is,
a certain number of evening practice sessions and weekend games.
Assuming nine two-hour sessions per week, this gives 144 users per
week, which is similar to that for tennis.

Squash courts

Squash courts are typically available for up to 90 hours per week. It would be very rare to achieve 100 per cent usage, but 70 per cent usage would involve some 250 individual users per week, assuming 30-minute bookings.

Sports hall

A 'two-court' hall can accommodate two tennis, basketball/netball or indoor soccer courts or eight badminton courts. It can also be used for activities such as aerobics. Assuming opening hours of 90 per week, 100 per cent usage for badminton with half singles and half doubles would provide for 2160 players with one-hour bookings. In fact, a hall would not be programmed entirely for badminton and would be unlikely to achieve 100 per cent usage. Some of the time a hall would be un-used; some of the time it would be used by 32 people an hour (all badminton, doubles); some of the time it might be used by 150 people an hour (aerobics), some of the time by only 20 per hour (basketball/netball, two-hour booking). Careful management and marketing, including sessions for the elderly or for 'mothers and babies', during the day-time, should be able to achieve 2000 users a week. However, this might only be achievable with school bookings. Non-school capacity could therefore be put at, say, 1500 per week.

Community halls and scout halls may be capable of accommodating some of the sporting activity indicated. Such halls are likely to be of 'one-court' size at most. Such halls are generally not managed for maximum opening hours, are sometimes available only to certain groups, and are less flexible in use. The capacity of a one-court hall is therefore likely to be less than half of that of a two–court hall. For the purposes of this exercise it is therefore assumed that such halls accommodate 350 visits per week.

Weights room

The capacity of a weights/exercise room will of course depend on its size and the amount of equipment. Such a room would be open for some 90 hours per week. Supposing a typical room has a maximum capacity of ten but a typical use-level of five people and 70 per cent capacity is achieved, using one-hour bookings, gives a capacity of 330 per week.

Golf course (18-hole)

Assuming a course is open for seven days a week, eight hours a day on average (up to 12 in summer, down to six in winter), and assuming one person can tee off every four minutes, gives 120 rounds a day – say 800 per week.

Bowling green

Assuming three sessions a day on six days a week, during the season, with 15 participants in each session, gives a total of 270 visits per week.

Athletics track

Bearing in mind that we are dealing with public use only, and any purpose-built track would probably be used during school time by schools, public use might be for, say, 30 hours a week (summer and winter average). Assuming 25 people using the facility for 90-minute sessions, gives 500 visits per week.

Informal open space

The idea of capacity for informal open space is almost a contradiction in terms, since there is almost no limit to the amount of open space which the individual can enjoy. Nevertheless, it is possible to argue that for certain types of open space experience people expect to look outside their immediate urban area – to state and national parks and the coast.

Within walking distance of their homes people might expect to find areas for day-to-day walking and informal outdoor games and not too far away they might expect to find 'district' level open space for such walking and perhaps for picnicking and public events. A reasonable approach would seem to be to take a well-used park and examine its use levels. The figure in Table 6.2 is based on the use of a large park in Sydney, Australia.

Theatre (400 seat)

Assuming six evening performances and one matinee with two-thirds of seats sold, gives a realistic capacity of almost 2000 visits per week.

Appendix 6.2: Measuring levels of use

The aim here is not to devise total management appraisal systems, but merely to consider the question of use as against capacity.

Grass playing pitches

Where formal bookings are required these can be used as a guide, but if clubs are given season-long bookings for a very low fee, there may be no incentive to use the pitch fully, so sample observations of actual use levels may be advisable. In any case, a club booking is not necessarily a good guide to *numbers* of users. Some clubs may pack more activity – and more users – into a booking period than others. In addition, pitches located in parks may attract informal use, which can only be ascertained by observation. Sample spot counts of use over a period of time may therefore be necessary (see Veal, 1992: ch.7).

Measures might be:

- number of booking as a percentage of the maximum possible number of bookings
- absolute number of bookings (differentiates between well-drained and floodlit facilities which have a higher capacity than others)
- number of users per annum as percentage of the theoretical maximum (see Appendix 6.1)
- absolute number of users per annum

Hard courts, outdoors

The same considerations apply as for grass pitches, although informal use may be less of an issue. While tennis courts are used less by clubs, there is still a need for sample counts to discover the average number of players per booking. Measures are as for grass pitches.

Squash courts

Measures:

- bookings as a per cent of slots available
- number of bookings per week

Sports hall

The question arises here as to whether to use bookings or use levels or both. The variety of activities possible in a hall presents problems. It is assumed that full data is available to compile any chosen measure, but in some situations, organisational bookings may mean that management does not have a record of numbers attending; this would need to be overcome by sample counts.

Measures:
- bookings as a percentage of booking slots available
- absolute number of bookings per annum
- users per square metre of space per annum
- absolute number of users
- number of different activities catered for

Weights room

Measures
- number of visits per annum per square metre
- number of visits per major piece of equipment
- absolute number of visits per annum

Golf course

Since golf courses are such a 'standard' facility, the number of rounds per annum is an adequate measure. 18-hole and 9-hole courses would need to be considered separately.

Bowling green

Same considerations as for grass pitches.

Athletics track

Same considerations as for grass pitches.

Informal open space

As the discussion of capacity indicates, this is much more difficult than the more formal facilities. Assessment of use levels on the basis of counts is now a well-established technique. The problem arises in evaluating the results. When is a park 'under-used' as opposed to offering a quiet uncrowded experience? When is a park 'over-used and crowded' as opposed to offering a lively, vibrant recreational experience for users? While quantitative information is useful, it is clear that, in this case, a great deal of qualitative judgement is needed to decide whether provision in an area is adequate or not.

Theatre

Data are readily available from ticket sales.

7 ESTIMATING AND FORECASTING LEISURE DEMAND

Introduction

It is argued in chapter 5 that planning for leisure should be on the basis of demand. This chapter focuses on demand – estimating its current nature and dimensions and predicting its future nature and dimensions. The term leisure *demand* is used in the economist's sense – that is, the amount of a service people consume or are predicted to consume at a given level of supply and price. As far as leisure services are concerned, therefore, demand is equated with participation. In the private sector this would be equivalent to sales. In fact, there is a range of measures which are used in leisure demand analysis. They are as set out in Table 7.1.

There has been considerable discussion in the literature over the appropriateness of participation levels as a measure of demand. Burton, for example, classifies demand into:

- *Existing demand* (as above)
- *Latent demand* – demand frustrated by lack of facilities
- *Induced or generated demand* – demand which only materialises when facilities are provided (eg the person who never considered playing squash until the leisure centre was built in their neighbourhood)
- *Diverted demand* – demand transferred from an old facility to a new one
- *Substitute demand* – demand transferred from one *activity* to another as a result of a new facility or service becoming available

(1971: 26; see also Gratton and Taylor, 1985: 99–100)

It is considered necessary to consider these various types of unmet or contingent demand because, for most people, what they would like by way of leisure goods and services is severely constrained by, among other things, money and the availability of, or access to, facilities. So what people *actually* do (expressed need/demand) is not necessarily what they would *really* like to do if some of these constraints were

Table 7.1 Measuring leisure demand

Measure	Definition	Example
A Participation rate	The proportion of a defined population which engages in an activity in a given period of time	6 per cent of the adult population of community X go swimming at least once a week
B Number of participants	Number of people in a defined community who engage in an activity in a given period of time (A × population or C ÷ frequency of visit)	20,000 people in community X swim at least once a week
C Volume of activity (visits)	The number of visits made or games played by members of a defined community or visits to a defined geographical area in a specified time period (B × visits/games per time period)[1]	There are 1.2 million visits to swimming pools in community X (1 million by residents) in a year
D Time	The amount of leisure time available to the individual in a defined community, over a specified time period – or time spent on specific activity (C × time per visit)[2]	The average retired person has 5 hours leisure time per day/ spends an average of 3 hours watching television per day
E Expenditure	The amount of money spent per individual or by a defined community on leisure goods or services over a specified time period (C × spend per visit)	Consumer expenditure on leisure in Britain is over £50 billion a year

Notes: [1]In tourism a further distinction is made between 'trips' (eg a complete holiday) and visits (ie places visited during the holiday). [2]In tourism the measure 'bed-nights' is often used.

removed. In particular, if prices for some activities were reduced, or transport access were improved, or there was more capacity at peak periods, demand (participation) would probably be higher than is currently observed. So, a statement such as 'the demand for cinema visits in this community is 50,000 visits a year', should really be qualified to say: 'given current prices and availability of cinemas, demand for cinema visits in this community is 50,000 visits a year'. This is true of any good or service in the economist's sense: the classic economist's demand curve shows a particular level of 'equilibrium' consumption/demand at the point where the demand and supply curve intersect (see Figure 7.1). The demand curve extends to the right of this point, indicating that, if prices were lower, people would buy more.

Figure 7.1 Demand and supply

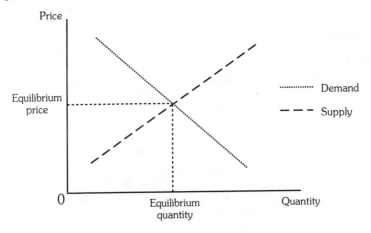

In this classic economic model, latent, induced, diverted and substituted demand are not ignored – they all come into play when a shift occurs in the demand or supply curve. Thus 'existing' demand increases if the supply curve moves downwards (there is an overall reduction in prices) or if it moves to the right (there is an increase in supply). Since a demand/supply curve for a particular leisure activity is only one of many which the consumer faces, for the many products and services available (it is one element in the economist's 'general equilibrium system'), diversion and substitution are built into the system (eg in the form of the economist's 'cross-elasticities').

As shown in using the Clawson method in chapter 8 and in relation to various spatial planning techniques in chapter 6, planning is very much about estimating the extent to which these various forms of *unmet* demand are transformed into *actual* demand in various supply scenarios.

Estimating current demand

This discussion of the complexity of the demand concept illustrates why it is necessary to consider approaches to estimating *current* demand as well as future demand. Some approaches to this issue have already been examined in chapter 6. It was noted there that public bodies such as local authorities are often not aware of the scale of demand with which they are dealing because of absence of data. The 'gross demand' approach is suggested as a means of estimating demand levels for various activities in a community, using secondary data sources. Direct community surveys could also be used.

Even when data are available they are often misinterpreted – for example, a community with a population of, say, 100,000 could have a swimming pool which attracts, perhaps, 200,000 visits a year and, because the number of visits is twice the level of the population, the impression is given that the community is being well served by the provision of the swimming pool. But if *every* member of the community visits the pool equally, this represents only two visits per person per annum – hardly a very impressive figure. In practice, most users of swimming pools are fairly regular users, the average user visiting probably once a week. Allowing for holidays, illnesses, etc., if it is assumed that the average user visits 40 times a year, then 200,000 visits are made by only about 5000 people – that is, only 5 per cent of the population. This means that 95 per cent of the population are *not* using the pool – again, a less than impressive statistic. Numbers of admissions or visits are therefore not an adequate measure of demand upon which to base policy: information is required on frequency of visit to establish the actual number – and proportion – of the community involved.

Thus, as suggested for the 'grid approach' in chapter 6, a community survey to establish how many people are using what services and how many are not (and their socio-economic characteristics), would seem to be an obvious starting point for any public organisation wishing to understand demand in its area.

Future demand

All policies and plans are concerned with the future, whether the future extends over days, months or years. Typically, the policy and planning activity discussed in this book is focused on a time period of several years. When built facilities are involved, the consequences of decisions can remain with a community for decades. Many policies and plans are concerned with meeting current deficiencies and solving current problems, but even then it is necessary to include a future-orientated perspective to ensure that the proposed solutions do not have unacceptable long-term consequences. The successful leisure service organisations will surely be those which plan for the future rather than for the problems of the past – while of course learning from the past.

In this chapter the aim is to consider ways in which the future can be considered by policy-making and planning agencies. The techniques discussed vary considerably. They include relatively technical approaches designed to produce quantified forecasts and less technical approaches concerned with qualitative issues and the 'big picture'.

The discussion of strategic planning in chapter 5 emphasised the need for leisure provision organisations to be forward looking. This need is ever more apparent as the rate of social and technological change accelerates. This sort of remark is virtually a cliché, but the irony is that, in the area of public planning for leisure, forecasting has taken a back seat in recent years because of the *lack* of social change. In the 1960s there were at least four major sources of social change which forced the public sector to engage in leisure demand forecasting. They were: the growth of leisure time, the growth of population, the growth of car-ownership and the growth of real incomes. In all four cases, in Britain and much of the rest of Europe, these are no longer sources of growth in demand for leisure. This is in contrast to many other parts of the world, where rapid growth in these factors is the norm, as industrialisation, urbanisation and migration proceed apace. In Britain and elsewhere in Europe the sources of change are now more qualitative than quantitative.

It is not the amount of leisure time that is changing but its distribution over the life-time and its distribution between different social groups; in fact, there is considerable debate in the literature over the extent to which leisure time has increased in the western world and over what time period (see Gershuny, 1992; Schor, 1991). It is not the size of the population that is changing but its composition, particularly the ageing of the community. It is not the level of income that is changing but its distribution, with, in many countries, an increasing polarisation of the prosperous and the poor. As far as car-ownership is concerned, major changes which might affect leisure demand seem unlikely.

However, all this could change during the professional life-times of people reading this book. If periods of sustained economic growth were to return, real incomes could rise again. Rising real incomes would af-fect other factors, including the level of car-ownership, and it is during periods of growing prosperity that workers are able to negotiate reduc-tions in working hours. Birth rates *could* rise again leading to popula-tion growth, but this seems unlikely. The process of larger proportions of women entering the paid workforce over recent decades has tended to reduce average leisure time per head because women in the paid workforce tend still to carry the bulk of the burden of domestic and child-care duties, so they are the group in the community with the least amount of leisure time. As the proportion of women in the paid workforce stabilises, this effect on overall leisure time will also stabilise.

There are, however, other sources of change which give rise to the need for forecasting. These include changing technology, the product life-cycle effect, changing tastes and the activities of producers.

Technological change is now endemic to the capitalist system, with billions of pounds being spent on research and development by indus-try, governments and universities throughout the world. While relatively little of this effort is explicitly aimed at leisure and leisure products, its effects do, as past experience has shown, inevitably have an impact on leisure. Thus in the past, technology such as transistors and computers, lightweight materials and satellites, often developed initially for military purposes, have become the basis of significant leisure industries. Many of the scientific and technological breakthroughs which will impinge on leisure in the future have already been made, but are still confined to laboratories and such television programmes as *Beyond 2000*. 'Tech-nological forecasting' is an art in itself – the skill being to predict which items of technology will translate into products or services which people will want, and at a price they will be prepared to pay (Quin, 1967). Over and above the purely technical questions is a broader issue about whether the introduction of new technologies is demand driven or sup-ply driven – that is, as discussed in chapter 3, whether the *producers* determine what happens or the *consumers*.

The product life-cycle is a marketing term referring to the way products are taken up by innovative consumers, achieve a period of sales growth and then go into decline. Here it is used in a modified form, focusing on the proportion of households, or individuals, who own the product. As illustrated in Figure 7.2, ownership often develops slowly when products are new and expensive. Often there is then a period of rapid growth, followed by a peak or 'saturation' level. This process takes several years. From the point of view of the producers, reaching the peak presents a problem since sales are then primarily for replacement purposes only, and this will represent a dramatic slowdown in sales unless the product can be rejuvenated in some way. Given the pace of technological change and the efforts of designers, it would seem that persuading consumers that they should replace technologically based goods for a newer, superior product has become routine, as any owner of a personal computer will know to their cost! In the 1960s this process was sometimes referred to as 'built in obsolescence' – a phenomenon, particularly related to cars, where quality and surface design changes were apparently manipulated to persuade people to replace vehicles unnecessarily. While this practice is no doubt still a factor, genuine technical improvements to products over, say, a five-year period, now seem common.

Figure 7.2 Product life-cycle/market penetration

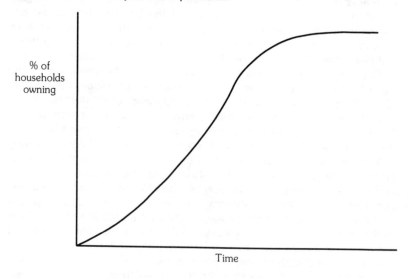

From a leisure behaviour point of view, however, the decline in product sales does not represent a decline in participation in the associated leisure activity. For example, in the case of television set manufacture, the rapid growth phase took place in the 1950s and 1960s as sets were purchased by households for the first time; the product was then given a second lease of life by the introduction of colour television in the 1970s. But once virtually all households were equipped with colour sets sales fell because only replacement sets and the slow growth of two-set households produced sales – hence the decline of the British television set manufacturing industry in the late 1970s. But television *watching* – the associated leisure activity – while it would have followed the same growth and peak, did not experience the same subsequent decline. A similar pattern would have been seen with video-cassette recorders more recently – the sale of equipment goes into decline once saturation ownership is achieved, but the leisure activity and any services associated with it, such as television show production or video hire, carries on. Indeed, the associated leisure activity and services associated with it develop a product life-cycle of their own – for example the growth of television channels, and changes in viewing habits over the years.

For forecasting therefore, the product life-cycle and the associated patterns of participation are of interest. For years after a product has been introduced, and even after it has passed its very rapid growth phase, there may be significant growth still feeding through the system and leisure participation patterns to be plotted and predicted, as shown in Figure 7.2.

Changing tastes are the most difficult of all the factors to predict (Bikchandani *et al.*, 1992). Some changes are long term, for example the decline in theatre-going and cinema-going, or the trend away from traditional team sports to more individualistic sports. Others can be short-term and move into the area of 'fads'. In the fashion industry changing taste is institutionalised: designs are changed each season. This industry highlights the issues associated with the phenomenon of changing tastes. As with the production and sale of technologically-based products, the question arises as to who is making the decisions: is it the industry itself or the consumer or are the people in between – the media, communicators, critics, 'culture brokers' – an independent force, with manufacturers and ordinary consumers running along behind, trying to keep up with the 'latest thing'? Just how consumer taste arises is a matter of some sociological debate (Featherstone, 1991; Tomlinson, 1990). While some products and designs may be foisted onto a gullible public, successful products and designs are, it can be argued, those which strike a chord with the public, reflect the mood of the buying public, and meet their – often psychic – needs.

Sometimes fashion, technology and culture meet and it is difficult to disentangle them. For example, 'surfing sub-cultures' in places such as California, Australia, and even Cornwall, can be partly related to the advent of the lightweight fibreglass surfboard, partly to commercial promotion by music and clothing industry and sports sponsors, and partly to a hedonistic sub-culture with its own dynamic (Pearson, 1979). A similar analysis might be made of the craze for skateboards and 'in-line' skating (Davidson, 1985).

Since fads, fashions and crazes are, by definition, fickle, it is almost impossible to predict them, although they also tend to have product life-cycles like consumer goods, often extending over a number of years. But longer-term change in taste patterns may be mapped, monitored and even predicted. It might be thought that consumer taste and fashion are a private-sector concern and therefore of little interest to the public sector. However, the private and public sectors are competing for the public's time and, to some extent, their money. The public sector has a range of 'products' which it wishes the public to 'consume'. Admittedly, in many cases the public-sector product has its own unique image and competition with the private sector is not an issue – for example the traditional urban park. In other instances, for example leisure services for young people, the private sector tends to set the pace and the public sector must adapt accordingly if it is to stay 'competitive'.

The activities of producers, and the issues to which they give rise, have already been discussed in relation to technological change and changing tastes, particularly in relation to the activities of the private sector. Thus the future, it can be said, is partly – but we do not know to what extent – determined by the activities of producers of goods and services: how they decide to research, to invest, to produce and to market. But this is, as discussed above, also true of the public sector. Campaigns such as 'Sport for All' (McIntosh and Charlton, 1985) are designed to influence people's behaviour – in so far as they are successful they influence the future. In the last 30 years in Britain, some 2000 indoor leisure centres have been built by the public sector: if they had not been built in the way that they were, from public funds, it is most unlikely that they would have been built on anything like that scale with private or voluntary resources. Therefore the millions of sporting and other leisure activities which they now accommodate each year would not have happened. The activities of public providers *determined* the future.

Local–Regional–National–International

Most leisure demand forecasting exercises, as reported in the literature, have been carried out at the national level (eg Kelly, 1987; Leisure Consultants, 1990; Veal, 1991a). This is perhaps curious considering that, as far as the public sector is concerned, the major providers of leisure facilities and services are local authorities. Part of the explanation for the lack of forecasting activity at local level may be that the data requirements of leisure demand forecasting and the perceived complexity of many of the techniques used may have suggested that forecasting at local level was not possible. However, as this chapter indicates, most techniques are useable at any level of government and if transport and shopping demand can be forecast at local, or sub-regional, level then so can leisure. A further reason for the lack of forecasting activity at local level would, however, appear to be related to the planning and policy-making process which, as discussed in chapter 5, has not generally faced up to the idea of demand, or participation, either in the present or the future.

Techniques

Some of the factors reviewed above remain resistant to systematic forecasting techniques, but they must be borne in mind nevertheless. There are, however, many influences on the future of leisure which can be addressed in a more or less systematic manner and the techniques available for such a task are outlined below. They fall into nine groups: 1 informed speculation; 2 asking the public; 3 asking the experts (the Delphi technique); 4 scenario writing; 5 time series analysis; 6 spatial models; 7 cross-sectional analysis; 8 comparative analysis and 9 composite methods. Each of these techniques is examined in turn; examples are given in the Further Reading section.

1 Informed speculation

Many essays and concluding chapters of leisure texts consist of speculation about the future. Such speculations are not based on any specific techniques or analysis, but represent a distillation of the thoughts and impressions of the authors. Their value therefore arises from the wisdom and experience of the writer. Often they are not intended to present forecasts or predictions as such, but to open up issues for thought and discussion. There is no methodology to be described for these exercises, but their value is often substantial, since they represent the product of considered thought. They are therefore an invaluable element of the leisure forecasting literature.

2 Asking the public

Many leisure participation surveys go beyond asking what people currently do in their leisure time and ask what they would like to do or are planning to do in future. This sort of question is often designed to assess expressed needs or demands, but they can also be seen as indicators of future behaviour patterns. Responses to such questions cannot be relied on as even approximate indicators of future demand since they often reflect wishful thinking which is never in fact acted upon. But they can be seen as indicators of sentiment, of what people may be drawn to do in favourable conditions, of what the popular and unpopular activities currently are. They provide useful market information. The approach is used in short-term economic forecasting for which regular surveys of business and consumer confidence are undertaken and the results used as 'leading indicators' of likely changes in business investment or consumer demand. In so far as the information is acted upon by providers, the popular activities are facilitated by the provision of venues and services, and people's aspirations become self-fulfilling prophesies.

3 Asking the experts – the Delphi technique

The Delphi technique exploits the fact that experts of various sorts may have insight into future developments in their field of expertise. The term 'Delphi' relates to the Greek mythical Delphic Oracle, a priestly entity who, in return for petitioning and often generous payment, could be persuaded to foretell people's future fortunes – often expressed in cryptic manner. The modern Delphi technique involves asking a panel of experts to express their views of the future and distilling this information into a forecast or forecasts. The number of experts involved could be as few as a dozen or so, or could number several hundred; they can be assembled in one place, as at a conference (eg Seeley *et al.*, 1980; Jones, 1990) or, more commonly, they can be contacted by mail. In a questionnaire, the experts may be asked a question of the form: 'What are the major changes you expect to see in your field of expertise over the next five/ten/twenty/etc. years?' Alternatively, they may be presented with a list of possible future events and asked when, if ever, they expect to see them happen.

In the first 'round' of questioning it could be expected that a range of experts is likely to produce a wide range of differing opinions. The technique then involves the collation of this information and feeding it back to the panel of experts for the 'second round'. In the second round the panel are asked the same question, but they have available the collated views of their colleagues; for example, the average date by which the panel members expect certain events to happen. The panel members are then invited to revise their opinions, if they wish, in the light of the information on their colleagues' opinions. The second-round information is then collated and the process could even be repeated again, for additional rounds. The collated views of the panel from the final round then provide the basis of the forecast.

One of the earliest uses of the technique in the leisure area was by Shafer *et al.* (1975), who asked a panel of 400 American recreation professionals and academics to indicate the most significant future events likely to take place in the area of outdoor recreation. Among those predicted were:

- By 1985:   Most people work a four-day, 32-hour week.
- By 1990:   US Census of population includes questions on recreation.
            Most homes have video-tape systems.
- By 2000:   Small recreational submarines common.
            Average age of retirement 50 years.
- After 2050: First park established on the moon.
            Average worker has three-month annual vacation.

Clearly the experts do not always get it right. However, much of the value of the technique could be said to lie in its ability to open up debate and promote thought, rather than in the precise accuracy of its predictions.

4 Scenario writing

Scenario writing is a technique which involves the devising of alternative pictures of the future as characterised by alternative values of key variables and the relationships between them. For example, alternative political scenarios for Britain for the end of the century could be a continuing of a right-wing Conservative government or its replacement by a centrist Labour government. Economically, there could be continuing high unemployment or the unemployment problem could have been solved, with a return to low unemployment. These two dimensions offer four alternative 'scenarios', as indicated in Figure 7.3.

Figure 7.3   Scenarios for Britain in the year 2000: two-dimensional

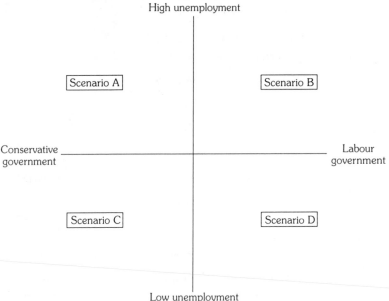

Scenario A, with high unemployment and a Conservative government, could be characterised by low public-sector spending and minimal unemployment benefits, whereas Scenario B, with a Labour government, might be characterised by higher government spending and more generous unemployment allowances, but possibly more economic crises as government attempted to solve the unemployment problem by spending money. Scenario C would be characterised by a prosperous private-enterprise culture with low taxes and low government spending, whereas Scenario D would probably involve a more substantial role for public enterprise with higher taxes and government spending.

Once the general characteristics of the scenarios had been worked out, any more detailed forecasting of leisure demand would now be undertaken (using other techniques) in the context of the scenarios, so that four sets of alternative forecasts would be produced instead of one.

It is possible that the leisure demand forecasts produced would not be very sensitive to the change in scenarios and the organisation commissioning the study could be so advised. However, if leisure patterns varied substantially between scenarios, then a range of demand forecasts could be presented.

The development of scenarios need not be restricted to two variables and two dimensions. For example, a third variable could be introduced into the above example. Growth in leisure time might be proposed as zero, moderate or substantial. The resultant 12 scenarios would then be as shown in Figure 7.4. It would become unmanageable to produce 12 sets of forecasts, so in practice just a selection of scenarios would be chosen for more detailed study, representing the widest range of possibilities and/or those considered to be most likely. Thus, for example, in Figure 7.4 the starred scenarios might be selected.

Figure 7.4   Scenarios for Britain in the year 2000: three-dimensional

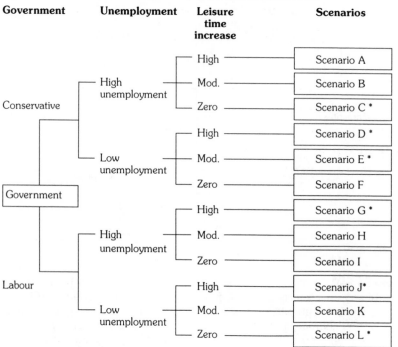

5 *Time-series analysis*

Time-series analysis is the most commonly used technique in tourism forecasting. It is a process in which the future is predicted on the basis of past or current trends in the phenomenon being studied. A prerequisite for the technique is the availability of data extending over a substantial time period. The technique is therefore most well developed in the area of international tourism because information on tourist arrivals and departures is available extending back over many years. This cannot be said of other forms of leisure activity.

At its simplest the technique can be seen as the visual extension of a trend line, as shown in Figure 7.5. A more sophisticated approach would be to 'fit' the line mathematically, by means of regression techniques, so that a formula could be used to produce the forecast, as shown in Figure 7.6.

Figure 7.5 Simple trend analysis

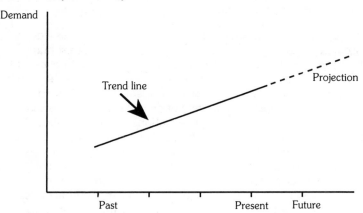

Figure 7.6 Trend line using regression

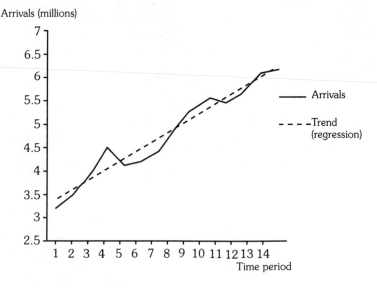

In this instance the regression line, shown as a broken line in the diagram, has the equation:

$Y = 3.15 + 0.21X$ ($r^2 = 0.95$)

or,

Arrivals (millions) = $3.15 + 0.21 \times$ Time period

In time period 20, therefore, for example, arrivals would be:

$3.15 + 0.21 \times 20 = 7.35$ million

In fact, rather than simply relating trends to the passage of time, researchers have found that the best predictor of tourist numbers over the short term is the last available figure, so that the forecast of tourist arrivals in year x is based on an equation involving the number of arrivals in year x–1. In practice, tourism arrivals do not carry on increasing at a constant rate; they often move in cycles, as suggested in Figure 7.6. It is possible to build equations which simulate such cycles, by taking account not just of the previous year's figure, but, say, the previous ten year's figures. Sophisticated modelling techniques, such as the ARIMA (Auto-Regressive Integrated Moving Average) technique, have been developed to capture these trends, in both annual and more frequent time-series, such as quarterly and monthly arrivals, and to produce forecasts based on them. These techniques are described by Archer (1976), Athiyaman and Robertson (1992) and Witt and Witt (1992), and computer packages are available, for example within SPSS, to carry them out.

An alternative time-series approach is to explore the possibility that the past trend in demand is related to some underlying factor, such as trends in real incomes, prices or exchange rates. The model is referred to as a 'structural' one, because it reflects an understanding of the underlying structure of relationships between the phenomenon's causal factors. For example, Figure 7.7 shows that the demand trend very much follows the trend in real incomes. Forecasts of demand for the leisure activity in question might therefore be based on forecasts of real income, which are widely available, although notoriously subject to fluctuation. In fact, such a model need not be restricted to a single structural variable. Crouch and Shaw (1991), for example, review a wide range of international tourism forecasting studies, involving as many as 25 different structural variables.

Figure 7.7 Structural trend line

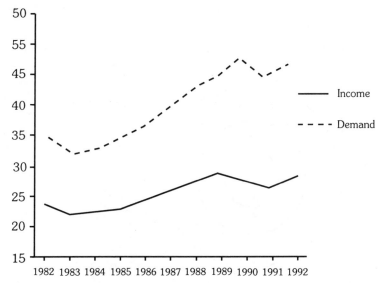

6 Spatial models

The idea of spatial models of leisure demand is explored as a planning technique in chapter 6 and in the 'Clawson' technique of cost-benefit analysis outlined in chapter 8. These techniques rely on the observed fact that, where fixed facilities are involved, people's patterns of leisure demand are influenced by the locations of those facilities. These patterns are not random but are sufficiently systematic to provide the basis for prediction. Basically, the further people live from a facility, the less likely they are to visit it. Visitation falls off with increased distance either because of the additional cost and effort in travelling or because of time availability.

In Figure 7.8, X marks the location of a hypothetical leisure facility and the rings are at one-kilometre intervals. Area A is likely to have the highest level of use, followed by areas B and C, and then D. For some types of facility this phenomenon is not marked, or the effect is only apparent over quite substantial distances – for example live theatre, where people generally expect to have to travel long distances. In other cases, such as swimming pools, or libraries, the effect is quite marked, over even very short distances. The effect is also noticeable in country-side recreation, as discussed in chapter 6.

These patterns are relevant to forecasting because the *future* patterns of demand will be affected by the decision whether or not to provide an additional facility, for example in area D. If a facility is provided participation in area D will rise, since people who would be interested in using a facility but have been hitherto prevented from doing so by the distance factor, become potential users of the new facility. If a new facility is not provided then participation will remain low in area D.

Thus 'the future' in this instance is not some uncontrollable phenomenon 'out there', but can be partly determined by the decision of providing agencies.

Figure 7.8   Hypothetical facility catchment area

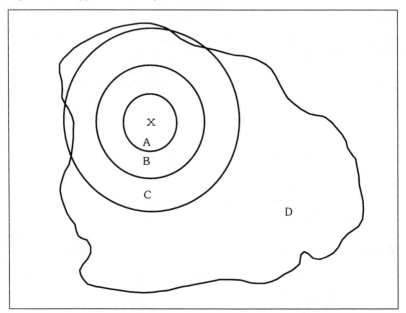

The process of quantifying the potential demand for prediction purposes is examined in chapter 6. The Clawson method, as outlined in
chapter 8, is a method for relating patterns of demand to economic
factors. In addition to its cost-benefit analysis role, the technique can be
used for predicting the impact of new facilities or the effect of price
rises.

7 Cross-sectional analysis

The cross-sectional technique is based on analysis of the variation in
leisure participation within – or across – the community. Participation
in most activities is known to vary according to certain factors, such as
age, occupation and income. As the structure of the population changes
with regard to these underlying variables so, it might be expected, will
leisure participation. Two approaches can be used in cross-sectional
analysis – the 'cohort' method and regression-based techniques. These
are discussed in turn below.

   The cohort method can best be demonstrated by an example, as
shown in Table 7.2. The table gives data from a hypothetical community in which surveys show that activity X is participated in primarily by
young people (column A). Applying the survey participation rates to
current age cohorts of the population (column B) gives an estimate of

the current numbers of participants by age group (column C). Applying the same participation rates to a population forecast, in this case for the year 2006 (column D), gives an estimate of future participation numbers (column E). It can be seen that, because the 2006 population forecast shows a reduction in the young, active, age groups and an increase in the older, less active, age groups, an overall fall in numbers of participants in activity X is predicted, even though there is a slight increase in the total population. If the activity had been one with high participation among older age groups the analysis would of course have shown a significant increase in the number of participants. Thus the predicted participation level depends on the cross-sectional pattern of participation and the predicted pattern of cross-sectional change in the underlying variable, in this case age.

Table 7.2 Cohort method for a hypothetical community

Age groups	A Participation in activity X: % per month	B Current population	C Current number of participants per month	D Population in year 2006	E Number of participants in year 2006
Data source:	Survey	Census	$(A \times B)/100$	Planning Dept.	$(A \times D)/100$
14–19	14.9	15,600	2,324	12,000	1,788
20–24	11.5	15,200	1,748	12,100	1,391
25–29	7.4	11,360	841	10,000	740
30–39	5.2	16,880	878	17,100	889
40–49	4.8	7,200	346	10,300	494
50–59	3.5	6,160	216	9,200	322
60+	2.5	7,600	190	9,800	245
Total	8.2	80,000	6,543	80,500	5,870

The weakness of the approach is that the basic cohort-specific participation rates (column A) are not assumed to change. But this is not intrinsic to the method. If different participation rates can be established using other methodologies, for example time-series analysis, then such rates could be used for the prediction.

Underlying variables other than age could be used, for example, occupation or incomes. However, predictions of such variables are less readily available than for age, particularly for local communities. The technique could, however, be used in combination with the scenario method, where hypothetical projections of the underlying variables could be used. For example, the impact of alternative income growth and distribution patterns on participation could be explored.

Ideally, more than one underlying variable should be examined. For example, it might be predicted that not only will there be more older people in a community, but that they will be relatively better off financially, because of improved superannuation provisions. Age-income cohorts would therefore reflect these changes. While current participation rates for such cohorts may be readily obtained from surveys, forecasts would generally be difficult to obtain, although, as discussed above, hypothetical predictions could be utilised for scenario purposes.

Regression-based techniques can cope more readily with a number of underlying variables because the activity forecasts are based on predictions of mean values rather the size of cohorts. The regression technique can be applied initially to cohorts, or to individuals. Applying regression to the cohort data in Table 7.2 involves the calculation of a regression line to represent the distribution of the data shown in Figure 7.9. The regression equation (calculated in this case using SPSS for Windows, with each age-group weighted by population size) is:

$$Y = 16.11 - 0.24X$$

or,

% Participation $= 16.11 - 0.24 \times$ Age

This equation can be applied to the average age of the population to produce an average participation rate. Thus, in the hypothetical case in Table 7.2, the current average age is approximately 33.1, whereas the predicted average age for the year 2006 is 36.6. Applying these averages to the equation gives the following estimates:

Current: % Participation $= 16.11 - 0.24 \times 33.1 = 8.2\%$
$= 6560$ participants

Year 2006: % Participation $= 16.11 - 0.24 \times 36.6 = 7.3\%$
$= 5900$ participants

As can be seen from Figure 7.9, the straight-line regression is not necessarily the best representation of the data, and a curved line would be better. This can be achieved by transforming the data into logarithmic form, but this is not illustrated here.

Rather than deal with individuals in cohorts with average ages and average participation rates, it is possible to perform the analysis using data from individuals, from a survey. The participation variable for each individual can either be a 'yes-no' variable, with the individual scoring one if they have participated in the activity and zero if they have not, or it can relate to the frequency of participation in a given time period. The age variable is then the individual's age. The analysis presents particular statistical problems, since most leisure activities are very much minority activities, so most respondents in a survey are non-participants, and score zero. The technicalities are beyond the scope of this text, but are discussed elsewhere, for example, by Ewing (1983).

Figure 7.9 Participation by age – curved relationship

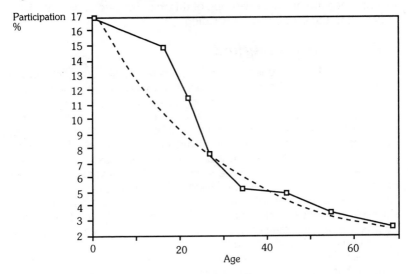

The regression approach lends itself more readily to incorporation of multiple underlying variables, because only a mean for each variable is required for forecasting purposes. Thus an equation involving age and income would be of the form:

% Participation = a + b × Age + c × Income

Here the values of a, b and c would be determined by the multiple regression analysis.

The number of 'independent' variables could be increased, subject to data availability and statistical validity. Such multi-variate analysis begins to resemble the methods used in economic or econometric forecasting, which is based on an individual, or household 'consumption function'. The consumption function is an equation which relates purchasing patterns to income and other characteristics of the household or individual. The advantage of this economic approach is that it has been developed to consider the whole of the individual or household budget and is not confined to single products or activities. Such consumption function equations may be developed in isolation, or they may be associated with equations related to other parts of the economy, such as government, private investment and imports and exports, which constitute a model of the whole economy. Such models are developed by national Treasuries and by economic consultants and academic economists. While some are based on equations as discussed here, others use the 'input–output' modelling technique.

The disadvantage of the economic approach is that leisure activity is not always well reflected in terms of expenditure. The potential exists, however, to apply the econometric approach, with its multiple expenditure choices and financial budget constraints, to choices in allocation of time, with *time* budget constraints. The technicalities of the econometric approach are beyond the scope of this text, but reference material is indicated in the list of Further Reading.

8 Comparative method

Dumazedier (1974) argued that a given society might consider futures for itself by examining the experiences of more advanced societies, particularly more economically advanced societies. In particular, societies approaching the 'post-industrial' phase of development could examine its impact and the ways of coping with it as experienced by the most economically and technologically advanced countries, particularly the USA. Such an approach to considering the future has certain similarities to scenario writing, with the scenarios being provided rather than having to be devised. It was not developed in detail by Dumazedier, and such factors as cultural and climatic conditions would seem to raise considerable problems in its application. The approach is used informally by forecasters, and may offer potential for developing countries, wishing to consider alternative models of development.

Dumazedier proposed the comparative method in an international context, but it has been applied most successfully intra-nationally, in the USA, by John Naisbitt, the author of *Megatrends* (1982). Naisbitt's technique involves examination of social trends in different parts of the USA, via content analysis of local media: certain states are then identified as 'bell weather' states, which set the pace for social change, which other states follow. While Naisbitt's 'megatrends' for the 1980s virtually ignored leisure, his 1990s version included 'Renaissance in the Arts' as one of ten 'megatrends', prompting the following assertion:

> In the final years before the millennium there will be a fundamental and revolutionary shift in leisure time and spending priorities. During the 1990s the arts will gradually replace sport as society's primary leisure activity. (Naisbitt and Aburdene, 1990: 53)

The basis of the claim that sport is currently society's 'primary leisure activity' is not clear.

9 Composite approaches

Many leisure forecasters tend, in practice, to utilise a combination of techniques rather than rely on any one. One method can be used to complement or to overcome the weaknesses of another. Thus the mechanical nature of some of the more quantitative techniques can be modified by results of Delphi exercises, and the broad brush results of national forecasts can be combined with spatial analysis for application at local level. Martin and Mason (1981), also known as Leisure Consultants (1990), use a combination of time-series, cross-sectional and scenario-writing techniques in their forecasting of UK leisure patterns. Kelly's (1987) study of recreation trends in the USA utilised cross-sectional 'cohort' methods, time-series analysis and consideration of trends in lifestyles and 'leisure styles'. In a study of Australian leisure futures, a basic cohort-based cross-sectional analysis was complemented by consideration of such factors as 'product life-cycles' and the effects of changing household composition (Veal, 1991a).

Conclusion

In the recent period of economic stagnation and zero population growth, leisure demand forecasting has not attracted the attention of academics as it did in the 1960s and 1970s. But, as the work of Leisure Consultants (1990) and the Henley Centre for Forecasting (Quarterly) demonstrates, there is still interest in and a need for demand forecasts among the commercial sector. In the public sector, individual local authorities faced with particularly rapid change in population or the local economy, are forced to consider the medium- to long-term future, but, for the most part, political horizons are limited. There is therefore, arguably, a role for academics and others involved professionally in the leisure field to develop the skills and demonstrate the value of a future-orientated perspective.

Further reading

For discussion of various aspects of forecasting, see the following sources:

Leisure forecasting techniques: Field and MacGregor, 1987; Gratton and Taylor, 1985: 99–114; Veal, 1987; Burton, 1989.

Tourism forecasting techniques: Smith, 1989; Archer, 1976; 1994; Witt and Witt, 1992.

Informed speculation: Pigram, 1983; Jackson and Burton 1989; Mercer and Hamilton-Smith, 1980; Burton, 1970; Jennings, 1979; Asimov, 1976; Kelly and Godbey, 1992: 479–512.

Asking the people: Coppock and Duffield, 1975: 84.

Asking the experts – Delphi: Chai, 1977; Jones, 1990; Kaynak and Macaulay, 1984; Linstone, 1978; Moeller and Shafer, 1983, 1994; Ng et al., 1983; Green et al., 1990.

Time-series analysis: Hill, 1978; Stynes, 1983; Athiyaman and Robertson, 1992;

Scenarios: Miles et al., 1978; Martin and Mason, 1981; Henry, 1988.

Spatial techniques: Coppock and Duffield, 1975; Smith, 1989: 111–20; Ewing, 1983.

Cross-sectional technique: Coppock and Duffield, 1975; Veal, 1980; Young and Willmott, 1973.

Econometric methods: Adams, 1986; Ewing, 1983.

Comparative method: Dumazedier, 1974; Naisbitt, 1982.

Composite techniques: Leisure Consultants, 1990; Martin and Mason, 1981; Kelly, 1987; Veal, 1991a; Henley Centre for Forecasting, Quarterly.

8 ECONOMIC EVALUATION

Introduction

In this chapter two forms of economic evaluation are considered: cost-benefit analysis and economic impact analysis. Cost-benefit analysis seeks to replicate for public-sector investment projects or services the sort of financial evaluation which is usually undertaken for private-sector investment projects. But in addition to the financial outlays and incomes which are taken account of by a private-sector enterprise, the public enterprise must consider the many additional, non-market, costs and benefits of the sort discussed in chapter 4. Economic impact analysis relates particularly to the 'economic management/development' criterion for government activity (see chapter 4); governments at all levels feel justified in becoming involved with various projects if they will create jobs and incomes – economic impact analysis seeks to quantify the impact of a project on the local community, in terms of jobs and incomes.

Both techniques assume the acceptability of the basic capitalist market framework for analysis and that the market process generally is an acceptable way of ordering economic affairs. For those who believe that the market system is fundamentally flawed or, for instance, that the distribution of incomes in society is fundamentally unjust, the techniques are largely irrelevant. However, even if it is believed that the market system is flawed but capable of being reformed, the techniques may be useful tools, because they use market-based thinking and analysis to justify non-market, government, activity, and thus the implementation of the results of cost-benefit or economic impact analysis generally leads to a shift of resources away from the market in favour of the public sector – a move which most reformists would see as beneficial.

Cost-benefit analysis

1 Introduction

There has been increasing interest in cost-benefit analysis in recent years as economic policy based on liberal principles has sought to cut back the size of the public sector, and those involved with public services have been required to account for their activities in economic terms. Thus cost-benefit analysis has been used to evaluate sporting and cultural events and environmental and heritage projects. There are, however, also objectors to the use of cost-benefit analysis.

Even if the basic market framework is accepted for most things, there are those who object to the use of cost-benefit analysis in certain areas, on the grounds that the value of certain things is 'beyond measure' or 'intangible' and that economics has no role to play in such valuations. In fact, the public does put a value on 'priceless' things, for example, when money is raised by public appeal to buy a major painting for the public collection, to prevent it being sold overseas. Occasionally the required amount of money is *not* reached for such purchases, implying that the price asked for the 'priceless' painting is too high. At a more mundane level, when local councils decide on the level of grant to give to the local repertory theatre or the budget for the municipal museum, they are indicating some sort of monetary valuation of those services. Private individuals also make decisions on what to spend on 'intangible' things such as the enjoyment of a Beethoven Symphony, when they decide whether or not to pay the required price for a recording or to attend a concert. It might be argued that in such circumstances the community or the individual is not placing a value on the intangible benefits but simply indicating what they can afford. The argument then becomes semantic: the economist's definition of *value* is what someone or some organisation will pay for something. The term 'the amount the community is willing or able to pay' could be used, but 'value' is more succinct.

Defenders of cost-benefit analysis do accept that there are limitations to the technique, pointing out that in practice there are often costs and benefits which, for various reasons, *cannot* be measured; the technique seeks to put monetary values on those things which *can* be valued economically, so that decision-making of a more qualitative kind can concentrate on those elements which cannot be valued in money terms. The process can be an aid to clarifying decision-making procedures by distinguishing between those aspects of a project which can be valued in money terms and those which cannot.

Four types of cost and benefit are therefore involved in any project. As shown in Figure 8.1, they are: A costs which can be measured, B costs which cannot be measured, C benefits which can be measured and D benefits which cannot be measured. Cost-benefit analysis involves *identifying* all the above, but it concentrates on quantifying the measurable aspects, A and C, only. Whether or not C exceeds A, the decision makers must still decide whether C+D is greater than A+B, and that will still involve an element of qualitative judgement. However, if there are no unmeasurable costs of type B, and if the measurable benefits (C) can be shown to be greater than the measurable costs (A), then the project has been shown to be viable without having to consider the unmeasurable benefits (D).

Figure 8.1 Measurable/Non-measurable costs and benefits

	Costs	Benefits
Measurable	A	C
Non-measurable	B	D

It should perhaps be noted that whereas cost-benefit analysis is very often scorned or suspected by enthusiasts for such areas as the arts, heritage, the environment or sport, because they feel that their area of interest is threatened by it, it is usually the case that analyses are carried out by economists who are also enthusiasts for the particular area. Economists who specialise in studies of the arts, sport or the environment are often personally committed to the field. And more often than not the analysis demonstrates that the benefits from the phenomenon being studied are being grossly under-valued by the decision-makers. It is rare for a cost-benefit analysis of a public leisure project to find that a project is poor value for the community.

There is a great deal of literature on the application of cost-benefit analysis to leisure, especially to outdoor recreation/tourism. However, there is very little evidence of its serious use as a tool for investment decision-making. One of the areas where the technique *is* actively used in this way is in transport, particularly road building. New roads produce savings in terms of travel time savings and reductions in accidents (whose costs can be measured). These savings can be compared with the costs of construction and maintenance and various road proposals can then be ranked in order of the levels of net benefits they are expected to produce. Many highway authorities in the western world adopt this approach, but there is no comparable use of the techniques in the leisure area. While cost-benefit analysis is sometimes used for investment appraisal where leisure is an adjunct to an economic product, such as in recreational use of reservoirs or forests, generally the examples of its use in leisure are *post hoc*: they are conducted to demonstrate the value of a project which is already up and running.

2 The cost-benefit analysis approach

In the private sector the main criterion generally used to determine whether an operation or project is viable is whether it can generate sufficient income to pay its costs and provide an acceptable return on the capital employed – whether it is profitable. If this cannot be done then the facility or service will not be provided in the first place or will, sooner or later, disappear from the market place or be sold at a loss to another owner who can then run it at a profit because of reduced capital costs. The investment market in the private sector is competitive, so that entrepreneurs only put their money into projects which they think will produce profits at least equal to the 'going rate of return'. The level of this rate of return will vary with the degree of risk associated with the project, and must be higher than the rate of interest investors would obtain by, for example, depositing their money in a bank (where there is very little risk). The combination of perceived risk and expected level of return must be acceptable to the investment market. Generally, leisure and tourism projects are seen as *high*-risk areas (compared with, say, retailing or food manufacture), so the rate of return demanded is comparatively high.

In the public sector different criteria apply; facilities frequently 'make a loss' financially. With few exceptions, there is generally a subsidy to the users of the service. This makes sense in terms of the various non-market social benefits which public services are believed to provide, as discussed in chapter 4; if a service is profitable then it might be expected that a private-sector operator could and would run it. There are very few truly financially profitable public sector operations which cover all their operating costs *and* provide a return on *realistically valued* capital resources. The question then arises as to how to decide which proposed projects in the public sector are worthwhile. How can alternative projects be compared and the best selected? How can we ensure that the money spent in one area of public expenditure, say roads, is as effective in producing benefits as money spent in another sector, such as leisure? If less benefits are being obtained from one area than another then, as in the market situation, it would seem sensible to transfer resources until some sort of balance is achieved.

Indeed, it should also be possible to demonstrate that money spent in the public sector is producing benefits at least as great as would be obtained from returning the money to taxpayers' pockets and allowing them to spend the money themselves in the market place. In the end the political decision-makers must make these decisions, as far as possible reflecting the preferences of the public; cost-benefit analysis is a technique to aid in that decision-making process and to make at least parts of it more 'rational', and more reflective of public preferences than they would otherwise be.

In the private sector a firm assesses a project's viability in terms of:

Expenditure vs Income

In the public sector, the corresponding terms are:

Costs vs Benefits

In the private sector income must exceed expenditure by the required amount; in the public sector benefits must exceed costs by the required amount. For example, a private sector resort development might be proposed as follows:

a.	Capital costs	£10 million
b.	Annual sales	£4 million
c.	Annual costs	£3 million
d.	Annual profits (b – c)	£1 million
e.	Return on capital employed (d/a)	10%

The investor would assess the anticipated 10 per cent return in the light of the level of risk involved and decide whether to invest.

In the public sector, if there were a proposal to build, say, a museum for a similar sum, the figures might be as follows:

a.	Capital costs	£10 million
b.	Annual sales	£1 million
c.	Annual running costs	£3 million
d.	Annual capital charges	£1 million
e.	Annual net cost/loss (b – c – d)	£3 million

Note that in the public-sector project, the £10 million is assumed to be entirely borrowed money, so there are interest and repayment charges (capital charges). In the private-sector case it is assumed that all the capital was provided by the risk-taking investor. In practice, the private-sector operation may also involve borrowed money and the public sector may involve money which is not borrowed, but the above examples ignore these variations for the sake of simplicity.

How can such a public-sector project be justified, when there are investment projects in the private sector, which could, on the face of it, make better use of the £10 million by investing it in a commercial project, providing a service which people are willing to pay for, and returning a profit? The answer is that it is believed that the museum produces social benefits – as discussed in chapter 4 – which are not reflected in the above, purely financial, figures. The purpose of cost-benefit analysis is to identify these *social benefits* and to assess whether they are worth the money – in this case £3 million each year.

Cost-benefit analyses can be used in three different situations: (a) study of a single proposed project; (b) comparison between alternative proposed projects; (c) study of an existing project or projects. Situations (a) and (b) would be used as an aid to decision-making on whether to embark on a project. Situation (c) is part of the process of evaluating on-going projects.

Cost-benefit analysis is therefore comparable to the project appraisal which any private firm must conduct before taking the step of investing shareholders' funds. Some costs and benefits of public-sector projects are exactly the same as those of private-sector projects. In the museum example discussed above, the construction and set-up costs are represented by the capital costs; the running costs are the costs of wages, materials, and so on; and ticket sales and other income are partial indicators of benefits received by the users. But what of the 'social benefits' (and costs)? How do they arise and how can they be identified?

By and large social or non-market costs and benefits correspond to the examples of 'market failure' discussed in chapter 4. The first five forms of market failure identified were: public goods, externalities, mixed goods/services, merit goods and option demand. Each of these implies some sort of benefit accruing to the community at large or to particular third-party groups in the community, with externalities being capable of also imposing costs on third parties. The task of cost-benefit analysis is to identify and quantify these costs and benefits in relation to specific projects and bring them into the assessment process. The best way to bring them into the process is considered to be, if possible, to express them in the same terms as the tangible costs and benefits, namely in money terms.

Among the other arguments for government involvement put forward in chapter 4 were: infant industries, size of project, natural monopolies, economic management/development and incidental enterprise. If a project is justified on these grounds then economic impact rather than cost-benefit analysis would be the appropriate technique for evaluation, as discussed in the second half of this chapter. The 'tradition' argument for government involvement is not easily susceptible to economic analysis unless the sense of tradition is itself seen as a public good.

The remaining argument discussed in chapter 4 was equity. Equity issues are not intrinsic to cost-benefit analysis, since, in mainstream economic analysis of the market, no distinction is generally made between groups of consumers, it being assumed that the question of equitable income distribution has been dealt with through taxation and welfare policies. However, 'distributional' effects of projects can be taken into account – that is, it is possible to indicate which socio-economic groups will reap the benefits of a project and which groups will bear the costs. These factors can then be taken into account by decision-makers.

The cost-benefit process involves three stages: identifying and measuring the costs of a project; identifying and measuring the benefits; comparing the costs and benefits. The measurement of costs is discussed in section 3 below. Measurement of benefits is discussed in sections 4–6. Comparison of costs and benefits is discussed in sections 7 and 8.

3 Identifying and measuring costs

The question of identifying and measuring costs would seem to be straightforward, and indeed, it is more straightforward than measuring benefits. In fact, many studies in the literature involve only benefit measurement because the measurement of costs is seen as unproblematical or because, when comparative studies are being conducted, the costs of two or more projects may be similar and the study is then concerned only with identifying which project produces the most benefits. Costs can be of four types: a. capital costs, b. running costs, c. externalities and d. opportunity costs. These are discussed in turn below.

a. Capital costs
Capital costs are those costs which are necessary for the purchase, construction and equipping of a project and generally getting it started – in other words, the 'investment'. These costs can be measured in two ways: either as a lump sum or as an annual cost. The lump sum is easy enough to understand: if a project costs a million pounds to start up then that is its capital cost. But if, to set up the project, a million pounds is borrowed at an interest rate of 10 per cent per annum, the annual cost will be £100,000 in interest. Since it will also be necessary to pay back the million pounds over, say, ten years – a mortgage – then the annual costs will be somewhat more than £100,000 a year. Of course, this might be off-set by the value of the asset acquired which, at the end of ten years, might be worth more than a million pounds.

b. Running costs
Running costs are a relatively simple concept. The costs of staffing, materials, heating, lighting, transport and so on are easily envisaged and often relatively easy to estimate.

c. Externalities
While there is much theory on negative externalities – costs accruing to a third party – there is little empirical data. This is largely because most public projects are aimed primarily at producing benefits and externalities of a negative type are generally seen as insignificant or ignored. A study of the Adelaide Grand Prix is a rare example of research on such negative externalities as traffic congestion (Dunstan, 1986), noise and property damage (McKay, 1986) and accident costs (Fischer *et al.*, 1986).

Four specific examples of negative externalities are discussed in turn below; they are: traffic congestion, noise and accidents.

Traffic congestion is an inevitable consequence of some leisure phenomena, such as special events or tourism. A new project can increase traffic congestion in its vicinity. This imposes costs on local residents, who now take longer to get from A to B. Surveys can be conducted to establish how many vehicles are involved and the time delays they are suffering. Thus, for instance, if, as a result of the event, a million vehicles experience delays of 15 minutes each on average, then this represents a 'time loss' of 250,000 hours. If all the time is lost by people working at paid jobs, then the 'value' of this lost time could be estimated from the average wage rate. If this is, say, £8 per hour, the value of the lost time is £2.0 million. If, as is likely, some of the travel time is lost by people not working in paid jobs, the valuation of their time is more complex, and this is discussed in more detail below under benefits. In addition to time loss, congestion causes vehicles to use more fuel; however, if each vehicle used, say, an extra 5 pence worth of fuel per trip because of the delays, this would amount to only £12,500 – a small sum compared with the time costs.

Noise is another negative externality which may be caused by leisure facilities and events. One way of valuing the 'cost' of noise to the sufferers is to estimate the cost of sound-proofing their homes. This is, for instance, done in cost-benefit studies of airports, in relation to houses under the flight path. It may, however, be only a partial solution in that people are still inconvenienced in the use of their gardens and in not being able to leave their windows open. In this instance some estimate of the compensation for loss of amenity might be assessed, of the sort that might be awarded by a court.

One way in which the monetary value of the cost of noise pollution might be assessed is by examining property prices. The difference between the price or rent of identical houses under and not under a flight path indicates the value that house buyers or renters place on peace and quiet. Note that in this case, the cost is a 'one- off' cost imposed on the owner at the time the airport is built. When the house is sold, the new owners are already compensated for the noise by the fact that they have bought a cheaper house. Interview surveys of affected people may also be used to assess the extent of noise inconvenience.

Major events and tourism can cause significant increase in traffic in an area, resulting in increased accidents. Although in one sense a money cost cannot be put on death and injury caused to humans by accidents, people nevertheless do frequently associate such phenomena with money. The courts, for instance, award financial damages for everything from death to minor injury. There is a 'going rate' in insurance cases for such things as loss of limbs, macabre though it may seem. Two inputs are made into assessment of these costs: medical costs and loss of income/output by the victim. Distress to victims and families is more difficult to assess in money terms, although again, compensation ordered by the courts can give some guide.

d. Opportunity costs

The 'opportunity cost' of something is measured by the value of that something in its best possible alternative use. It is a measure of benefits foregone and underlies cost throughout economic theory. It is particularly important in cost-benefit analysis and perhaps particularly so in leisure and tourism. The idea is best explained by an example.

Large city centre parks are dedicated to recreational use, but the cost of the decision to dedicate that land to recreation can be measured by considering the value of the land in its next best alternative use. The land occupied by Central Park in New York, or Hyde Park in London, would be worth billions of pounds if sold on the open market for development. The community is foregoing that income as the price of providing the open space. Thus, if the going rate of interest is 10 per cent per annum then a park which could, in theory, be sold for £100 million is 'costing' £10 million a year in income foregone – £10 million is its annual 'opportunity cost'.

The opportunity cost of resources, especially land, arises frequently in the case of leisure/tourism because such phenomena as urban parks, national parks, coastline and prestige city sites tend to feature prominently. Since these resources have often been in the public domain from time immemorial and have not recently involved any cash outlay, they are popularly considered to be costless. But the economist would argue that it is wrong to consider them so. Even where costs have been incurred, for instance in recently acquired land, there may be a temptation to ignore the cost of acquisition, assuming it to be a 'sunk' cost. Again the economist would say this is erroneous. If 'opportunity cost' is ignored then projects which do have 'real' capital costs rather than opportunity costs are disadvantaged.

4 Identifying and measuring benefits

It is in the area of benefits that the links back to public-sector rationale can be made most clearly. The aim of cost-benefit analysis is to try to identify the people who benefit from a public project and then to find out how those people value the benefits. The benefits arising from the various forms of market failure, as discussed in chapter 4, are discussed in turn below.

a. Public goods

The classic type of public provision is the 'public good' – which is non-rival and non-excludable. Examples include firework displays, public broadcasting, preservation of the landscape and marine navigational assistance such as marker buoys. The firework display is the easiest of these to examine. Suppose it costs £100,000 to mount a firework display: how do we know this is worth it? The benefits are enjoyed by the people who watch the display. If the display is in a public area, such as the Thames Embankment, then these people are unable to actually pay for the experience, but they are obtaining a benefit. How do we find out what the value of this benefit is to them and therefore whether the total value of the benefits enjoyed is greater than the £100,000 spent? In the case of maintenance of heritage, where on-going, 'vicarious' enjoyment or national pride is involved, a cost-benefit analysis would seek to discover the value placed on these sentiments by the general public. The most common approach to measuring these benefits is the 'willingness-to-pay' or 'contingency' method.

In the case of a public event, a social survey could be mounted, after the event, which would ask people whether they saw it, and how much they would have been prepared to pay if asked. If it was found that, say, 200,000 people had seen the event and would, on average, have been prepared to pay £1 each, then the valuation of the users, at £200,000, is greater than the £100,000 cost, so the display is justified. If the exercise was being done before the event, people could be asked whether they intended to watch and if so what they would, in theory, be prepared to pay.

There are problems with the approach because, if people thought they might *actually* be charged for the display, they might be tempted, in their response to the survey, to deliberately underestimate the amount they would be prepared to pay. On the other hand, if they thought that there was no prospect of being charged and the question was entirely hypothetical, they might exaggerate the amount they would be willing to pay. It is possible that these two tendencies cancel each other out in 'willingness-to-pay' surveys, thus giving, on average, a true figure. But there is some doubt about the validity of the technique generally, given its hypothetical nature.

A similar approach can be used to place a value on the 'psychic' benefit or income of the vicarious user, as discussed above. The general public could be asked what they would be prepared to pay per annum, for example, to preserve the Lake District, or the Parthenon or the Pyramids.

An alternative method is to base the valuation on the amounts which people pay for similar events or services which are charged for. This would not be suitable for the 'psychic income' example discussed above, but it would be possible for the firework display example.

The *Adelaide Grand Prix* study (Burns *et al.*, 1986) came up with an ingenious inferential method of measuring the psychic income which the residents of Adelaide gained from having the Formula One Grand Prix in their city. It was found from surveys that 20 per cent of the population experienced extra travel costs because of the Grand Prix, amounting in aggregate to $6.2 million. Nevertheless, 90 per cent of these same people were still in favour of the Grand Prix being held. This suggests that, for those people, the enjoyment of the Grand Prix must at least have compensated for the extra travel costs, of $5.6 million (90 per cent of $6.2 million). So this was seen as a minimum measure of the 'psychic benefit' for that group. It was argued that the 80 per cent of the population who did not experience extra travel costs would have enjoyed a similar level of psychic benefit. The study concludes that, since '... one fifth of the population had benefits of $5.6 million then, extrapolating to the total population ... total benefits are at least $28 million' (p. 26). Thus the total 'psychic income' to the population of Adelaide from holding the Grand Prix was $28 million (about £14 million), far outweighing the various costs identified in the rest of the study.

Where the public good involves direct enjoyment by users and the users have to travel to a specific site or area, as in the case of a public event or visiting a park, it is possible to assess valuations on the basis of travel patterns and costs. This methodology is discussed below under the heading 'Measuring private benefits'.

b. Externalities

Externalities are one of the most important types of benefit associated with public leisure facilities; they are similar to public goods, except that the beneficiaries are identifiable third parties, rather than the public at large.

The existence of a public leisure facility can often give rise to increased trade for neighbouring businesses – for example nearby pubs and restaurants benefiting from the presence of a theatre; the value of this externality would be reflected in property values or rents or in the turnover of these businesses. The expenditure, the increased business, and the increased property values or rents are all indicators of the same thing; so in a cost-benefit study care must be taken to count this phenomenon only once.

A further factor to be considered in relation to this type of externality is whether it represents a real net benefit of the project, or whether it results from a transfer of activity from elsewhere. For example, if the increased business of restaurants and pubs is counterbalanced by a decrease in the business of restaurants and pubs elsewhere in the city then there is no net benefit. On the other hand, if the concentration of facilities causes an overall increase in pub and restaurant spending, or attracts more visitors from outside of the city, then there can be said to be a net increase in economic activity and therefore a net benefit to the community.

A large public organisation can provide externality benefits to smaller organisations in an industry. For example, a large public cultural organisation such as a national theatre or opera or broadcasting organisation will often provide training and professional experience for workers in the industry and will underpin a technical support industry which others can make use of. While the training costs of such organisations can be estimated, the value of the other externalities which they produce can be difficult to estimate.

c. Mixed goods/services

In nearly all cases of public leisure provision, there are private consumer benefits involved in a project as well as public benefits. Very often that private benefit is not reflected in the price paid by the consumer of the service – as it would be in the private sector – because the price has been reduced, sometimes to zero, in order to achieve other social objectives. Reducing the price of something means that more people are able or willing to buy more of it. In addition to the wider social benefits (eg public good aspects enjoyed by non-users, externalities, merit good or economic aspects), the users are obtaining an individual benefit which should also be taken into account. Examples are outlined in Table 8.1.

In these instances the public and the private benefits must be measured for the purposes of the cost-benefit analysis. The public or social benefits are all examples of public goods, externalities, merit goods, etc., which are discussed under the appropriate headings. The measurement of private benefits is a major issue which is discussed in section 5.

Table 8.1 Benefits from mixed goods/services

Examples	Public good and other social benefits	Private benefits
Performing arts	Cultural spin-off Tourist attraction	Enjoyment of performance
Urban parks	Amenity for local properties and passers-by Pollution dispersal	Enjoyment of the park
National parks	Merit good, option demand, vicarious enjoyment, amenity for properties and passers-by	Enjoyment of the park
Sports facilities	Health effects, enjoyment of sporting success	Enjoyment of participation Health benefits
Youth facilities	Reduction of anti-social behaviour	Enjoyment of facilities
Facilities for elderly	Physical and mental health effects	Enjoyment of facilities Health benefits

d. Merit goods

Merit good arguments would appear to be unquantifiable. It is not the general public or the leisure facility user who make such judgements but professional groups, pressure groups or politicians. However, in a democratic society, it might be expected that such decisions would be approved of by a majority of the general public. The value of the merit good dimension of a service might therefore be assessed in a similar manner to that of public goods, primarily by means of the 'willingness-to-pay' or contingency method.

e. Option demand

Option demand, or existence value – where people are willing to see government expenditure on something to ensure its availability for possible future use – can be evaluated by surveys using the 'willingness-to-pay' or contingency method.

5 Measuring private benefits

In private-sector leisure facilities, and in a few public-sector facilities, the 'market price' for the service is charged and, in economic terms, this is seen as an indicator of the value of the benefits enjoyed. For example, if 100,000 people a year pay £5 each to visit a leisure facility then they are said to be placing a collective value of at least £500,000 on the experience. In the case of public leisure facilities which are mixed goods, and in some cases of public goods, the price of entry is either zero or subsidised, in recognition of the public good, externality or other dimension, so the price paid for entry is not a reflection of the value the user attaches to the experience. How are the user benefits to be measured in such cases? The 'willingness-to-pay' approach, and its limitations, have been considered in the discussion of public goods above. Two alternatives discussed here are the travel cost or 'Clawson' method, and the idea of 'switching values'.

The travel cost or Clawson method

A common approach to measuring private benefits is to measure the 'consumer surplus'. Consumer surplus arises in any market situation. When a price is set by the provider of a service the same price is paid by all. But some would be willing to pay more if they had to. In Table 8.2 hypothetical data illustrate this idea. This is the essence of the economic demand curve, as shown in Figure 8.2.

Table 8.2   Price vs sales (hypothetical)

Price	Sales
£2	500
£5	300
£7	200
£10	100
£15	50
£17	0

Figure 8.2   Demand curve

Price £

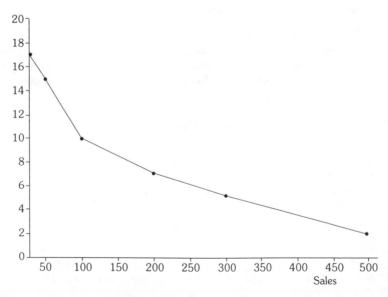

Sales

Suppose, in this example, the price charged is £5 – sales are then 300, and 200 potential customers, who would have been prepared to pay between £2 and £4.99 do not buy. The 300 customers are all charged £5. But of those, 50 would have been prepared to pay at least £15; 50 would have been prepared to pay between £10 and £14.99; 100 would have been prepared to pay between £7 and £9.99; and 100 would have been prepared to pay between £5 and £6.99. Most of these people – all except those who were prepared to pay *just* £5 – are getting a bonus – they are getting the item for less than they would have been prepared to pay for it: they enjoy a 'consumer surplus'. The total 'consumer surplus' can be estimated as in Table 8.3. It assumes that the purchasers can be divided into four groups:

A the 50 prepared to pay at least £15 (assume £16.00 average)
B the 50 prepared to pay between £10 and £14.99 (assume £12.50 average)
C the 100 prepared to pay between £7 and £9.99 (assume £8.50 average)
D the 100 prepared to pay between £5 and £6.99 (assume £6.00 average)

Table 8.3 Estimate of consumer surplus

Group	Price would have paid	Price paid	Difference (a–b)	Number of customers	Consumer surplus (c×d)
	a	b	c	d	
	£	£	£	N	£
A	16.00	5	11.00	50	550
B	12.50	5	7.50	50	375
C	8.50	5	3.50	100	350
D	6.00	5	1.00	100	100
Total	-	-	-	300	1375

The £1375 total is the value of the consumer surplus and is a measure of the benefit which the buyers are getting over and above what they paid. It can be represented diagrammatically as the shaded area in Figure 8.3.

Figure 8.3 Consumer surplus

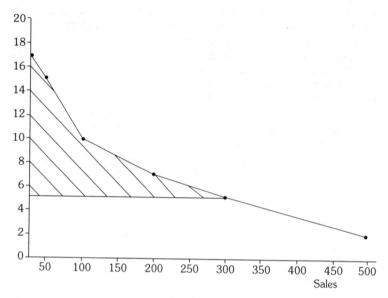

Price £

The consumer surplus is seen as a useful measure of the benefit users obtain from a leisure service. If, as is the case with many public facilities, the price charged were reduced to zero, it would still be possible to estimate the consumer surplus because it is based on what people would be *prepared* to pay. The question is, how can this be established in practice? Two methods economists use to finding out what people might be prepared to pay to use a facility are, firstly, asking them – the 'willingness-to-pay'/contingency method as already discussed – and secondly, the 'travel cost' or 'Clawson' method (Clawson and Knetsch, 1962). The latter was developed particularly in the context of leisure/tourism trips. It is based on the idea of deriving a *demand curve*, and hence the consumer surplus, from a study of the costs which users of a leisure/tourism site incur in travelling to the site.

Suppose that the travel catchment area of a site can be divided into four zones, A, B, C and D, as shown in Figure 8.4. For each zone there are different travel costs to the site. A user survey could establish how many people travelled from each zone and the population Census could be used to find out the resident population of each zone, to produce data of the sort given in Table 8.4. It can be seen that the level of visits per 1000 of population falls as the travel costs increase, as shown in Figure 8.5. It is assumed that entry to the site at present is free. How do we use this information to estimate the level of use for different price levels – that is, determine a demand curve?

Figure 8.4 Leisure site with travel zones

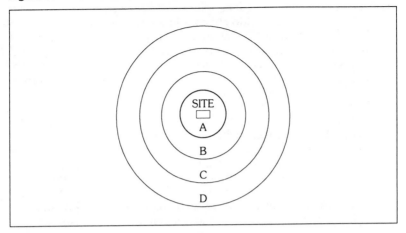

Table 8.4 Hypothetical leisure/tourism site

	Source of information	Zone				Total
		A	**B**	**C**	**D**	
a. Travel costs £ per head	Survey	£5	£10	£15	£20	
b. No. of visits p.a.	Survey/counts	40,000	60,000	25,000	0	125,000
c. Population '000s	Census	20	40	50	60	170
d. Visits per 1000 population per annum	Calculated (b/c)	2000	1500	500	0	

Figure 8.5 Costs vs visit rates

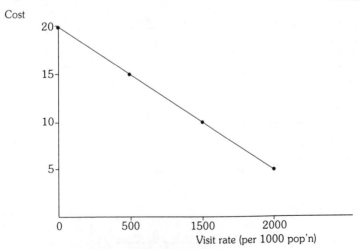

The process proposed by the Clawson method is set out in Table 8.5. It uses the information on how people react to changes in *travel costs* to infer how they would react to changes in *entry charges*. The effects of a range of hypothetical entry charges are explored. For example, if an entry fee of £5 were introduced, people in Zone A would be faced with total costs of £10 (£5 travel and £5 entry). This is the same as the travel costs for Zone B. If people react to entry charges as they do to travel costs – that is, if Figure 8.5 could be said to relate to aggregate travel and entry costs, rather than just travel costs – then it might be expected that the visit rate for Zone A would fall to 1500 per 1000, the level that Zone B residents produced when faced with total costs of £10. Similarly, with an entry charge of £5, Zone B costs would rise to £15 per head and their visit rate would fall to 500 (the visit rate which Zone C originally had) and Zone C costs would rise to £20 and their visit rate to zero, since Zone D had zero visits when faced with costs of £20. A similar analysis could be done for a £10 and £15 entry fee as shown in Table 8.5. (Zone D is omitted because it generates no trips.)

Table 8.5   Travel cost analysis

	Source of information	Zones			Total visits
		Zone A	Zone B	Zone C	
a. Population '000s	Census	20	40	50	
Entry charge nil – as in Table 8.4					
b. Total cost	Survey	£5	£10	£15	
c. Total visits	Survey/counts	40,000	60,000	25,000	125,000
d. Visits/1000 pop'n	c/a	2000	1500	500	
Entry charge £5					
e. Total cost	b + 5	£10	£15	£20	
f. Visits/1000 pop'n	d	1500	500	0	
g. Total visits	f × a	30,000	20,000	0	50,000
Entry charge £10					
h. Total cost	b + 10	£15	£20	£25	
i. Visits/1000 pop'n	d	500	0	0	
j. Total visits	i × a	10,000	0	0	10,000
Entry charge £15					
k. Total cost	b + 15	£20	£25	£30	
l. Visits/1000 pop'n	d	0	0	0	
m. Total visits	l × a	0	0	0	0

The resultant price/visits schedule is as shown in Table 8.6 and constitutes a demand schedule, upon the basis of which a demand curve could be drawn. From this schedule we can see that 10,000 visitors would be prepared to pay a £10 entry charge, but not as much as £15. Assuming they would, on average, be prepared to pay £12.50, and making similar assumptions about the other price groups, it is possible to calculate the consumer surplus as follows:

10,000 @ £12.50 (ie between £10 and £14.99)	£125,000
40,000 @ £7.50 (ie between £5 and £9.99)	£300,000
75,000 @ £2.50 (ie between 0 and £4.99)	£187,500
Total	£612,500

Table 8.6 Price/visit (demand) schedule

Entry price	Visits (demand)
0	125,000
£5	50,000
£10	10,000
£15	0

This means that the 125,000 visitors to the site are obtaining £612,500 of benefits, even though they are not paying for them. Such a sum could be entered on the benefit side of a cost-benefit analysis.

The travel cost/Clawson method is not without its critics, since it makes a key, challengeable assumption: that people would react to entry charges as they react to travel costs. Nevertheless, it is one of the few alternatives to the 'willingness-to-pay' method, which is also subject to criticism.

Switching values

The 'switching values' approach avoids the problem of direct measurement of user benefits. Rather than measuring benefits it suggests to decision-makers the minimum value which the benefits would have to have if a project is to be approved. This is illustrated by the example in Table 8.7. In this case the net annual costs of the project are £200,000 and the number of visits is 400,000, suggesting that the project is worthwhile if each visit is deemed to be worth at least 50 pence. The decision-makers (eg councillors) make the decision as to whether visits are worth that level of subsidy (Manidis, 1994).

Table 8.7 Switching values (hypothetical)

Annual costs of project	£3 million
Annual measured income of project	£2.8 million
Net annual costs	£200,000
Number of visits per annum	400,000
'Switching value' – £ per visit	£0.50

6 The value of time

Another type of benefit which arises in mixed goods situations is the saving of leisure time. This arises when recreation or tourist traffic is a significant factor in new road schemes, but the value of time can also be incorporated into the 'travel costs' element of the Clawson method – that is, travel costs can include time as well as such things as fuel and vehicle wear and tear.

In cost-benefit studies of road developments the value of time savings by travellers is usually the major benefit arising. Thus, if a proposed road scheme costing, say, £1 million a year (in maintenance and capital charges) saves, say, 15 minutes of travel time for 2 million motorists a year (ie 500,000 hours), and if time is worth £8 an hour, the saving would be £4 million a year – far in excess of the road costs.

Leisure enters into the road cost-benefit analysis, since a proportion of the motorists using the road will be at leisure or on holiday – is their time worth anything? For someone involved in paid work – truck drivers or couriers, for example – their time (and time savings) can be said to be valued at the wage rate. This, incidentally, means that the value of time savings of highly paid workers is higher than that of lower paid workers; so road schemes which save more time of the former will produce more savings and more economic benefits than those which save more time of the latter. Some would say that leisure time should be valued at the wage rate because, at the margin, workers can be said to value their leisure time at the wage rate. If they valued it less they should, in theory, work longer hours; if they valued it more, it would make sense for them to work shorter hours. Others would argue that this sort of analysis suggests that it is the overtime rate rather than the normal hourly pay rate which should be used. Or it could be pointed out that the existence of collective bargaining and fixed working hours means that the individual has little choice about working hours, so this is not a useful basis for valuation.

There are, however, instances where individuals can be seen to pay to save their own leisure time. In such situations people appear to put a value on their leisure time for themselves. Examples where this can be observed is in the choice of travel mode – people fly rather than drive to a holiday destination to save time – at what cost? People also pay tolls on motorways and bridges rather than take the slow road or the long way round. Studies have been conducted in such situations and have usually come up with leisure time valuations somewhat less than the wage rate – usually between half and two thirds of the wage rate, in fact.

This raises an important equity issue. Wealthy people are able to place a higher monetary value on their leisure time than poor people. The leisure time savings of a road scheme which affected residents of a wealthy area would therefore be valued more highly than the leisure time savings from a road scheme serving residents of a poor area; so the former scheme would be favoured. But it is generally accepted that this would not be appropriate and so all leisure time savings are valued at an average rate.

7 The timing of costs and benefits

In the discussion above it has been assumed that the costs and the benefits from a project are constant from one year to the next and can be estimated on an annual basis. This makes for simple calculations, but is not realistic for most projects. In fact, very often, costs are high early on and benefits are initially low, but increase over time. Rather than a single annual cost and annual benefit figure, therefore, it is necessary to examine the *flow* of annual costs and benefits over the life of the project – that is, over a reasonable time period, by which time major replacement or rebuilding might be expected.

The simple approach would be to add the flow of, say, 20 annual costs and benefits, and compare the two totals. However, two projects could have the same aggregates arising from very different sequences of costs and benefits. For example, in Table 8.8, it can be seen that, although both projects have the same aggregate net benefits, Project A has more net benefits early on in its life, but Project B's net benefits are not produced until later. Project A would therefore be preferred because, generally, other things being equal, people would prefer to obtain benefits earlier rather than later. This is reflected in the realities of interest payments which must be paid on borrowed money. Project A is 'in the black' from year 2, when the £1 million first-year deficit has been paid off. But Project B is 'in the red' until year 7, when the net benefits cancel out the accumulated deficits. This sort of consideration is applied by accountants to projects in the private sector. Even though, in a public-sector cost-benefit analysis, the costs and benefits may not represent cash, but estimated *social* costs and benefits, economists argue that they should be treated in the same way when evaluating projects.

Accountants overcome the problem of uneven flows of income and expenditure (costs and benefits) over the life of the project by use of a 'discount rate', which is the other side of the coin, as it were, to interest rates. If the current rate of interest is 10 per cent, then £100 invested for a year will be worth £110 in a year's time. Looked at another way, £110 in a year's time is worth £100 at present.

Table 8.8 Two projects compared over 10 years

Year	Project A			Project B		
	Costs	Benefits	Net benefits	Costs	Benefits	Net benefits
	£m	£m	£m	£m	£m	£m
1	10	9	–1	11	8	–3
2	8	9	+1	10	8	–2
3	7	10	+3	9	7	–2
4	7	10	+3	9	8	–1
5	6	11	+5	9	9	0
6	8	12	+4	8	12	+4
7	9	11	+2	7	12	+5
8	10	10	0	7	14	+7
9	9	9	0	7	13	+6
10	8	9	+1	8	12	+4
Total	82	100	+18	85	103	+18

The flow of net benefits can be 'discounted' to the present to give the 'net present value' (NPV) of the project. At an interest rate of 10 per cent, the NPV of project A is £11.3 million, whereas the NPV for project B is £7.6 million.

8 Presenting the cost-benefit analysis

The results of a cost-benefit analysis exercise must be drawn together in a summary table. The data may be in terms of annual amounts or net present values; in Table 8.9 the former is used.

Table 8.9 Summary cost-benefit analysis (annual flows) (hypothetical)

Costs	£'000 p.a.	Benefits	£'000 p.a.
Capital charges	1500	User benefits paid for (sales)	1750
Opportunity costs	400	User benefits not paid for (consumer surplus etc.)	750
Running costs	1800	Non-user benefits (may be various categories: public good, option demand, externalities, etc.)	1800
Externalities	450		
Total costs	4150	Total benefits	4300
		Surplus	+150

Economic impact analysis

1 Introduction

While cost-benefit analysis is concerned with the overall viability of an investment project, economic impact analysis is more limited in scope, being concerned mainly with the extent to which the project generates jobs and incomes, and not with other benefits or with detailed examination of costs. Thus, giving everybody £100 cash from the government coffers to spend as they please would have a measurable *economic impact*, but it is unlikely to be seen as wise use of funds in cost-benefit terms.

In terms of the economic arguments for state involvement in leisure, as discussed in chapter 4, economic impact analysis is linked to the *economic development* argument; government activity is justified in terms of its impact on jobs and incomes, in contrast to cost-benefit analysis, which is related to the market failure arguments, such as public goods and externalities.

If government activity is to be justified in terms of economic development then the main criterion for decision-making should be to obtain the maximum impact in terms of increased incomes and employment per pound (or million pounds) of government expenditure. Economic impact studies are therefore designed to produce statements of the form: 'The outlay of X pounds of government money on this project will produce Y pounds of increased income and/or Z new jobs.'

Economic impact studies may be undertaken:

- before initiating a project, as an aid to decision-making;
- after completion of the project, as a form of evaluation;
- after one event (eg a festival) in order to persuade government to continue to support future events.

Studies may be undertaken by government for its own needs, or by an interest group or organisation (including a Quango, such as the Arts Council) to persuade government and/or the community of the worth of a project or sector. One particular form of economic impact study examines the significance of a whole sector, such as the arts or sport, to the economy. Such studies might be better termed *economic significance* studies and are discussed separately below.

Often an economic impact study is concerned primarily with private-sector activity – for example studies of tourism or of a privately run sporting event – but the motivation for doing the study is invariably related to government and its role. The private sector does not undertake economic impact studies for its own use. Economic impact studies are undertaken to convince *government*, from an economic management point of view, to support a project. Often an event cannot run profitably and requires a subsidy from government; the latter is justified by demonstrating the amount of additional income which the event generates. For example, the report on a study of the Australian Formula One Grand Prix states that the Grand Prix '... regularly makes a financial operating loss of from £1m to £2.6m, but generates over £20m in extra income in South Australia' (Burgan and Mules, 1992: 708).

2 Counting the cost

The initial stage in economic impact analysis is to identify and quantify the expenditure items which are to be counted and the study area to which the analysis is to relate. The definition of study area is of key importance for the analyses discussed below. The net economic impact of a project is affected by the flows of money which it generates, into and out of the study area. Thus, if the study area is small, such as a local government area, the impact of a project is diminished by the considerable sums of money generated by the project which will inevitably flow to firms and individuals located outside the area. The larger the area the less chance there is of these 'leakages' occurring, since a project will be able to source its supplies and labour needs from within the area. The extent to which an area can do this, and therefore retain the maximum proportion of the income generated, depends not only on the size of the area but its overall economic structure. Thus an area with a furniture manufacturing industry, or high-tech design capabilities would not need to 'import' these goods and services and so would retain the benefit from expenditure on such items. However, a small study area can appear to benefit when visitor or customer flows and expenditure are involved, since more of the visitors or customers are then counted as coming from outside the area and therefore as bringing benefits into the area.

The smaller the study area the greater the proportion of money generated that 'leaks'. For example, if the study area is a single city the leakages are likely to be substantial; if it is a region the leaks will be less because more supplies will be sourced from within the region. If the study area is a whole country the leakages include only imports and overseas holiday expenditure. The level of leaks is also affected by the diversity of the economy. For example, an area with very little manufacturing will, in effect, 'import' most of its material supplies. At national level, small countries are likely to need to import more supplies than large countries.

As with cost-benefit analysis, part of the data requirements relate directly to the project under study: its construction and running costs. However, in the case of economic impact analysis we are not concerned with opportunity costs or non-financial aspects such as public good or externality effects.

It is, however, necessary to know something about the structure of the local economy, particularly how firms and other organisations, and private individuals, spend their incomes – for example, how much private individuals save, spend on food, housing and so on, and how much firms spend on wages, materials and rent. Surveys of organisations and private individuals could be conducted in the study area to discover this, or use could be made of existing data, for example national surveys of consumer and industry expenditure patterns. However, in small study areas the vital information on how much expenditure is allocated locally could only be gathered by survey. In the case of firms, they might be divided into different sectors, such as construction, services, retailing and so on.

3 The multiplier

The multiplier idea applies to any form of expenditure, but is usually applied to expenditures which represent net increases in demand for goods and services within an economy. Thus it is usually applied to any increase in expenditure from *outside* the area of study – for example export income, visitor expenditure, investment by firms from outside the area, or expenditure by a higher tier of government. However, it can also be applied to new investment expenditure by local firms or increased expenditure by the local tier of government, as long as it is not funded by increased taxation (eg it is funded by borrowing or by using reserves). It can be seen, therefore, that, in the area of leisure, the main area where this sort of analysis would apply is that of tourism, since tourism brings expenditure into an area from outside. Non-tourism examples do, however, exist. For example, day-visitors from outside the study area have the same effect as tourists; this applies to coastal and rural areas which attract day-visitors from urban settlements, and also urban centres which attract visitors from suburban and rural hinterlands for cultural, sporting and entertainment purposes. Investment by private firms or governments in leisure projects, such as sports or entertainment facilities, have multiplier effects.

The multiplier idea is that the initial expenditure of a sum of money is just the start of a process, not the end. For example, an investor who spends £1 million on building a leisure complex spends that money on the wages of construction workers and supplies of building materials and equipment. The construction workers spend their money on food, transport, housing and so on, and the suppliers of building materials and equipment spend the money they receive on wages for their workers, further supplies and so on. And so the process continues, with more and more 'rounds' of expenditure spreading throughout the economy. So does the original £1 million multiply endlessly, to produce an *infinite* 'multiplier'? The answer is 'no' – because of the phenomenon of 'leakages'. The firms and workers who receive payments in the various 'rounds' do not spend all the money they receive in the local area – much of it 'leaks' out. Some is spent directly outside the study area – for example by construction firms, equipment suppliers and retailers buying in supplies from outside the area and workers and their families going on holiday or buying mail-order. Some of the money is not 'spent' at all, but is deducted as income tax or VAT, or is retained as savings. So, on each 'round' of expenditure the amount of money circulating within the local economy is reduced.

The aim of multiplier analysis is to quantify these effects so that the overall net effect of project expenditure can be quantified. There are basically two ways in which this is done in such studies. One is by special surveys and the other is by means of an economic technique known as input-output analysis. We consider the use of special surveys here.

To simplify the explanation we will assume that surveys have established that firms in the area are fairly similar in their patterns of local and non-local expenditure. Suppose the survey reveals that firms, on average, spend 25 per cent of their income with other local firms, 40 per cent on wages and payments of profits to local residents, and 35 per cent outside the study area, in terms of imported supplies and taxes. And suppose that a resident survey establishes that the average resident spends 50 per cent of their income locally and 50 per cent goes in non-local expenditure or taxes. We are now in a position to trace what happens to project expenditure, and this is shown in Figure 8.6 in relation to a 'typical' £1000 of expenditure. (Note that these calculations can be relatively easily done by computer using a spreadsheet.)

After 15 rounds the sums involved become very small, so this analysis has been terminated at that stage. It shows that, as a result of the initial £1000 expenditure, local businesses experience an increase in turnover of £1817.64, including the initial £1000. Private individuals – wage-earners and business shareholders – experience an income increase of £726.90. The business turnover figure calculated in this way should be treated with some caution. It does not, in the economist's terms, represent 'value added' – there is a certain amount of 'double counting' in the figure. For example, if a leisure centre cafe buys pre-cooked meals from a catering company, which has in turn bought supplies from a retailer in the area, who in turn bought them from a wholesaler in the area, the value of the original supplies is counted three times (including the final sale to the customer); only the 'mark-up' at each sale constitutes 'value added'. The totals in Figure 8.6 nevertheless mean that an investment project of, say, £1 million, would generate an estimated £1,817,640 of business turnover in the area and £726,900 of personal incomes.

Figure 8.6 Multiplier analysis

Round	Leaks	Local firms	Private residents	Leaks
		£1000 Expenditure		
1		£1000		
2	£350	£250	£400	
3	£87.50	£200 + 62.5 = £262.50	£100	£200
4	£91.88	£50 + 65.63 = £115.63	£105	£50
5	£40.47	£52.50 + 28.91 = £81.41	£46.25	£52.50
6	£28.49	£23.13 + 20.35 = £43.48	£32.56	£23.13
7	£15.22	£16.28 + 10.87 = £27.15	£17.39	£16.28
8	£9.50	£8.70 + 6.78 = £15.48	£10.86	£8.70
9	£5.42	£5.43 + 3.87 = £9.30	£6.19	£5.43
10	£3.26	£3.10 + 2.32 = £5.42	£3.27	£3.10
11	£1.90	£1.86 + 1.36 = £3.22	£2.17	£1.86
12	£1.13	£1.08 + 0.81 = £1.89	£1.29	£1.08
13	£0.66	£0.64 + 0.47 = £1.11	£0.76	£0.64
14	£0.39	£0.38 + 0.28 = £0.66	£0.45	£0.38
15	£0.23	£0.22 + 0.17 = £0.39	£0.26	£0.22
Total		£1817.64	£726.90	

'Multipliers' are ratios relating the initial rounds of expenditure to aggregate effects. There are various multipliers which can be calculated. The 'business turnover' multiplier relates the initial business turnover to the overall business turnover; the more important income multiplier relates the initial income figure in round 2 to the overall income effect.

- Business turnover multiplier: $1817.64 \div 1000 = 1.82$
- Income multiplier: $726.90 \div 400 = 1.82$

The above is known in the tourism literature as the 'orthodox' income multiplier. An alternative, 'unorthodox' income multiplier relates the increase in income to the initial, round 1, expenditure:

- 'Unorthodox' income multiplier: $726.90 \div 1000 = 0.73$

The multiplier can be used to calculate the effect of projects of various size. Thus the impact of a £15 million project would be:

- Business turnover impact: £15,000,000 × 1.82 = £27,300,000
- Income impact: £15,000,000 × 0.73 = £10,950,000.

The calculations illustrated in Figure 8.6 can be repeated with varying levels of 'leakage' to show the effects of an economy with low leakage as opposed to one with high leakage, as shown in Table 8.10.

Table 8.10   High leakage and low leakage multipliers

		High leakage situation	Low leakage situation
	Expenditure item	**Proportion of expenditure**	
Firms	Wages etc.	0.3	0.4
	Local suppliers	0.2	0.4
	Leakage	0.5	0.2
Private residents	Local firms	0.4	0.7
	Leakage	0.6	0.3
Business turnover multiplier		1.5	3.1
Income multiplier (unorthodox)		0.4	1.2

Often the interest in the economic impact of a project is in its job-generating effect. The income effect can be translated into a measure of the employment effect by use of an average wage or income rate. Thus, in the example given above, where a £15 million project produced a total increase in incomes of £10,950,000, if the average income is £10,000 per annum, the number of full-time equivalent jobs created is:

$$10,950,000 \div 10,000 = 1095 \text{ full-time equivalent jobs}$$

It should be noted, however, that such estimates rarely translate directly into full-time jobs. For some businesses the effect of the project will be only very small and will not justify employing additional staff; it might result in increased overtime for existing staff, or, if there is spare capacity, an increase in profits for the owners of the firm. Often, jobs will be short-term or part-time. The estimate of the employment effect is therefore very approximate.

An alternative method of calculating multipliers, especially for large projects, is via an economic technique known as *input-output* analysis. This is a form of economic modelling which seeks to emulate the inter-relationships among the various sectors of the economy. Detailed discussion is beyond the scope of this book; for more information readers are referred to any introductory economics textbook.

4 Economic significance studies

In times when 'economic rationalism' is guiding government policy over-all, representatives of certain industry sectors feel compelled to justify their existence in economic terms. This is especially true of areas of leisure which have, in the past, been viewed primarily as a 'cost' to the community – a 'consumption item', as 'non-essential' or, as in the case of tourism, simply not recognised as a 'serious' industry sector. To some extent all service industries in modern developed countries suffer from this problem of perception. Despite the fact that services constitute as much as three quarters of a modern economy, including a significant proportion of international trade, the perception persists in the com-munity that the *real* business of the economy lies in such activities as agriculture, mining and manufacturing. Service industries suffer from an 'image' problem. Organisations representing sport and the arts have seen it as necessary to draw the attention of government to the dimen-sions of these areas *as industries.*

Such studies involve collation of statistics on turnover of various sectors of the economy and government and consumer expenditure. This often entails considerable effort since 'official' statistics do not always identify leisure expenditure as such. For example, a considerable proportion of transport and clothing expenditure is for leisure purposes.

Examples of such studies include the study of *The Economic Impact and Importance of Sport in the UK*, commissioned by the Sports Council from the Henley Centre for Forecasting (1986). This estab-lished that sport accounted for £5.6 billion of 'value added' in the UK economy in 1985, and supported 376,000 jobs. A study of *The Economic Importance of the Arts in Britain* was commissioned by the Gulbenkian Foundation, the government Office of the Arts and Libraries, the Museums and Galleries Commission, the Arts Council of Great Britain and the Crafts Council from the Policy Studies Institute and published in 1988 (Myerscough et al., 1988). It estimated that, in 1985, the turnover of the arts sector in Britain was some £10 billion, with 'value added' of £4 billion, and 486,000 jobs supported. Similar studies have been conducted by the government in Australia (DASETT, 1988, 1988a).

Figure 8.7 shows the findings of a study conducted in the state of Michigan in the USA in relation to the arts (Touche Ross, 1985). The aim was to show the relationship between the government inputs into the arts, in the form of grants and tax concessions on gifts, and the size of the industry as a whole. As the diagram shows, in 1983, $55 million of 'gifts and grants' went to arts organisations which earned additional income, mainly from the box office, of $78 million, and spent a total of $133 million in the local economy, mainly in the form of wages to artists. A multiplier effect of 1.5 transforms this into a 'total economic impact' of $195 million. The aim of the exercise was to demonstrate to government that the $55 million of grants and gifts underpinned an industry with a much larger economic significance. It should not, of course, be assumed that withdrawal of the $55 million would result in a total loss of $195 million to the Michigan economy, since some of the $55 million might be spent elsewhere and have similar effects, and the money earned at the box office would probably also be mostly still spent in the local economy. The purpose of such an exercise should therefore be to demonstrate that activities such as the arts do play, like other forms of economic activity, an economic role in society, as well as a cultural one.

Figure 8.7   Arts industry in Michigan

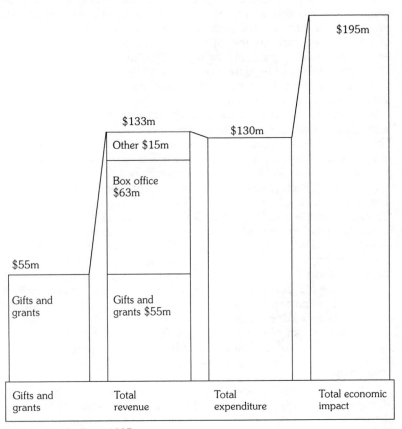

Source: Touche Ross, 1985

Further reading

Willingness to pay: Peterson, Driver and Gregory, 1988.

Travel cost/Clawson method: Clawson and Knetsch, 1962.

Tourism impacts: Faulkner, 1993; Mathieson and Wall, 1982; Frechtling, 1994, 1994a.

The arts: Baumol and Bowen, 1976; Myerscough *et al.*, 1988; Touche Ross, 1985; Throsby and O'Shea, 1980.

Sport: Gratton and Taylor, 1985, 1991.

Outdoor recreation: Peterson, Driver and Gregory, 1988.

Multiplier: Bull, 1991; Smith, 1989.

9 PERFORMANCE EVALUATION

Introduction: Evaluation in context

The logic of formal models of the planning/management process is that outcomes of public policy programmes or projects should be evaluated – they should be subject to 'performance appraisal'. That is, they should be examined to see to what extent they are achieving what they were intended to achieve (effectiveness), and whether they are doing so at an acceptable cost (efficiency). Evaluation can be seen as an important part of the cycle of decision-making, as illustrated in Figure 5.1 (see page 51). Decisions on what to do next are made to a large extent on the basis of experience of current and past policies and their outcomes, so evaluation of current and past activities feeds into subsequent rounds of decision-making.

One key method of evaluation, which has recently grown in importance, is economic evaluation. In this context two techniques have already been examined, namely cost-benefit and economic impact analysis. As indicated in chapter 8, these techniques can be used to evaluate projects *before* they happen, when they might be viewed as part of the planning process, or they can be used to evaluate projects *after* they have been implemented, when they become part of the evaluation process. However, in most areas of public policy such techniques tend to be used for major, high-cost, high-profile projects and are treated as research or inquiry techniques rather than everyday tools of management. For day-to-day, or year-to-year decision-making public organisations tend to use less formalised and less expensive techniques.

Most observers would agree that, in the western world, there will continue to be pressure on public-sector organisations to evaluate their activities in a formal manner, and leisure service organisations will not be exempt from this trend. Pressures will come from outside of leisure service organisations – mainly from governments which provide the money – and from inside organisations, as staff with professional management skills, and who are familiar with the processes, gain ascendancy.

It might be thought that privatisation and Compulsory Competitive Tendering have simplified the evaluation process by reducing it to financial considerations only. But this is not the case. If the management of a service is contracted out then the public body must decide what terms to include in the management contract and must decide whether or not the resultant service is worth the management fee. Even where a service is apparently financially self-sufficient, it is rarely the case that capital or opportunity costs are covered. Thus the authority still has to decide whether the service provided is worth the allocation of land and buildings, or whether the community would be better off if the land were sold to the highest bidder. In fact, Compulsory Competitive Tendering has, if anything, focused attention on objectives and, consequently, on evaluation.

The results of evaluation can take a variety of forms. Firstly, they may be a routinised element in the organisation's 'management information system', so that the performance of particular programmes or departments can be evaluated on a regular basis. This is comparable to the regular financial reports which managers receive on 'profit centres' in private-sector organisations. Secondly, evaluation can take the form of *ad hoc*, one-off exercises – reports commissioned by senior management or external authorities, as required. Thirdly, evaluation may appear in the *Annual Report* which most public organisations are required to produce. Many governments are now attempting to influence the form and content of such annual reports to ensure that they contain evaluative information, linked to strategic Corporate Plans. Corporate Plans require organisations to follow the conventional management/planning model involving the setting of objectives and evaluation of outcomes.

Evaluation can be seen as either *operational* or *comparative*. *Operational evaluation* is designed to assess the performance of a programme or project in its own terms – it is a self-contained exercise. For example, if a programme was established to spend £5 million to increase the numbers of a certain category of visitor to a site by 25 per cent in a given time period, the programme would be evaluated in those terms – that is, whether it stayed within budget and resulted in the requisite increase in visitors in the time period specified. Operational evaluation has the advantage that the criteria for success are decided by the organisation or section of the organisation which is responsible for the programme and which should therefore be most familiar with it. The same feature can, however, also be seen as a disadvantage because it can be abused by those individuals or organisations who may choose unambitious targets or criteria, so that, in effect, they cannot fail. This is overcome to some extent by comparative evaluation.

Comparative evaluation is more difficult to implement because it involves deciding how one programme is performing compared with another. This is manageable when dealing with similar types of programme/facility with similar objectives – for example comparing the performance of two or more swimming pools. This idea is sometimes referred to as 'benchmarking', a process by which external 'benchmark' performance measures are established for certain types of management unit. Of course, certain differences, for example in the age of the facilities, public transport access, or the nature of the local neighbourhood population, may produce differences which make comparisons of performance difficult if not impossible. At a higher level, government may wish to evaluate across a number of totally different programme areas, for example they may wish to decide whether a museums service is performing as well as a national parks service, or how arts programmes compare with health programmes in terms of value for money. In the private sector this common 'benchmarking' is achieved by means of the financial 'rate of return' on capital.

Effectiveness versus efficiency

Evaluation is usually concerned with both effectiveness – the extent to which the programme has achieved what it was intended to achieve – and efficiency – the cost per unit of output. It is here where evaluation often becomes particularly threatening to the public service, because, even if measures of effectiveness can be agreed and a programme or project is evaluated as being very successful in terms of its effectiveness, it can still be seen as inefficient.

The public-sector professional is often motivated by professional values concerned with quality of output and standards appropriate to the culture of the service involved; so talk of efficiency, particularly if associated with cost-cutting, can be seen as a threat to all that – indeed, as a threat to the very substance of the professional's judgement. By contrast, in the commercial sector, where making profit is the main aim, cost-cutting is more likely to be seen in a positive light, especially if things are arranged so that the person or department achieving the savings is seen to get the credit for doing so. This, however, does not preclude problems in the private sector, where certain groups in an organisation may be less profit-orientated and more 'quality'-orientated than others – for example the design, engineering or research sections of a manufacturing company or the creative workers in the broadcasting or entertainment sector.

Despite fears and misgivings, the pressure is on to measure efficiency as well as effectiveness. This requires public organisations to measure *outputs* as well as *inputs*. In Figure 9.1, as output (effectiveness) increases, an organisation would expect to move along a line such as A – that is, costs would rise also. Staying on the one line would, however, imply that efficiency (costs per unit of output) was remaining constant. Increasing efficiency involves moving onto a lower line, such as B. While the proponents of corporate management and evaluation would claim to be attempting to move organisations onto new efficiency lines such as B, others would claim that often the effect is simply cost-cutting, which moves the organisation back down along line A – thus reducing effectiveness.

Figure 9.1 Effectiveness vs efficiency

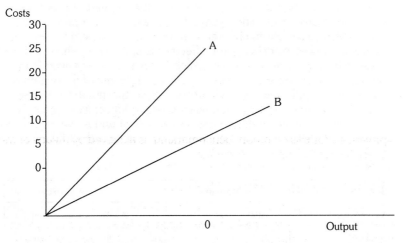

The evaluation process

How, then, does evaluation take place? The first step is to refer to the goals or objectives of the organisation, programme or facility, as discussed in chapter 5. Then indicators must be established which show the extent to which the programme or facility has reached or progressed towards its goals or objectives.

Gratton and Taylor (1988: 150, 152) contrast performance evaluation in the private and public sectors. In the private sector objectives are generally considered to be simpler than in the public sector – the objective is to maximise profits and/or growth. However, the range of 'performance ratios' devised by accountants to evaluate companies is considerable, including profits as a proportion of sales *and* as a rate of return on capital, liquidity measures, asset utilisation measures, capital structure (share capital vs loans) and investment measures (share price vs dividends). No single measure is adequate to evaluate a firm, although some measures may be considered more important than others. For public-sector leisure organisations Gratton and Taylor put forward a similarly extensive range of measures, which they divide into effectiveness, efficiency and economy measures. The discussion below considers effectiveness, efficiency and economy measures in turn.

Effectiveness measures

Examples of effectiveness measures for public leisure services given by Gratton and Taylor include levels of expenditure, levels of visits, participation rates, facility capacity utilisation and marketing expenditure. Bovaird (1992) takes the measurement of effectiveness one step further by suggesting that it involves not just *throughput*, such as numbers of users of a service, but also *impact*, meaning the qualitative effects of use of the service on the user – for example improved fitness.

Hatry and Dunn (1971) give an example of how such qualitative assessments might be incorporated, and how the evaluation process can be related to objectives. Their suggested objectives for a public recreation service are set out in chapter 5. Implicit in the statement on page 61 are a number of *criteria* for effectiveness, each of which can be assessed by means of *measures*, which in turn can be derived from a number of *data sources*, as shown in Table 9.1. Some of these items of data could be collected routinely (for example the number of attendances at swimming pools), but others would require special data-collection exercises (for example attendances at parks) and some would require quite detailed research (for example citizen or user attitudes).

Table 9.1 Community recreation performance criteria and measures

Criteria	Measures	Data sources
A Adequacy	A1 Attendances A2 Participants/non-participants A3 Persons living within x mins/y miles of facilities A4 User/resident perceptions	A1 Ticket sales or counts A2 A1 + user surveys (frequency of visit) + pop'n census (non-users) A3 Maps and population census A4 User/resident surveys
B Enjoyableness	B1 Attendances B2 Participants/non-participants	B1 As A1 B2 As A2
C Accessibility	C1 Persons living within x mins/y miles of facilities	C1 As A3
D (Un)crowdedness	D1 Crowdedness indices D2 Waiting times D3 Numbers turned away D4 Capacity utilisation D5 User perceptions	D1 Combination of D2–D5 D2 Management study D3 Management study/ records D4 Management study D5 User survey
E Variety	E1 Number of different activities catered for	E1 Inventory
F Safety	F1 Accidents	F1 Management records
G Physical attractiveness	G1 Index of attractiveness	G1 Special study + user/ resident survey
H Crime reduction	H1 Crime rates	H1 Police records
I Health enhancement	J1 Illness	J1 Local health records or special study
J Economic well-being	K1 Business income, jobs, property affected	K1 Cost-benefit study (see chapter 8)

Source: Hatry and Dunn, 1971

The Hatry and Dunn exercise involves a four-step process: 1 examining the statement of objectives; 2 isolating from it criteria for evaluation; 3 devising ways to assess/measure those criteria; 4 carrying out the data collection and evaluation.

In the course of this book a wide variety of goals and objectives for leisure facilities have been alluded to. Some arise from political philosophies and some are implicit in the planning and evaluation techniques discussed. Table 9.2 summarises these various goals and objectives and relates them to appropriate measures of effectiveness. This appears to be a very daunting list, but many, such as the political values, are alternatives, and others, such as economic development or the encouragement of infant industries, only apply in special circumstances.

Table 9.2 points to a need for substantial data collection on a regular basis. Some of this data collection relates to the 'environmental appraisal', as summarised in Table 5.2 (see page 54). But what is being suggested here is that, rather than being 'one-off' data-collection exercises for the purpose of establishing the plan or strategy, they need to be repeated on a regular basis if policies are to be evaluated. In practice, however, the cost of collecting some of the data specified may be considered excessive and they may be ignored or undertaken only rarely – this applies particularly to those items requiring research. Public-sector agencies tend to see evaluative and market research as major, exceptional undertakings, whereas many private-sector organisations see continuous user and market research (for example, annual market surveys) as a normal activity. Following discussion of the question of efficiency and economy, Table 9.2 draws together the data-collection requirements of the environmental appraisal and the evaluation tasks.

Efficiency measures

Efficiency involves a ratio – of outputs to inputs. Gratton and Taylor (1988: 152) give examples as follows:

- net running costs per head of population
- gross operating costs per visit
- net operating costs (subsidy) per visit
- income vs gross costs (cost recovery)
- income per member of staff
- visits per staff-hour (productivity)

All except the last of these are financial measures, but non-financial resources can also be involved, particularly space. Thus visits per square metre or, in an auditorium, per seat, might also be used. Table 9.2 links efficiency measures with corresponding goals (as discussed at various points in the book), effectiveness measures and data sources. Again, this exercise points to the need for a substantial data-collection requirement – particularly the ability to allocate service costs to particular facilities and programmes and to link this with visitor numbers.

Table 9.2 Goals and measures of effectiveness and efficiency

Goal	Measures of effectiveness/ efficiency	Comm. survey	User surveys	Ticket sales	User counts	Inven-tory	Service costs	Own records	Census	Special study
						Data Sources				
Access to facilities for chosen leisure activities for all	*Effectiveness* Proportion of pop'n participating	•								
	Proportion of popn within reach of facilities	•				•			•	
	Proportion of pop'n satisfied with service	•	•							
	Efficiency Net cost per visit/participant			•	•		•			
Provision for need for all	*Effectiveness* Extent to which needs (eg. see Social priority analysis) are met (eg see grid method)	•	•							
	Efficiency Net cost per visit/participant						•			
Maintain existing provision	*Effectiveness* Qualitative measures					•				
	Efficiency –									
Promote excellence	*Effectiveness* Excellence: medals, awards, records, etc.									•
	Efficiency Costs per medal etc.						•			
Minimise state role	*Effectiveness* Short-term: extent of privatisation Long-term: quantity and quality of service	•					•	•		
	Efficiency Public/private service costs						•	•		
Extend state role	*Effectiveness* Growth of facilities/staff/user numbers				•			•		
	Efficiency Costs per visit/participant			•	•		•			
Promote equality of opportunity	*Effectiveness* Proportion of different social groups participating (eg see grid)	•	•						•	
	Efficiency Costs per visit by target group	•	•				•			
Promote democratisation	*Effectiveness* Representation on governing bodies									•
	Efficiency –									
Provide facilities and opportunities which counter commercial exploitation	*Effectiveness* Qualitative measures									•
	Efficiency –									
Promote facilities/ programmes which counter patriarchy	*Effectiveness* Qualitative indicators of change	•	•							•
	Efficiency –									

Objective	Measures							
Promote access to facilities by women	*Effectiveness* Number of facilities/ programmes — Female participation levels	●	●	●	●	●		
	Efficiency Cost per visit/female participant	●	●	●	●		●	
Child-care provision	*Effectiveness* Number of child-care places and utilisation			●		●		
	Efficiency Cost per child place/visit			●		●	●	
Promote environmentally friendly activities	*Effectiveness* 'Environmental audit' of programmes							●
	Efficiency Cost per user compared with others							●
Protect the natural environment	*Effectiveness* Area protected				●			
	Qualitative review							●
	Efficiency –							
Provide services which provide public good, externality, mixed good, merit good and option demand benefits	*Effectiveness* Willingness-to-pay surveys	●	●				●	●
	Measure health etc. benefits	●	●					●
	Clawson method			●				
	Efficiency Costs per visit/rate of return				●	●	●	
Promote economic activity through leisure	*Effectiveness* Profit — Economic impact – jobs, incomes	●					●	●
	Efficiency Cost per job created					●		●
Promote equity	*Effectiveness* Visits by deprived groups	●	●				●	●
	Efficiency Costs per visit	●	●				●	●
Meet standards (various)	*Effectiveness* Facility inventory				●			
	Efficiency –							
Raise demand at least to the national/regional average	*Effectiveness* Participation levels	●					●	
	Efficiency Costs per visit/participant					●		
Serve all areas	*Effectiveness* Catchment areas, access and usage in different areas	●	●					
	Efficiency Costs per visit in different areas	●	●			●		
Ensure full range of facilities	*Effectiveness* Facility inventory for each level of community				●			
	Efficiency –							

Goal	Measure	1	2	3	4	5	6	7	8	9	10	11	12
Meet needs of target groups in specified areas	*Effectiveness* Access and facilities in target areas	•	•										
	Efficiency Costs per visit/target participant	•	•							•			•
Provide full range of experiences	*Effectiveness* Inventory of facility/ resource types							•		•			
	Consumer reaction	•	•										
	Efficiency Cost per visit/experience type	•	•	•	•	•	•						
Appropriate provision for all groups	*Effectiveness* Participation levels by all groups	•	•									•	
	Efficiency Costs per visit/target participant	•	•	•	•					•			
Serve all areas	*Effectiveness* Facility catchment areas		•										
	Efficiency Costs per visit/different areas			•	•					•			
Maximise utilisation of facilities	*Effectiveness* facility utilisation			•	•	•						•	•
	Efficiency Costs per unit of capacity												•
Meet community wishes	*Effectiveness* Community satisfaction	•											•
	Efficiency –												

Economy measures

Economy is related to the purchase of materials and services. Improvements in economy are achieved through reducing the prices paid for inputs. It has to be assumed that this is generally achieved by such methods as 'shopping around', buying in bulk and so on, rather than buying inferior products. However, there may be situations where a reduction in quality of input is justified if it does not detract from the quality of the end-product.

In general, improved economy assists efficiency, since it affects the costs of inputs; there could, however, be situations where improved purchasing practices result in the buying of better quality inputs, which improve effectiveness.

Operationalising evaluation

While the Hatry and Dunn statement is useful for illustrating the connection between goals and performance evaluation, in practice, goal statements, through the planning process, lead to the establishment of individual services, facilities and programmes, each with their own sets of specific goals and objectives and it is these which form the basis for the evaluation exercise.

In essence, therefore, the evaluation process involves, for every policy, facility, service, programme or sub-programme, the following steps:

1 identification of goals
2 specification of objectives (targets)
3 devising measures of effectiveness (in achieving objectives)
4 devising efficiency measures
5 specification of data-collection methods
6 collection of base-line data
7 data collection at specified times (eg weekly, quarterly, annually)
8 comparison of base-line data with current data and with targets or external benchmark data
9 delivery of verdict

Further reading

Programme evaluation in general: Shadish *et al.*, 1991; Quade, 1989.

Leisure programme evaluation: Hatry and Dunn, 1971; Torkildsen, 1993 (Guide 13); Theobald, 1979; Bovaird, 1992; Stabler and Ravenscroft, 1993.

10 POLICY AND PLANNING FOR PARTICULAR SECTORS AND GROUPS

Introduction

In the bulk of this book, while examples have been given of different aspects of leisure, the discussion and analysis have been conducted largely in terms of leisure as a whole. In fact, as has also been noted, leisure is a diverse and multi-faceted phenomenon. While the *common* elements in the various aspects of leisure have been stressed in most of the book, in this chapter the diversity, and the implications of that diversity for policy and planning, are examined. While 'leisure' has been considered in general terms, so have 'people'. The differing needs and demands of various social groups within the community are therefore also considered here. The examination is necessarily brief; more specialised and detailed sources are listed in the Further Reading.

Sectors

There are many ways in which leisure might be divided: including along geographical, temporal, institutional and experiential dimensions, as indicated in Table 10.1.

For the purposes of this chapter a hybrid categorisation is used, combining a number of the above dimensions, to identify five sectors: 1 sport and physical recreation, 2 the arts, 3 outdoor recreation in natural areas, 4 urban outdoor recreation and 5 tourism.

The discussion of each sector is under four headings: the scope of the sector, the rationale and goals of policy within the sector, institutional factors, and planning. The rationale for public involvement in the sector and the consequent goals which are generally pursued, and planning, relate directly to the issues addressed in this book. Institutional aspects have not, however, been discussed in great detail in the rest of the book; one such aspect, which is common to all five sectors, is the 'Quango' phenomenon.

Table 10.1 Classification of leisure

Geographical	Temporal
• Home-based activities • Neighbourhood trips • District or city trips • Regional/state-wide trips • Nation-wide trips • International trips	• Day-to-day • Weekly/fortnightly • Irregular • Seasonal • Annual • Life-cycle related • Once-in-a-life-time events
Institutional	**Experiential**
• Family-based • Community-based • Work or school-based leisure or: • Commercially provided – home-based • Commercially provided – out-of-home • Public-sector provided • Voluntary-sector provided	• Rest and relaxation • Entertainment • Socialising • Cultural activity • Physical recreation • Environmental experience • Travel • Educational

Leisure is, *par excellence*, the field of the 'Quango' (Quasi-Autonomous Non-Governmental Organisation). These are organisations established by governments and funded by governments and whose members are appointed by governments, but which are seen as being, to some extent, separate from and independent of government. One reason for the use of such an organisational device is referred to in the arts in particular as the 'arm's length' principle: the idea that government should not be seen to be directly interfering with such matters as the arts or sport or heritage – that policy should be in the hands of disinterested experts. An alternative reason is that, in these specialised areas, a more flexible organisational structure is required than the traditional, bureaucratic government department; this argument is more likely to be applied in more commercially orientated areas such as tourism.

Thus in a number of leisure sectors the most important single public organisation is usually the national Quango - the Sports Council, the Arts Council, the Countryside Commission, the Tourism Commission, and so on. Such organisations are extremely important to the field, because of the financial resources they command, because of their connection with national government and because of their ability to conduct research, launch campaigns and generally influence the direction of the field. However, it should be borne in mind that such organisations, however influential, are only one 'player' in the field. Often the *collective* importance of other organisations is greater, particularly in the financial sense; thus, for example, local authorities collectively spend far more money on sport, the arts and the countryside than do the Sports Council, the Arts Council and the Countryside Commission respectively, and voluntary organisations in these areas are often equally important. While the 350 British local authorities and thousands of voluntary organisations may have a lower profile and be less easy to study than national organisations, their activities – or inactivity – can be far more significant for leisure.

1 Sport and physical recreation

Scope
Sport is fairly easily defined as competitive or challenging physical, ludic activity, and as such involves a variety of activities ranging from informal individual, family or community-based activity to highly competitive and commercialised phenomena of world-wide proportions. Physical recreation encompasses those activities which are physical in nature and leisure-orientated, but not necessarily competitive or organised – typical activities being walking, non-competitive cycling and some forms of water-based recreation.

Rationale and goals
Sport and physical recreation is generally the focus of public policy because of the health benefits it brings, together with such features as the fostering of community cohesiveness and pride, and economic factors such as the attraction of industry or the economic impact of major events, for example the Olympic or Commonwealth Games. In general, therefore, the aim of public policy is, on the one hand, to maximise participation in sport and physical recreation among the general population ('Sport for All'), and on the other hand to promote maximum high-level achievement in competitive sport, both locally and internationally. Those involved in sport, however, tend to enjoy it for its own sake and may be somewhat bemused at others' need to justify support in instrumental terms. As a result, much political support for sport may arise as a result of the lobbying activity of sporting organisations and their associates, rather than from some appraisal of the benefit of sport to the wider community.

To some extent the two goals of sports policy – high-level performance and 'Sport for All' – are complementary and to some extent they are in competition, if not in contradiction. One view is that sport thrives on a sort of 'pyramid' model, as shown in Figure 10.1. A strong, broad, mass participation base should provide the breeding ground for talent to produce the elite athletes for international competition. Conversely, a successful elite and a strong local and national competitive structure should provide interest and inspiration to encourage the base.

Figure 10.1   Sports participation pyramid

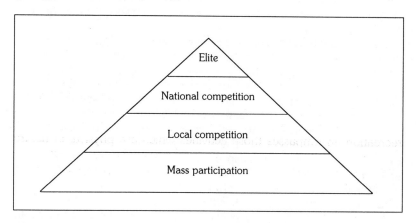

Institutional factors

While the 'pyramid' scenario may indeed work, the planning and management of organisational structures to achieve it can be extremely difficult. At each level there is involvement of public, private and commercial organisations, with different sets of goals and different modes of operation. Those professional and voluntary managers and policy-makers involved in opposite ends of the pyramid often do not subscribe to, or even understand, the 'pyramid' philosophy: they have their own, very different perspectives. Indeed, someone involved in elite sports competition may have a low opinion of recreational sport and resent the resources devoted to it, while someone involved in community recreation may be philosophically antagonistic towards the very concept of elitism, and resent the resources being devoted to the support of elite sport.

At the 'community' level in the pyramid the distinction between sport, physical recreation and social recreation becomes blurred: the community recreation manager may feel that it is just as useful, or even more useful, to provide opportunities to enable elderly people to get 'out of the house' for a game of bingo at the leisure centre, or to get teenagers to exercise through attendance at a discotheque, as it is to provide for more conventional sports activities. On the other hand, the desire to reach as wide a cross-section of the community as possible and to max-imise attendances at leisure facilities may, in the view of some, lead to over-concentration on superficial 'dabbling' in sporting activity and neglect of facilities, resources and organisational structures for those who wish to progress or improve.

At the elite level questions can arise over just how far individuals should push themselves, or be pushed, to excel and win for the benefit of national pride, if this is at the expense of long-term physical and mental health. Further, while public resources are provided to support the development of athletes in the context of an amateur ethos, increasing commercialisation and professionalisation of sport results, ultimately, in great personal financial rewards for some and raises questions of 'who pays?'

The concept of elitism raises issues related to amateurism, professionalism and commercialism. In sport, professionalism usually implies financial self-sufficiency: that is, those sectors where the athletes are professional do not generally look to the public sector for subsidy; they derive their income from spectators, television fees and sponsorship. In traditional sports different relationships have grown up between the publicly funded amateur part of the sport and the commercially funded professional part, although the relationship has not always been amicable, as witness the relationship between Rugby League (professional) and Rugby Union (amateur). On the other hand, in the case of boxing, the limited facilities required for training have enabled the sport, even at amateur level, to be fairly self-sufficient. Tennis has relied on private clubs, sometimes helped by public funds and sometimes using public facilities. In the case of golf, amateurs pay their way and use the same facilities as the professionals, while publicly provided facilities also tend to be financially self-sufficient. In the case of soccer, the amateur game is extensively supported through subsidised access to publicly provided playing pitches.

Planning

As chapter 6 indicates, planning for sport facilities for the community on the basis of standards of provision for playing fields is a long-established tradition. Since its establishment in the early 1970s, the British Sports Council has been instrumental in widening the scope of public planning to include such facilities as sports centres and swimming pools, dual use of education facilities, the utilisation of more sophisticated planning techniques and the development of inter-linked national, regional and local strategies (Sports Council, 1972, 1975, 1978, 1982, 1988, 1991, 1991a, 1993).

Planning for the promotion of mass participation by means other than the provision of facilities is a less certain process. Direct promotion by means of publicity campaigns has been difficult to evaluate, as have education programmes (McIntosh and Charlton, 1985).

Planning for the top part of the pyramid is complicated by the involvement of numerous national and international governing bodies of sport, commercial promoters, professional players' organisations, media interests and, in the public-sector corner, the Quangos, often with ministers, despite the 'arm's length' principle, looking closely over their shoulders. The core of planning at this level is the formal strategic plan of the governing body; such a plan is a necessity if the aspirations of the sport are to be supported by public funds (Elvin, 1990: 73).

2 The arts

Scope
The arts cover a wide spectrum of human activity, including the performing arts, of theatre, music, opera and dance; painting and sculpture and their exhibition in galleries; craft activities; museums and other forms of heritage conservation; literature and poetry; libraries; architecture and design; and film, television and radio.

Rationale and goals
Public subsidy of the arts, particularly the performing arts, has traditionally been justified on the grounds of the wider cultural benefits which they bring to the community (Baumol and Bowen, 1976). Other arguments relate to their growing economic importance (Myerscough *et al.*, 1988; Wall, 1983) and, especially in relation to galleries, museums and libraries, their educational value (Baumol and Bowen, 1976).

The arts have certain similarities with sport and certain stark differences. The similarities lie in the duality of objectives: excellence versus mass involvement. The differences lie in the structure of the industry and its relationship with the public. The irony is that the elements of the arts industry which are financially self-sufficient tend to be classified as 'entertainment' rather than the arts. Thus those areas which make money – film, the commercial theatre, recorded music, commercial television, and publishing – are classified as 'entertainment' or 'popular culture', and it would seem that, to exaggerate only a little, only if an activity does not make money can it be classified as 'art'. However, whereas in sport public resources are required to enable direct participation by members of the public in the activity, and professionals are largely self-supporting, in the case of the arts, public resources are required to support *professionals*, with the public role being largely that of audience only.

The area of the arts which corresponds to grass-roots sports participation is 'amateur theatre', 'amateur music', etc. Whereas the 'amateur' is a celebrated phenomenon in sport, in the arts amateur activity is looked down upon. Active participation in the arts is either left to voluntary effort (for example amateur music and drama), to the public or commercial education sector (for example adult education classes in painting or pottery, or commercial dance studios), or to self-help (for example, amateur rock and jazz bands). When the arts community itself ventures into the area or participation – in the form of 'community arts' – it is often controversial (Kelly, 1984).

There is a further difference between sport and the arts which is worth noting, since it leads to a particular difficulty in arts policy and management which does not arise in sports policy and management. This is that, in the arts, the concept of excellence is often disputed, whereas it is not in sport. There is generally no dispute about who is the number one ranking tennis player, or what team won the World Cup. In particular, there is a consensus between athletes, sports administrators and the general public about what excellence is. This is not the case in the arts:

what artists or administrators think of as excellence is often at variance with the tastes of the general public. While there are exceptions, in general the public will flock to performances of the familiar and the 'unchallenging', but will stay away in droves from productions which are new or 'difficult'. Hence arts managers are often faced with trying to balance artistic challenge and integrity with commercial 'realities' – getting 'bums on seats'.

Libraries are often neglected in discussion of the arts, and yet they are the most pervasive and significant of the publicly funded arts/cultural services; Waters reports that in the late 1980s, of the £1000 million of national and local expenditure on the arts in Britain (although this excludes the BBC), almost £500 million was spent on libraries, of which over £400 million was spent by local authorities (Waters, 1989: 68). Of course, public libraries have an educational and information-providing role, but most of their use is for leisure purposes (Taylor and Johnson, 1973). While it is, no doubt, their educational and information roles which provide much of the basis for their continued political support as free public services, the leisure function of libraries offers an interesting case-study of public provision. Lending libraries are obviously socially desirable since, possibly, several hundred people can read one book, compared with only a few in the case of private ownership. But why should the borrower not pay? Private lending libraries existed into the 1950s, where people paid a small sum to borrow books, in the same way that they currently hire film video-cassettes. But they were eventually undermined by the arrival of the cheap paperback. The free public lending library has the advantage of making a wider range of titles available to the reader (not all books are available in cheap paperback editions) and makes books available to those for whom even paperback prices would be a deterrent. As a leisure service, therefore, the public lending library is both efficient and equitable. Against this must be balanced the financial interests of publishers and authors, which have been addressed to a certain extent by the Public Lending Right Act, 1979.

Similar arguments apply to art galleries and museums: an infinite number of people may enjoy works of art and heritage items in galleries, compared with just a few if they were privately owned. To this extent galleries and museums meet the 'non-rival', although not the 'non-excludable', criterion for public goods, as discussed in chapter 4. In addition, the 'natural monopoly' criterion applies in relation to single works of art, or collections of national or even world cultural importance.

Broadcasting is a quintessential public good even if provided entirely for leisure purposes and even if commercially supported through advertising. It is likely, however, that public broadcasting bodies, such as the BBC, generally receive their political support not because of their leisure role but because of their educational, information and national cultural identity role. Like libraries and museums, their primary *function*, as leisure services, is not necessarily the basis of their continued *funding*.

Institutional factors

Because of the need to support professional performers in a subsidised environment the central preoccupation of much of the arts management community would appear to be funding. In the performing arts, a large proportion of funding is generated from the box office and other entrepreneurial activities, while the balance comes in the form of grants from local or central government. It is the latter which attracts the most debate and controversy. Clearly, if governments would provide more money the arts would have more freedom to pursue their artistic aims, and would be less constrained by the discipline of the box office. The controllers of the public purse strings might, however, look askance at such a proposition: surely 'less dependence on the box office' means fewer people attending performances – surely that would not be achieving the public objective of bringing the arts to the people! Of course, the arts organisations *could* be saying: if we had more money we could mount more lavish productions, provide more variety and put on more performances in more locations – this would bring the arts to more people. In so far as the public funding bodies are suspicious of the earlier argument but are sympathetic to the latter, they have an interest in knowing just how any additional funding will be used. Hence they may become embroiled in arguments about interference with artistic freedom.

In the case of other art forms, notably galleries and museums, the preoccupation with funding is equally prevalent. While 'blockbuster', money-making exhibitions and entrance fees are becoming more common, galleries and museums are usually even more dependent on public subsidy than are the performing arts. This has traditionally been justified on the educational grounds discussed above. The demand for additional funding is nevertheless endemic. Museum trustees and managements always need money for acquisitions, for expansion to exhibit the artefacts they have stored away, or for staff to pursue research and conservation activities. Galleries always require more money for acquisitions.

Planning

With the exception of libraries, planning for the arts can best be described as an *ad hoc* process. Since the *Housing of the Arts* reports of the 1960s (Arts Council of Great Britain, 1959, 1961), there has been no apparent national strategic planning comparable to the Sports Council's own detailed plans for sport and the guidance it offers to other organisations. At the local level, again with the possible exception of libraries, planning for the arts would appear to be more a matter of municipal pride rather than assessment of community need. The principle seems to be that any urban authority of any size feels that it should have a theatre, probably as part of a 'civic centre', a museum, and possibly an arts centre – indeed, the philosophy might well have been summed up by the title of one of the early, and few, books on arts centres, which was: *Every Town Should Have One* (Lane, 1978).

3 Outdoor recreation – natural areas

Scope

Outdoor recreation in natural areas takes place in national and country parks, in forests, on the coast and on footpaths and, through the phenomenon of 'driving for pleasure', throughout the countryside.

Rationale and goals

As with sport and the arts, public policy with regard to outdoor recreation in the natural environment – in national parks, country parks and the coast – is faced with two potentially conflicting goals. They are conservation and recreational access. Conservation of flora, fauna and heritage seems a clear enough mandate, until it is realised that, in the case of Britain, hardly any area of the country has been untouched by human activity over the centuries. Before human beings made their mark the whole of Britain was covered in forest, but now even the national parks are grazed by sheep! So what is 'natural' and to be conserved? In some areas abandoned mines, which would, in modern times, be seen as a desecration, have become part of the heritage. But the real problems arise when considering recreational access. For virtually any eco-system, human activity, certainly on any scale, poses a threat. Walking trails, car-parks, toilet blocks and camp-sites usurp space which might have been used by flora and fauna and their use inevitably disturbs flora and fauna: true conservation implies the exclusion of the species *homo sapiens* in its modern form.

And yet national parks authorities are required by law to facilitate recreational access. And facilitating such access is a necessary part of their continued community and political support. But the overt promotional and marketing activity of the sports and arts sectors is not part of the countryside recreation scene. In natural areas a balance has to be struck between recreational access and conservation. One way in which policy-makers seek to do this is by designation and zoning processes. Thus, at one end of the spectrum nature reserves and, in some countries, wilderness areas, are established, from which humans are virtually excluded. Within national parks, efforts are made to concentrate high-volume visitation in limited areas, where services can be provided and the impact on the natural environment can be contained. At the other extreme, country parks are created which are primarily devoted to recreation and can sometimes be indistinguishable from larger urban parks.

Institutional factors

A unique feature of countryside recreation – particularly in Britain – is that much of it takes place on private property, with the public role being to ensure and to manage rights of access. This is true of large parts of Britain's national parks, of footpaths, and coastal access (although beaches themselves are in the public domain). While initial campaigns for public access were organised by voluntary effort (Glyptis,

1991: 28), today the public's interest in recreational access to the countryside is represented by elected councils and Quangos (such as Regional Councils of Sport and Recreation and the Countryside Commission), although voluntary organisations remain politically important.

Providing for countryside recreation faces the further special problem that, typically, the population being planned for is not the resident population, but the nearby urban population. Consequently, rural rate-payers are seen to be paying to provide for the recreational needs of urban residents. Of course, this might be seen as a balance to the cultural and other services provided by urban areas to rural residents, but things are rarely seen in such a light, especially given that the rural population is generally small compared with the urban population. This financial imbalance is, of course, an argument for national and regional government providing financial support for local rural councils and for national park organisations – and this does take place.

Planning

The fact that the 'clients' for countryside recreation are urban residents is the key feature of planning for countryside recreation. This means that, ideally, planning should be undertaken on a regional rather than local basis. Thus, for example, planning for outdoor recreation in the various counties in the South East of England is dominated by demands of the population of London; any one individual county cannot be expected to encompass this process in its entirety – researching and planning for the phenomenon must be a cooperative, regional, process. However, the need for this sort of approach to planning has become less urgent as static or declining populations and economic recession have slowed the rate of growth of recreation demand and in some cases put it into reverse (Rodgers, 1993). Planning for outdoor recreation, in a no-growth situation, can become more 'resource-based' and less concerned with demand pressures.

4 Urban outdoor recreation

Scope

Urban outdoor recreation takes place primarily in parks, playing fields and playgrounds. The provision of such facilities constitutes the largest single public leisure service sector, in terms of expenditure, land allocation and staff, and is the longest established. Parks include formal and informal landscaped areas for walking and relaxation and specific-purpose facilities designed for more physically active recreation, including boating facilities, playgrounds, hard sports areas such as tennis courts, and grass playing pitches. And they may contain catering facilities and performance spaces. Parks accommodate events, such as music performances, sports matches, demonstrations and rallies, and peripatetic phenomena such as funfairs and circuses. Other forms of urban public open space should not be ignored, including public squares, market places, village greens and, indeed, streets, especially where they have been pedestrianised.

Rationale and goals

This sector does not face the conflicting goals of recreational access versus conservation to anything like the extent that they are faced by its countryside counterpart. Urban parks can, however, extend to the urban fringe, where environmentally sensitive areas can be involved, and even within urban areas, parks may encompass areas which are valued for their nature conservation value rather than their direct recreational value. In addition, parks can include natural or built items of heritage value, such as mature trees, or monuments and buildings, the conservation of which may conflict with some recreational objectives. In general, however, parks have been planned, designed and developed by human beings specifically for recreational purposes.

Nevertheless, there is an 'excellence' factor in park management which parallels that in sport or the arts, and that is horticultural values. The horticulturalist has a set of professional values which may or may not be compatible with the needs and demands of the recreational user. In general, the horticulturalist wants to 'do things with plants'; elaborate floral displays are, in fact, popular with one section of the public, but they are expensive.

Parks for informal recreation offer the same sorts of community benefits as natural areas, in the form of opportunities to relax, 'commune with nature' and take mild exercise. Generally, the aim of the providers of such facilities is to 'provide opportunity' rather than to actively promote or maximise participation. In so far as parks contain sports facilities, the goals should, logically, be similar to those discussed under sport and physical recreation, and therefore a more proactive approach to promotion of participation is appropriate. There should therefore be a difference between the resource-based focus of informal recreation area management and the people-based, promotional orientation of sports facilities.

Institutional factors

Generally, urban open space is in the ownership and control of local government. In large urban centres, however, other agencies may be involved, such as the Royal Parks in London, run by the Department of the Environment. Often parks have been maintained in local government as a service separate from other leisure services. In such a situation it is likely that the dual approach to management discussed above is not implemented, the resource-based, facility maintenance approach tending to win out.

Planning

As indicated in chapter 6, planning for open space in urban areas on the basis of standards is a long-established practice. In Britain the opportunity to develop new parks, even in areas with very low levels of provision, is very limited. In fact, it is in the areas of greatest relative deprivation, in the centres of large cities, that the opportunities are most rare, because of the price of land. Planning of these areas today is therefore much closer to management – the task is to determine how to make the best use of the facilities available. Optimising use can involve management practices (for example increasing staff patrols in areas where usage is limited because of safety fears) or development work (for example improving the drainage of pitches or providing artificial surfaces).

5 Tourism

Scope

Tourism is defined differently by different writers and agencies. Definitions of 'a tourist' generally involve an overnight stay away from home somewhere other than the person's normal place of residence. Some definitions distinguish between those who travel for leisure purposes and those who travel for other purposes, such as business, and yet the business traveller's requirements overlap considerably with those of the leisure traveller. Similarly, the requirements of the day-tripper to a holiday area (who would not normally be included in the strict definition of 'tourist') are often similar to those of the staying tourist in all respects except the requirement for accommodation. While the high-profile sector of tourism is international travel, in most developed countries *domestic* tourism – people taking holidays in their own country – is larger in both number of trips and financial turnover.

A benefit of tourism which is often mentioned by policy-makers but has rarely been quantified is that visitor expenditure can make viable certain facilities and services, which would not be viable if they were dependent on local residents alone. This applies to transport infrastructure and to many leisure facilities. Quite small communities can enjoy – in season and sometimes out of season also – a range of leisure facilities which would not exist without visitors. A human dimension of this is the idea of what might be called the 'VFR multiplier'. VFR stands for 'Visiting Friends and Relatives', and this is often a significant element of the tourist market, especially in large cities. The VFR multiplier arises as a result of local hosts needing to entertain their visiting friends and relatives – so they take them to all the local sites, such as museums, historic sites and historic pubs. Thus the existence of the visitor causes the local resident to visit places which they might otherwise not visit – especially if they are seen as 'touristy'. Thus at any site visitors can be seen as comprising four categories:

a. unaccompanied tourists
b. unaccompanied residents
c. VFR tourists accompanied by residents
d. residents accompanying VFR tourists

Category (d) can be seen as an effect generated by tourism which, while it is not a 'net economic benefit to the local community' (because the local residents would probably have spent the same money locally on something else anyway), it is a benefit to the leisure/tourist site operators. And, in so far as the places visited are of a cultural nature, social benefits are generated from locals visiting them. The VFR multiplier would be the ratio of expenditures: (c+d):(c).

Tourism is often viewed and analysed in terms of the *industry* rather than the *tourist*. The tourism industry is fragmented, not only in terms of the dominance of small businesses (such as hotels and camp-sites, restaurants and gift shops), but also in terms of the variety of sub-sectors involved, including travel agents, transport, the accommodation sector, cafes and restaurants and built and natural environment attractions. As with leisure generally, many sectors of the so-called tourism industry are only *partly* in the tourism industry – for example transport, catering and many of the attractions (when they are used by locals as well as visitors).

Rationale and goals
Public policy and planning for tourism has in common with countryside recreation planning the characteristic that it is *not* focused on the needs and demands of local residents. Thus, in so far as the public agency responsible for policy and planning is democratically elected or answerable to a democratically elected body, policy and planning are not directed at meeting the holiday-making needs and demands of the electorate; rather, they are generally aimed at maximising the benefits which local residents might obtain from *other people's* holiday-making and minimising the negative effects which they might generate. The benefits are seen almost exclusively as economic – the generation of jobs and incomes – and the negative effects are almost exclusively seen as environmental.

Paralleling the ambivalence of the dual goals of countryside recreation, tourism policy is generally juggling with two contradictory goals: the maximisation of tourist numbers and expenditure and the minimisation of their environmental impact. The *maximisation* part of the equation is much stronger. The conflict between the two goals is often resolved – or permitted to remain unresolved – by separating them institutionally, as discussed below.

The unique feature of tourism policy is the way public bodies intervene in what is essentially a private-sector industry. Public bodies generally undertake a marketing and promotional role on behalf of the industry. Public money is spent on generating customers for private industry with a view to reaping social benefits in the form of increased jobs and incomes (and tax income). Why does this sort of intervention happen in tourism and not in other industries, such as car-manufacturing? Two factors would seem to explain it: one is the fragmentary nature of the industry, as discussed above, and the other is the fact that the markets which must be addressed are, by definition, not local, and so are expensive for any one small business to access.

Another form of state involvement in tourism is not given a great deal of prominence in tourism policy or the literature, and that is the idea of 'social tourism' (Finch, 1975). Social tourism is the process by which deprived groups in the community are assisted to go on holiday, usually via some form of subsidy, but also by direct provision. The idea is particularly appropriate for 'carers' – generally family members who take care of people with severe disability or chronic illness. Provision of relief for such individuals, in the form of a holiday, is a humanitarian gesture, but can also be very cost-effective for the state in helping the carer to continue in that role, rather than the burden of care falling on the state.

Institutional factors

The contradiction between the maximisation of tourist numbers and minimisation of environmental impact has to a large extent been avoided, rather than confronted, at the national and regional levels as a result of the fact that the responsibility for tourism promotion lies in the hands of the private sector and a certain type of public body, namely Tourism Commissions and Associations, while the responsibility for environmental protection lies with local planning authorities. Thus the option of reducing or stabilising tourist numbers is not really available to the environmental planners – all they can do is seek to influence where tourists are allowed to go and what they are allowed to do where.

Planning

Planning for tourism is, like planning for countryside recreation, characterised by the fact that demand comes from outside the area. Planning activity is influenced by the institutional factors discussed above. Unlike many other fields of leisure planning, demand forecasting has played a significant role in tourism planning, but mainly at the national level. National Tourism Commissions and Ministries produce tourism demand forecasts and targets. On the basis of such forecasts and targets some attention is then given to the question of accommodation and airport capacity, but little attention is given to the capacity of the leisure environments and attractions which tourists come to see. That this is a problem is to some extent recognised in attempts by national and regional tourist bodies to spread the tourist load, both spatially and temporally – that is, it is recognised that certain places (eg London) become overcrowded at certain times (eg in summer). But by and large the regional and local tourism planning task is to cope with a level of demand which is seen as more or less 'given'.

Groups

Every individual is unique and so could be said to have unique leisure requirements. In family settings and some organisational settings this uniqueness can be catered for, but human beings are also social animals with interests, demands and needs in common. *Common* experiences can be as important as individual experiences – people want to belong and to share. Classifying people into groups and considering their common characteristics and needs is not therefore to deny their individuality; in fact, it has been the *failure* of providers to consider the common needs of some groups which has, in the past, denied members of such groups their individuality. As a result of campaigns, regulations, research and the spread of ideas such as 'market segmentation' and 'niche marketing', some of these problems are now beginning to be overcome. In this section six social groups with particular leisure needs are considered. They are: women and men, children, youth, the elderly, people with disabilities, and ethnic groups.

1 Women and men

Women comprise more than half the population, but early leisure research, policy and planning often gave the impression that women were at best a minority and at worst non-existent. In chapter 3 we have already considered how women's leisure needs are viewed from feminist perspectives. Here we consider the question from a narrower perspective, namely: how should policy and planning for leisure in contemporary society seek to incorporate the particular leisure needs of women? Such an approach is avowedly 'reformist' in feminist terms since, in a society of full equality between men and women there would be few, if any, 'women's needs' – all would be human needs. Thus, if child-care were shared equally, child-care facilities would be demanded by 'parents' rather than 'mothers'. If male violence were to be eliminated, then travel after dark for leisure or any other purpose would not be a problem experienced by women or men. If all sports were open to both sexes – for mixed or single-sex competition – then particular provision for 'women's sports' would not be necessary: access would be available to all. But society is not equal, so measures must be taken to redress the imbalances which exist and to put in place 'transitional arrangements', some of which would not be necessary in a fully equal society.

The main problem area in leisure policy and planning for women would appear to be the area of sport. This is reflected in the voluminous literature on women and sport. Women's comparatively low level of participation and the reasons for it are discussed in terms of cultural expectations and constraints (eg Scraton, 1993), media sports coverage (eg Brown, 1993) and lack of facilities (Mowbray, 1993), and is recognised in specific targets in the Sports Council's plans (1988).

Participation statistics suggest that in most other areas women's participation levels are greater than or equal to those of men. It is rarely suggested that, for example, the arts or entertainment sectors discriminate against female audiences, or that libraries, parks or countryside recreation facilities do not cater to the needs of women.

One non-sporting exception would appear to be pub-going, where males continue to predominate. This bears out the proposition that leisure reflects wider social conditions, in that it must be assumed that males have traditionally used pubs more than women because they have had more money and more freedom – culturally and physically – to go out as and when they please. Women's freedom to 'pop down to the local' for a drink is still constrained for a variety of reasons (Green *et al.*, 1990: 64). And in this case it would be difficult to blame the provider for the inequality since the industry-driven trend in British pubs is for that bastion of male chauvinism, the public bar, to be rapidly disappearing in favour of the 'uni-sex' lounge bar.

Increased access and provision for women's leisure has implications for men. If resources, for example of land, are limited, men may be required to give up some of the facilities which have hitherto been allocated, by default, to them. In theory, to meet equal demand for women, provision of facilities and services in some areas would need to be almost doubled – and men would have to share the cost through taxation and/or other revenue-raising methods, in the same way that women have shared the burden of funding men's public leisure provision to date. In fact, a more equal society could lead to qualitative changes in men's leisure, especially in the area of sport, and such ideas are already being addressed in literature on the topic of 'masculinity' (eg Miller, 1990; Lynch, 1993).

2 Children

While the origins of public leisure services can be traced to the early development of play facilities for young people, and children constitute a significant proportion, if not the majority, of the customers of public leisure facilities, children's leisure needs have been relatively neglected in discussion of leisure policy. Part of the reason for this is the difficulty of conducting research with children: for practical or ethical reasons it is difficult to administer questionnaires to young children, so that leisure participation surveys and facility user surveys omit children who are younger than about 12 years and often older. Research therefore tends to be conducted by means of observation, and is left to child psychologists who have an interest in children as individuals, but not necessarily as a social category.

When considering provision there is a tendency to think only in terms of (outdoor) playgrounds, ignoring the fact that children are the major customers of such facilities as swimming pools, commercial computer games, skating rinks and so on. There is an assumption that the leisure needs of children are attended to by schools and parents and therefore that relatively little attention is required from public bodies which carefully consider the needs and demands of all other 'market segments'. In addition to consideration of formal provision, for young children the home and neighbourhood is their informal leisure/play environment, yet children's needs are seldom taken into account in the design of such environments (Young, 1988).

3 Youth

Much of the political sentiment behind the support for public leisure services would appear to be based on the belief that approved leisure provision should be available for young people. Indeed, the very origins of modern public leisure services are often traced to the nineteenth-century provision of 'Mechanics' Institutes' (Cunningham, 1980). One belief is that provision of suitable leisure facilities for young people will prevent juvenile crime. The 1975 White Paper on *Sport and Recreation* stated:

> By reducing boredom and urban frustration, participation in active recreation contributes to the reduction of hooliganism and delinquency among young people. (Department of the Environment, 1975: 3)

At around the same time, a national organisation organised a conference entitled *Off the Streets: Leisure Amenities and the Prevention of Crime* (NACRO, 1975), which reflected the possibility of a link between crime prevention and leisure provision. In fact, there has never been any systematic research to test this proposition empirically.

A curiosity in Britain is that the main public leisure service directed explicitly at young people, the youth service, is not seen as part of leisure services at all, but as part of education. The youth service, like the adult education service, is run as an adjunct to education services and is therefore imbued with the education 'ethos'. Thus the training of youth leaders is closer to that of social workers and teachers than to that of leisure managers. The youth club, while using leisure as a *medium*, has therefore had other objectives, such as education or welfare work for 'at-risk' youth.

Youth and their leisure and sub-cultures have been the subject of considerable research over recent decades (eg. Roberts, 1983; Rapoport and Rapoport, 1975; Brake, 1980). The trouble is that, as with research on any social group in a changing society, this work has in many instances become dated as the economic and social environment of young people has changed. In the 1960s and 1970s young people were 'affluent'. In the 1980s, however, they bore the brunt of unemployment, so that most young people in their late teens were either in the education/training system or unemployed: relatively few were employed and 'affluent'. There is therefore a need for continual updating of research and the policies which flow from it.

For many public leisure services young people are simply one of a number of 'user groups' or 'market segments'. Designing programmes to meet the needs and demands of young people is therefore a challenge for the management of existing facilities. 'Multiple use' is not always ideal, of course. The atmosphere of facilities designed and managed exclusively or mainly for young people – for example skating rinks – is very different from those where other user groups must also be catered for. The commercial sector is generally highly successful at providing facilities which tap straight into youth culture and its styles (Smith, 1975).

4 The elderly

The aging of the population of western societies is a phenomenon with which most are now familiar. Much research has been done over the last decade and a half to remedy the neglect of the particular leisure needs and demands of this group. As with research on youth, there is a tendency for such research to become outdated in the light of changing social conditions. The elderly as a category are becoming younger, fitter and more affluent. They are becoming younger because of a tendency for earlier retirement, and often the definition of 'the elderly' includes 'the retired'. They are becoming fitter as a result of advances in medicine and also, possibly, a different outlook which encourages older people to be more active and to be more conscious of preventive 'lifestyle' factors. They are becoming more wealthy because of inheritance (particularly related to increasing levels of home-ownership) and superannuation. While a significant proportion of the elderly still suffer from financial and health/mobility problems, an increasing proportion do not. They present themselves to leisure providers as a 'market segment' like any other.

It might be said that, if the elderly are just another 'market segment', then 'the market' can meet all their leisure needs, but this would be an inappropriate conclusion. Younger age-groups also constitute 'market segments' and, while commercial provision plays its part for all age-groups, the state also has a role to play. As argued in the early parts of this book, equity and 'need' are only *part* of the argument for state provision – net community benefits can also arise even if services are provided for relatively affluent people. And in some cases – for example the provision of parks or swimming pools – the state has a virtual monopoly of supply, so, having got itself into that situation, it has an obligation to provide for all, regardless of socio-economic situation, and even if the service involves a significant element of 'user pays'.

The net benefits to the community from providing leisure opportunities for the elderly are likely to be even greater than from providing for younger age-groups. For both the 'young' elderly and 'old' elderly, the mental and physical benefits to the individual and to the wider community of staying active are obvious. The challenge is therefore very much one for management and it is one which has been widely taken up. Often the facilities are available: the task is to provide programmes at the right time, in the right place and at the right price to attract this 'market segment'. Fortunately, the elderly demand services at times when facilities are relatively under-used.

The 'continuity theory' suggests that the proportion of the elderly who take up new activities upon retirement is relatively low (Atchley, 1989). The implications of this are either that people must be attracted to the particular activity *before* retirement or that new ways of marketing the idea of experimentation to retired people must be found.

5. Ethnic groups

Ethnic groups are groups of people with a common culture – so everyone belongs to some ethnic group, whether it be a majority or minority in a particular society. While ethnicity is often associated with race, this need not be the case, as the experience of Northern Ireland illustrates. The challenge in most contemporary societies is to achieve racial equality while seeking to gain the cultural benefits which *ethnic diversity* can offer. Leisure service providers are at the forefront of both processes and, indeed, face the dilemmas which these objectives can bring. For example, is it wise to encourage ethnically based sports teams to bring different groups together in friendly competition, or will the rivalry actually damage community relations?

In Britain, most ethnic minority groups have their origins in immigration from various parts of the British Commonwealth/Empire. Often, immigrants were recruited by British employers specifically as cheap labour in periods of labour shortage. Whole groups of migrants therefore suffered from low incomes and, as a result of this and racial discrimination, also suffered from poor housing and a 'cycle of deprivation'. Policy for ethnic minority groups, including leisure policy, has tended to be orientated towards alleviating or compensating for general social deprivation. Such policies need to be handled sensitively, whether aimed specifically at ethnic minority groups or deprived groups in general since, while leisure services may be provided for reasons of equity, as discussed in chapter 4, such provision can appear to be viewed as a cynical exercise in placation if other services, such as housing, health and education, not to mention jobs, are not being attended to at the same time.

Another dimension of policy related to ethnic groups relates not to deprivation but to differences in social customs and values. In particular, as discussed by Green *et al.* (1990: 70–81) women and girls from Moslem or conservative Christian communities are restricted in terms of permitted public recreation behaviour. Such restrictions have been slowly recognised by public leisure providers and catered for by special programmes.

6 People with disabilities

Disabilities come in a variety of forms and degrees and affect a substantial proportion of the population at some time during their lives. Included are mental illness, physical disability (suffered from birth or as a result of illness or accident, and including deafness, dumbness and blindness), disabilities related to the nervous system and the muscular-skeletal system, and chronic conditions such as diabetes and asthma. Such a huge range of conditions calls for a correspondingly wide range of policy responses.

While the majority of people with severe disabilities lived in institutions, the question of leisure provision for them was largely an institutional task. In recent years a process of 'de-institutionalisation' has been taking place in the belief that people with disabilities can live more dignified lives in the community. Leisure services have a clear role to play in such a process since leisure activities can be not only therapeutic for the individual, but also a direct means of integration with the wider community.

Finally

Each of the leisure sectors and social groups discussed in this last chapter merits a book in its own right. Each could be examined in terms of the philosophical, ideological, economic, planning and demand issues raised in the bulk of the book. Few public policies relate broadly to *leisure* or to *the community*; they nearly all, when it comes down to it, relate to specific types of activity for specific groups of people. The challenge for the policy-maker and planner is to enhance the quality of life of real people by seeking to understand their leisure needs and demands in the context of an understanding of the economic, political and social processes which control the distribution of community resources.

Further reading

Sport and physical recreation: Department of the Environment, 1975, 1991; Gratton and Taylor, 1985, 1991; Hillman and Whalley, 1977; Kamphorst and Roberts, 1989; McIntosh and Charlton, 1985; Ministry of Housing and Local Government, 1966; Roberts and Brodie, 1992; Sports Council (various).

The arts: Waters, 1989; Baumol and Bowen, 1976; Baldry, 1976; Braden, 1979; Hawkins, 1993; Hantrais and Kamphorst, 1987; Kelly, 1984; Lane, 1978.

Outdoor recreation – natural areas: Coppock and Duffield, 1975; Glyptis, 1991, 1993; Groome, 1993; Patmore, 1983; Pigram, 1983.

Outdoor recreation – urban: Jackson, 1986; Lever, 1973; Ravenscroft, 1992; Welch, 1991.

Tourism: Bull, 1991; Finch, 1975; Mathieson and Wall, 1982; Smith, 1989; Johnson and Thomas, 1992.

Women: Deem, 1986, 1986a; Green et al., 1990; Henderson et al., 1989; Scraton, 1993; Wearing, 1990; Wimbush and Talbot, 1988.

Children: Ellis, 1973; Barnett, 1991.

Youth: Roberts, 1983; Brake, 1980; Rapoport and Rapoport, 1975.

The elderly: Atchley, 1989; Rapoport and Rapoport, 1975; Green et al., 1990: 82–4.

Ethnic groups: Green et al., 1990: 70–81; Kew, 1979; Pryce, 1979.

People with disabilities: Kennedy et al., 1991; Austin, 1987; Levitt, 1991; Stein and Sessoms, 1977.

BIBLIOGRAPHY

Adams, F.G. (1986) 'Forecasting – the econometric approach', Ch.4 of *The Business Forecasting Revolution: Nation – Industry – Firm*, New York: Oxford University Press, pp. 74–105.

Adams, I. (1990) *Leisure and Government*, Sunderland: Business Education Publishers.

Alt, J. (1979) 'Beyond class: the decline of industrial labor and leisure', *Telos*, Vol. 12, pp. 55–80.

Archer, B. (1976) *Demand Forecasting in Tourism*, Bangor Occasional Papers in Economics, No. 9, Bangor: University of Wales Press.

Archer, B. (1994) 'Demand forecasting and estimation', in Ritchie and Goeldner, *op. cit.*, pp. 105–114.

Arnstein, S. (1969) 'A ladder of citizen participation', *Journal of the American Institute of Planning*, July, pp. 216–24.

Arts Council of Great Britain (1959) *Housing the Arts in Great Britain: Part I: London, Scotland, Wales*, London: ACGB.

Arts Council of Great Britain (1961) *Housing the Arts in Great Britain: Part II: The Needs of the English Provinces*, London: ACGB.

Asimov, I. (1976) 'Future fun', in *Today and Tomorrow and ...*, London: Scientific Book Club, pp. 199–209.

Atchley, R. (1989) 'A continuity theory of normal aging', *The Gerontologist*, Vol. 29, pp. 183–90.

Athiyaman, A. and Robertson, R.W. (1992) 'Time series forecasting techniques: short–term planning in tourism', *International Journal of Contemporary Hospitality Management*, Vol. 4, No. 4, pp. 8–11.

Austin, D.R. (1987) 'Recreation and persons with physical disabilities: a literature synthesis', *Therapeutic Recreation Journal*, Vol. 17, pp. 38–43.

Bacon, W. (1989) 'The development of the leisure profession in the United Kingdom: a comparative analysis of development and change', *Society and Leisure*, Vol. 12, No. 1, pp. 233–46.

Bailey, P. (1979) *Leisure and Class in Victorian England*, London: Routledge and Kegan Paul.

Baldry, H.C. (1976) 'Community Arts', in Haworth and Veal, *op. cit.*, pp. 2.1–2.6.

Barnett, L.A. (1991) 'Developmental benefits of play for children', in Driver *et al., op. cit.*, pp. 215–48.

Baumol W.J. and Bowen W.G. (1976) 'Arguments for public support of the performing arts', in M. Blaug (ed.) *The Economics of the Arts*, London: Martin Robertson, pp. 42–57.

Bennington, J. and White, J. (eds) (1988) *The Future of Leisure Services*, Harlow: Longman.

BERG – *see* Built Environment Research Group.

Bickmore, D., Shaw, M.G. and Tulloch, T. (1980) 'Lifestyles on maps', *Geographical Magazine*, Vol. 52, No. 11, pp. 763–9.

Bikhchandani, S., Hirshleifer, D. and Welch, I. (1992) 'A theory of fads, fashion, custom and cultural change as informational cascades', *Journal of Political Economy*, Vol. 100, pp. 992–1026.

Bovaird, T. (1992) 'Evaluation, performance measurement and achievement of objectives in the public sector', in J. Sugden and C. Knox (eds) *Leisure in the 1990s: Rolling Back the Welfare State*, Conference Papers, Eastbourne: Leisure Studies Association, pp. 145–66.

Braden, S. (1979) *Artists and People*, London: Routledge.

Bradshaw, J. (1972) 'The concept of social need', *New Society*, No. 496, 30 March, pp. 640–43.

Brake, M. (1980) *The Sociology of Youth Culture and Youth Sub-Cultures*, London: Routledge.

Bramham, P. and Henry, I. (1985) 'Political ideology and leisure policy in the United Kingdom', *Leisure Studies*, Vol. 4, No. 1, pp. 1–20.

Bramham, P., Henry, I., Mommaas, H. and Van Der Poel, H. (eds) (1993) *Leisure Policies in Europe*, Wallingford, Oxon: CAB International.

British Standards Institution (1991) *Quality Systems* (BS5750), London: BSI.

Brown, P. (1993) 'Women, the media and equity in sport', in Veal *et al., op. cit*, pp. 160–63.

Brownlie, I. (ed.) (1992) *Basic Documents on Human Rights*, Oxford: Clarendon Press.

Built Environment Research Group (1978a) *Sports in a Jointly Provided Centre: A Study of Meadway Sports Centre, Reading*, Study 14, London: Sports Council.

Bull, A. (1991) *The Economics of Travel and Tourism*, Melbourne: Pitman.

Burgan, B. and Mules, T. (1992) 'Economic impacts of sporting events', *Annals of Tourism Research*, Vol. 19, pp. 700–10.

Burns, J.P.A. *et al.* (eds) (1986) *The Adelaide Grand Prix – The Impact of a Special Event*, Adelaide: Centre for South Australian Economics Studies.

Burton, T.L. (1971) *Experiments in Recreation Research*, London: Allen and Unwin.

Burton, T.L. (1970) 'The shape of things to come', in T.L. Burton (ed.) *Recreation Research and Planning*, London: Allen and Unwin, pp. 242–68.

Burton, T.L. (1989) 'Leisure forecasting, policymaking and planning', in Jackson and Burton, *op. cit.*, pp. 211–44.

Certo, S.C. and Peter, J.P. (1991) *Strategic Management: Concepts and Applications*, New York: McGraw-Hill.

Chai, D.A. (1977) 'Future of leisure: a Delphi application', *Research Quarterly*, Vol. 48, No. 3, pp. 518–24.

Chairmen's Policy Group (1982) *Leisure Policy for the Future*, London: Sports Council.

Chappelle, D.E. (1973) 'The 'need' for outdoor recreation: an economic conundrum', *Journal of Leisure Research*, Vol. 5, No. 3, pp. 47–53.

Clark, R. and Stankey, G. (1979) *The Recreation Opportunity Spectrum: A Framework for Planning, Management and Research*, General Technical Report PNW–98, Seattle, Washington: US Dept of Agriculture Forest Service.

Claxton, J.D. (1994) 'Conjoint analysis in travel research: a manager's guide', in Ritchie and Goeldner (eds), *op. cit.*, pp. 513–22.

Clawson, M. and Knetsch, J.L. (1962) *Economics of Outdoor Recreation*, Baltimore: Johns Hopkins Press.

Clarke, J. and Critcher, C. (1985) *The Devil Makes Work: Leisure in Capitalist Britain*, London: Macmillan.

Coalter, F. (with Long, J. and Duffield, B.) (1988) *Recreational Welfare*, Aldershot: Avebury/Gower.

Cooper, W.E. (1989) 'Some philosophical aspects of leisure', in Jackson and Burton, *op. cit.*, pp. 49–68.

Coppock, J.T. and Duffield, B.S. (1975) *Recreation in the Countryside: A Spatial Analysis*, London: Macmillan.

Cranston, M. (1973) *What are Human Rights?*, London: The Bodley Head.

Crouch, G.I. and Shaw, R.N. (1991) *International Tourism Demand: A Meta-Analytical Integration of Research Findings*, Management Paper No. 36, Clayton, Victoria: Monash University Graduate School of Management.

Cunningham, H. (1980) *Leisure in the Industrial Revolution*, London: Croom Helm.

Cushman, G. and Hamilton–Smith, E. (1980) 'Equity issues in urban recreation services', in Mercer and Hamilton-Smith (eds), *op. cit.,* pp. 167–79).

Dare, B., Welton, G. and Coe, W. (1987) *Concepts of Leisure in Western Thought*, Dubuque, Iowa: Kendall Hunt.

DASETT – *see* Department of the Arts, Sport, the Environment, Tourism and Territories.

Davidson, J.A. (1985) 'Sport and modern technology: the rise of skateboarding, 1963–1978', *Journal of Popular Culture*, Vol. 18, No. 4, pp. 145–57.

Deem, R. (1986) *All Work and No Play? The Sociology of Women's Leisure*, Milton Keynes: Open University Press.

Deem, R. (1986a) 'The politics of women's leisure', in F. Coalter (ed.) *The Politics of Leisure*, Conference Papers No. 24, London: Leisure Studies Association, pp. 68–81.

Department of the Arts, Sport, the Environment, Tourism and Territories (1988) *The Economic Impact of Sport and Recreation – Household Expenditure*, Technical Paper No. 1, Canberra: AGPS.

Department of the Arts, Sport, the Environment, Tourism and Territories (1988a) *The Economic Impact of Sport and Recreation – Regular Physical Activity*, Technical Paper No. 2, Canberra: AGPS.

Department of the Environment (1975) *Sport and Recreation*, Cmnd 6200, London: HMSO.

Department of the Environment (1977) *Guidelines for Regional Recreational Strategies*, Circular 73/77, London: HMSO.

Department of the Environment (1991) *Sport and Recreation,* Planning Policy Guidance Note 17, London: HMSO.

Department of the Environment and Department of Education and Science (1977) *Leisure and the Quality of Life: A Report on Four Local Experiments*, 2 volumes, London: HMSO.

Dower, M., Rapoport, R., Strelitz, Z. and Kew, S. (1981) *Leisure Provision and People's Needs*, London: HMSO.

Doyal, L. and Gough, I. (1991) *A Theory of Human Needs*, London: Macmillan.

Driver, B.L., Brown, P.J. and Peterson, G.L. (eds) (1991) *Benefits of Leisure*, State College, PA: Venture.

Drucker, P. (1990) *Managing the Non-profit Organisation*, Oxford: Butterworth-Heinemann.

Dumazedier, J. (1982) *The Sociology of Leisure*, The Hague: Elsevier.

Dunstan, G. (1986) 'Living with the Grand Prix: Good or Bad?', in Burns *et al., op. cit.*, pp. 105–23.

Edgell, D.L. (1990) *International Tourism Policy*, New York: Van Nostrand Reinhold.

Ellis, M.J. (1973) *Why People Play*, Englewood Cliffs, NJ: Prentice-Hall.

Elvin, I.T. (1990) *Sport and Physical Recreation*, Harlow: Longman.

Etzioni, A. (1967) 'Mixed scanning: a 'third' approach to decision-making', *Public Administration Review*, Vol. 46, No. 1, pp. 385–92.

Ewing, G.O. (1983) 'Forecasting recreation trip distribution behaviour', in Lieber and Fesenmaier, *op. cit.*, pp. 120–40.

Fain, G.S. (ed.) (1991) *Leisure and Ethics*, Reston, VA: American Alliance for Health, Physical Education, Recreation and Dance.

Faulkner, B. (1994) *Evaluating the Tourism Impacts of Hallmark Events*, Occasional Paper 16, Canberra: Bureau of Tourism Research.

Featherstone, M. (1991) *Consumer Culture and Postmodernism*, London: Sage.

Field, B.G. and MacGregor, B.D. (1987) 'Recreation', Ch. 7 of *Forecasting Techniques for Urban and Regional Planning*, London: Hutchinson, pp. 159–231.

Finch, S. (1975) 'Holidays: the social need', in Haworth and Veal (eds), *op. cit.,* pp. 6.1–6.8.

Fischer, A. *et al.* (1986) 'Road accidents and the Grand Prix', in Burns *et al., op. cit.*, pp. 151–68.

Fitzgerald, R. (1977) 'Abraham Maslow's hierarchy of needs – an exposition and evaluation', in Fitzgerald, R. (ed.) *Human Needs and Politics*, Sydney: Pergamon, pp. 36-51.

Frechtling, D.C. (1994) 'Assessing the impacts of travel and tourism – measuring economic benefits', in Ritchie and Goeldner, *op. cit.*, pp. 367–92.

Frechtling, D.C. (1994a) 'Assessing the impacts of travel and tourism – measuring economic costs', in Ritchie and Goeldner, *op. cit.*, pp. 393–402.

Friedman M. and Friedman R. (1979) 'The role of government', in *Free to Choose*, Harmondsworth, Middx: Penguin, pp. 47–58.

Galbraith, J.K. (1973) *Economics and the Public Purpose*, Harmondsworth, Middx: Penguin.

Garrett, T. and Spedding, A. (1977) *Guidelines for Community Recreation Planning*, Wellington, NZ: Ministry of Recreation and Sport.

Gershuny, J. (1992) 'Are we running out of time?', *Futures*, Vol. 24, pp. 3–22.

GLSECSR – see Greater London and South East Council for Sport and Recreation.

Glyptis, S. (1983) 'Business as usual? Leisure provision for the unemployed', *Leisure Studies*, Vol. 2, pp. 287–300.

Glyptis, S. (1991) *Countryside Recreation*, Harlow: Longman.

Glyptis, S. (ed.) (1993) *Leisure and the Environment*, London: Belhaven.

Gold, S.M. (1973) *Urban Recreation Planning*, Philadelphia: Lea and Febiger.

Gold, S.M. (1980) *Recreation Planning and Design*, New York: McGraw-Hill.

Gorz, A. (1980) *Farewell to the Working Class*, London: Pluto.

Gorz, A. (1980a) *Ecology as Politics*, Boston: South End Press.

Gratton, C. and Taylor, P. (1985) *Sport and Recreation: An Economic Analysis*, London: Spon.

Gratton, C. and Taylor, P. (1988) *Economics of Leisure Service Management*, Harlow: Longman.

Gratton, C. and Taylor, P. (1991) *Government and the Economics of Sport*, Harlow: Longman.

Gray, H.P. (1982) 'The contributions of economics to tourism', *Annals of Tourism Research*, Vol. 9, pp. 105–25.

Greater London Council Planning Department (1968) *Surveys of the Use of Open Space: Volume 1*, London: GLC.

Greater London and South East Council for Sport and Recreation (1982) *Prospect for the Eighties: Regional Recreation Strategy*, London: GLSECSR.

Greater London and South East Sports Council (1977) *A Playing Fields Strategy for Greater London*, London: GLSESC.

Green, E., Hebron, S. and Woodward, D. (1990) *Women's Leisure, What Leisure?*, London: Macmillan.

Green, H., Hunter, C. and Moore, B. (1990) 'Application of the Delphi technique in tourism', *Annals of Tourism Research*, Vol. 17, pp. 270–79.

Groome, D. (1993) *Planning and Rural Recreation in Britain*, Aldershot: Avebury.

Hall. P. (1980) *Great Planning Disasters*, London: Weidenfeld and Nicholson.

HALO – *see* Hertfordshire Association of Leisure Officers

Ham, C. and Hill, M. (1984) *The Policy Process in the Modern Capitalist State*, Brighton: Wheatsheaf.

Hantrais, L. and Kamphorst, T. J. (eds) (1987) *Trends in the Arts: A Multinational Perspective*, Voorthuizen, Netherlands: Giordano Bruno Amersfoort.

Harper, J.A. and Balmer, K.R. (1989) 'The perceived benefits of public leisure services: an exploratory investigation', *Society and Leisure*, Vol. 12. No. 1, pp. 171–88.

Harrington, M. (1974) 'Leisure as the means of production', in L. Kolakowski and S. Hampshire (eds) *The Socialist Idea: A Reappraisal,* London: Weidenfeld and Nicholson, pp. 153–63.

Hatry, H.P. and Dunn, D.R. (1971) *Measuring the Effectiveness of Local Government Services: Recreation*, Washington, DC: The Urban Institute.

Hawkins, G. (1993) *From Nimbin to Mardi Gras: Constructing Community Arts*, Sydney; Allen and Unwin.

Haworth, J.T. and Veal, A.J. (eds) (1975) *Leisure and the Community,* Conference Papers, London: Leisure Studies Association.

Heller, A. (1976) *The Theory of Need in Marx*, London: Allison & Busby.

Henderson, K.M., Bialeschki, D., Shaw, S.M. and Freysinger, V.J. (1989) *A Time of One's Own: A Feminist Perspective on Women's Leisure*, State College, PA: Venture.

Henley Centre for Forecasting (1986) *The Economic Impact and Importance of Sport in the UK*, Study 30, London: Sports Council.

Henley Centre for Forecasting (Quarterly) *Leisure Futures*, London: HCF.

Henry, I. (1984) 'The politics of the New Right: consequences for leisure policy and management', *Leisure Management*, Vol. 4, No. 9, September, pp. 10–11.

Henry, I. (1984a) 'Conservatism, socialism and leisure services', *Leisure Management*, Vol. 4, No. 11, November, pp. 10–12.

Henry, I. (1985) 'Leisure management and the social democratic tradition', *Leisure Management*, Vol. 5, No. 2, February, pp. 14–15.

Henry, I. (1988) 'Alternative futures for the public leisure service', in Bennington and White, *op. cit.*, pp. 207–44.

Henry, I.P. (ed.) (1990) *Management and Planning in the Leisure Industries*, London: Macmillan

Henry, I.P. (1993) *The Politics of Leisure Policy*, Basingstoke: Macmillan.

Henry, I. and Spink, J. (1990) 'Planning for leisure: the commercial and public sectors', in Henry, *op. cit.*, pp. 33–69.

Henry, I. and Spink, J. (1990a) 'Social theory, planning and management', in Henry, *op. cit.*, pp. 179–210.

Heritage, Conservation and Recreation Service (1979) *The Third Nationwide Outdoor Recreation Plan: Executive Report*, (United States Department of the Interior) Washington, DC: US Govt. Printing Office.

Hertfordshire Association of Leisure Officers (1978) *Leisure Planning: An Advisory Brief for District Appraisals*, Stevenage: HALO/Stevenage Borough Council.

Hill, K.Q. (1978) 'Trend extrapolation', in J. Fowles (ed.) *Handbook of Futures Research*, Westport, Conn.: Greenwood Press, pp. 249–72.

Hillman, M. and Whalley, A. (1977) *Fair Play for All*, London: PEP (now Centre for Policy Studies).

Hirsch, F. (1977) *Social Limits to Growth*, London: Routledge and Kegan Paul.

Howard, D.R. and Crompton, J.L. (1980) *Financing, Managing and Marketing Recreation and Park Resources*, Dubuque, Iowa: Wm C. Brown.

Iso-Ahola, S. (1980) *The Social Psychology of Leisure and Recreation*, Dubuque, Iowa: Wm C. Brown.

Iso-Ahola, S. (1989) 'Motivation for Leisure', in Jackson and Burton (eds), *op. cit.*, pp. 247–80.

Jackson, E.L. and Burton, T.L. (eds) (1989) *Understanding Leisure and Recreation – Mapping the Past, Charting the Future*, State College, PA: Venture.

Jackson, P. (1986) 'Adapting the R.O.S. technique to the urban setting', *Australian Parks and Recreation*, Vol. 22, No. 3, pp. 26–8.

Jansen–Verbeke, M. (1985) 'Inner city leisure resources', *Leisure Studies*, Vol. 4, No. 2, pp. 141–58.

Jenkins, C. *et al.* (1989) 'Making waves: the structure of the catchment area of a leisure pool', in D. Botterill (ed.) *Leisure Participation and Experience: Models and Case Studies*, Conference Papers 37, Eastbourne, UK: Leisure Studies Association, pp. 137–68.

Jennings, L. (1979) 'Future fun: tomorrow's sports and games', *The Futurist*, Vol. 13, No. 6, pp. 417–31.

Johnson, P. and Thomas, B. (eds) (1992) *Perspectives on Tourism Policy*, London: Mansell.

Jones, S. (1990) 'The Australian tourism outlook forum Delphi', in Horwath and Horwath Services (eds) *Australian Tourism Outlook Forum: Contributed Papers*, Sydney June, Canberra: Bureau of Tourism Research, pp. 51–5.

Kamenka, E. and Tay, A.E. (eds) (1978) *Human Rights*, Port Melbourne, Victoria: Edward Arnold.

Kamphorst, T.J. and Roberts, K. (eds) (1989) *Trends in Sports: A Multinational Perspective*, Voorthuizen, Netherlands: Giordano Bruno Culemborg.

Kaynak, E. and Macaulay, J.A. (1984) 'The Delphi technique in the measurement of tourism market potential', *Tourism Management*, Vol. 4, December, pp. 87–101.

Kelly, J. (1987) *Recreation Trends: Toward the Year 2000*, Champaign IL: Management Learning Laboratories.

Kelly, J. and Godbey, G. (1992) *The Sociology of Leisure*, State College, PA: Venture.

Kelly, O. (1984) *Community, Art and the State: Storming the Citadels*, London: Comedia.

Kelsey, C. and Gray, H. (1985) *Master Plan Process for Parks*, Alexandria, Virginia: American Alliance for Health, Physical Education, Recreation and Dance.

Kennedy, D.W., Smith, R.W. and Austin, D.R. (1991) *Special Recreation: Opportunities for Persons with Disabilities*, Dubuque: Wm C. Brown.

Kew, S. (1979) *Ethnic Groups and Leisure*, London: Sports Council/ SSRC.

Kingsbury, A. (1976) 'Animation', in Haworth and Veal, *op. cit.*, pp. 12.1–12.5.

Lane, J. (1978) *Arts Centres: Every Town Should Have One*, London: Paul Elek.

Leach, R. (1993) *Political Ideologies*, 2nd edn, Melbourne: Macmillan.

Leisure Consultants (1990) *Leisure Forecasts 1991–95*, Sudbury, Suffolk: Leisure Consultants.

Lever, W.F. (1973) 'Recreational space in cities – standards of provision', *Journal of the Royal Town Planning Institute*, Vol. 59, March, pp. 138–40.

Levitt, L. (1991) 'Recreation for the mentally ill', in Driver *et al., op. cit.,* pp. 161–78.

Lieber S.R. and Fesenmaier D.R. (eds) (1983) *Recreation Planning and Management*, London: Spon.

Limb, M. (1986) 'Community involvement in leisure provision – private enterprise or public interest?', in F. Coalter (ed.) *The Politics of Leisure*, Conference Papers Series No. 24, London: Leisure Studies Association, pp. 90–110.

Lindblom, C.E. (1959) 'The science of "Muddling through"', *Public Administration Review*, Vol. 19, No. 2, pp. 79–88.

Linstone, H.A. (1978) 'The Delphi technique', in Fowles, J. (ed.) *Handbook of Futures Research*, Westport, Conn.: Greenwood Press, pp. 273–300.

Logothetis, N. (1992) *Managing for Total Quality: From Dening to Taguchi and SPC*, New York: Prentice Hall.

London M., Crandall, R. and Fitzgibbons, D. (1977) 'The psychological structure of leisure: activities, needs, people', *Journal of Leisure Research*, Vol. 9, No. 4, pp. 252–63.

Lynch, R. (1993) 'The cultural repositioning of rugby league football and its men', *ANZALS Leisure Research Series*, Vol. 1, pp. 105–19.

MacFarlane, L.J. (1985) *The Theory and Practice of Human Rights*, London: Maurice Temple Smith.

Maddox, G. (1985) *Australian Democracy in Theory and Practice*, Melbourne: Longman Cheshire.

Manidis, P. (1994) 'Cost-benefit analysis in parks', in Royal Australian Institute of Parks and Recreation *Who Pays – Open Space and Recreational Facilities*, Seminar Proceedings, Canberra: RAIPR, pp. 45–53.

Marcuse, H. (1964) *One Dimensional Man*, London: Routledge & Kegan Paul.

Marriott, K.L. (1990) *Recreation Planning: A Manual for Local Government*, Adelaide: South Australian Department of Recreation and Sport.

Martilla, J.A. and James, J.C. (1977) 'Importance–performance analysis', *Journal of Marketing*, Vol. 41, No. 1, pp. 77–9.

Martin, W.H. and Mason, S. (1981) *Leisure and Work: The Choices for 1991 and 2001*, Sudbury, Suffolk: Leisure Consultants.

Maslow, A. (1954) *Motivation and Personality*, New York: Harper & Row (2nd edition 1970).

Matthieson, A. and Wall, G. (1982) *Tourism: Economic, Physical and Social Impacts*, London: Longman.

McIntosh, P. and Charlton, V. (1985) *The Impact of Sport for All Policy 1966–1984*, Study 26, London: Sports Council.

McKay, J. (1986) 'Some social impacts of the Grand Prix on residents closest to the circuit – noise and property damage', in Burns *et al., op. cit.*, pp. 124–50.

Mercer, D. (1975) 'The concept of recreational need', *Journal of Leisure Research*, Vol. 5, No. 1, pp. 37–50.

Mercer, D. and Hamilton–Smith, E. (eds) (1980) *Recreation Planning and Social Change in Urban Australia*, Malvern, Victoria: Sorrett.

Miles, I., Cole, S. and Gershuny, J. (1978) 'Images of the future', in C. Freeman and M. Jahoda (eds) *World Futures: The Great Debate*, London: Martin Robertson, pp. 279–342.

Miller, T. (1990) 'Sport, media and masculinity', in D. Rowe and G. Lawrence (eds) *Sport and Leisure: Trends in Australian Popular Culture*, Sydney: Harcourt, Brace Jovanovich, pp. 74–95.

Mills, P. (1992) 'BS5750 – a leisure perspective', in P. Mills (ed.) *Quality in the Leisure Industry*, Harlow: Longman, pp. 16–34.

Ministry of Education (n.d.) *Standards of Public Library Service*, London: HMSO.

Ministry of Housing and Local Government (1969) *People and Planning* (The 'Skeffington Report'), London: HMSO.

Ministry of Culture and Recreation (n.d.) *Culture and Recreation Master Planning*, Toronto: Ministry of Culture and Recreation.

Ministry of Culture and Recreation (1976) *Guidelines for Developing Public Recreation Facility Standards*, Toronto: Sports and Fitness Division, Ministry of Culture and Recreation.

Moeller, G.H. and Shafer, E.L. (1983) 'The use and abuse of Delphi forecasting', in Lieber and Fesenmaier, *op. cit.*, pp. 96–104.

Moeller, G.H. and Shafer, E.L. (1994) 'The Delphi technique: a tool for long-range travel and tourism planning', in Ritchie and Goeldner, *op. cit.*, pp. 473–80.

Mowbray, M. (1993) 'Sporting opportunity: equity in urban infrastructure and planning', *ANZALS Leisure Research Series*, Vol. 1, pp. 120–41.

Murphy, B. and Veal, A.J. (1978) *Community Use of Community Schools at the Primary Level*, Research Working Paper 5, London: Sports Council.

Musgrave, R.A. and Musgrave, P.B. (1980) 'The theory of social goods', in *Public Finance in Theory and Practice*, New York: McGraw-Hill, pp. 54–95.

Myerscough, J., *et al.* (1988) *The Economic Importance of the Arts in Britain*, London: Policy Studies Institute.

NACRO – *see* National Association for the Care and Resettlement of Offenders.

Naisbitt, J. (1982) *Megatrends: Ten New Directions Transforming our Lives*, New York: Warner Books.

Naisbitt, J. and Aburdene, P. (1990) *Megatrends 2000*, London: Pan Books.

National Association for the Care and Resettlement of Offenders (1975) *Off the Streets: Leisure Amenities and the Prevention of Crime*, London: NACRO.

National Capital Development Commission (1981) *Urban Open Space Guidelines*, Technical Paper 21, Canberra: NCDC.

National Playing Fields Association (1971) *Outdoor Play Space Requirements*, London: NPFA.

Nevill, A.M. and Jenkins, C. (1986) 'Social area influences on sports centre use, an investigation of the ACORN method of social area classification', in J.A. Mangan and R.B. Small (eds) *Sports, Culture, Society*, Proceedings of the VIII Commonwealth and International Conference on Sport, Physical Education, Dance, Recreation and Health, London: Spon.

Ng, D., Brown, B. and Knott, W. (1983) 'Qualified leisure services manpower requirements: a future perspective', *Recreation Research Review*, Vol. 10, No. 1, pp. 13–19.

Nicholls, M. (1975) *Recreationally Disadvantaged Areas in Greater London: Report of an Analysis of Provision for Sports and Active Recreation*, RM 467, Policy Studies Unit, London: Greater London Council.

O'Brien, S. and Ford, R. (1988) 'Can we at last say goodbye to social class? An examination of the usefulness and stability of some alternative methods of measurement', *Journal of the Market Research Society*, Vol. 30, No. 3, pp. 289–332.

Paddick, R.J. (1982) 'The concept of need in planning for recreation', in M.L. Howell and J.R. Brehaut (eds) *Proceedings of the VII Commonwealth and International Conference on Sport, Physical Education, Recreation and Dance: Vol. 4 (Recreation)*, Brisbane: University of Queensland, pp. 39–47.

Papadakis, E. (1993) *Politics and the Environment*, Melbourne: Longman Cheshire.

Patmore, A. (1983) *Recreation and Resources*, Oxford: Basil Blackwell.

Pearson, K. (1979) *Surfing Subcultures of Australia and New Zealand*, St. Lucia, Queensland: University of Queensland Press.

Perez de Cuellar, J. (1987) 'Statement', *World Leisure and Recreation*, Vol. 29, No. 1, p. 3.

Peterson, G.L., Driver, B.L. and Gregory, R. (eds) (1988) *Amenity Resource Valuation: Integrating Economics with other Disciplines*, State College, PA: Venture.

Pieper, J. (1965) *Leisure: The Basis of Culture*, London: Faber.

Pigram, J. (1983) *Outdoor Recreation and Resource Management*, London: Croom Helm.

Porritt, J. (1984) *Seeing Green: The Politics of Ecology Explained*, Oxford: Basil Blackwell.

Pryce, K. (1979) *Endless Pressure: A Study of West Indian Life-Styles in Bristol*, Harmondsworth, Middx: Penguin.

Quade, E.S. (1989) *Analysis for Public Decisions*, 3rd edn, New York: North-Holland.

Quin, J.B. (1967) 'Technological forecasting', *Harvard Business Review: Forecasting*, (Reprint No. 21215), pp. 39–56.

Rapoport, R. and Rapoport, R.N. (1975) *Leisure and the Family Life Cycle*, London: Routledge.

Ravenscroft, N. (1992) *Recreation Planning and Development*, Basingstoke: Macmillan.

Ritchie, J.R.B. (1994) 'The nominal group technique – applications in tourism research', in Ritchie and Goeldner, *op. cit.*, pp. 493–502.

Ritchie, J.R.B and Goeldner, C.R. (eds) (1994) *Travel, Tourism and Hospitality Research*, 2nd edn, New York: John Wiley.

Roberts, K. (1983) *Youth and Leisure*, London: Allen and Unwin.

Roberts, K. and Brodie, D.A. (1992) *Inner-City Sport: Who Plays and What are the Benefits?*, Voorthuizen, Netherlands: Giordano Bruno Culemborg.

Rodgers, H.B. (1993) 'Estimating local leisure demand in the context of a regional planning strategy', in Glyptis, *op. cit.*, pp. 116–30.

Schor, J.B. (1991) *The Overworked American: The Unexpected Decline of Leisure*, New York: Basic Books.

Scraton, S. (1993) 'Boys muscle in where angels fear to tread – girls' sub-cultures and physical activities', in J. Horne, D. Jary and A. Tomlinson (eds) *Sport, Leisure and Social Relations*, Keele: Sociological Review, pp. 160–86.

Sears D.W. (1975) 'The recreation voucher system: a proposal', *Journal of Leisure Research*, Vol. 7, No. 2, pp. 141–45.

Seely, R.L., Iglarsh, H.J. and Edgell, D.J. (1980) 'Utilizing the Delphi technique at international conferences: a method for forecasting international tourism conditions', *Journal of Travel Research*, Vol. 18, pp. 30–34.

Shadish, W., Cook, T.D. and Leviton, L.C. (1991) *Foundations of Program Evaluation: Theories of Practice*, Newbury Park, CA: Sage.

Shafer, E.L., Moeller, G.H. and Russell, E.G. (1975) 'Future leisure environments', *Ekistics*, Vol. 40, No. 236, pp. 68–72.

Shaw, M. (1984) *Sport and Leisure Participation and Lifestyles in Different Residential Neighbourhoods*, London: Sports Council/ SSRC.

Simpson, J.A. (1976) 'Notes and reflections on animation', in Haworth and Veal, *op. cit.*, pp. 13.1–13.6.

Smith, P. (1975) 'Comments from a commercial standpoint', in NACRO, *op. cit.*, pp. 17–19.

Smith, S. (1989) *Tourism Analysis*, Harlow: Longman.

Soper, K. (1981) *On Human Needs: Open and Closed Theories in a Marxist Perspective*, Brighton: Harvester.

Sports Council (1968) *Planning for Sport*, London: Central Council for Physical Recreation.

Sports Council (1972) *Provision for Sport: Indoor Swimming Pools, Indoor Sports Centres, Golf Courses*, London: HMSO.

Sports Council (1975) *Indoor Sports Halls: A New Approach to their Dimensions and Use*, London: Sports Council.

Sports Council (1977) *Capital Grants for Sports Facilities: A 5–Year Programme* (duplicated typescript), London: Sports Council.

Sports Council (1978) *Provision for Swimming: A Guide to Swimming Pool Planning*, London: Sports Council.

Sports Council (1982) *Sport in the Community: The Next Ten Years*, London: Sports Council.

Sports Council (1988) *Sport in the Community: Into the 1990s*, London: Sports Council.

Sports Council (1991) *The Playing Pitch Strategy*, London: Sports Council.

Sports Council (1991a) *District Sport and Recreation Strategies – A Guide*, London: Sports Council.

Sports Council (1992) *Provision for Swimming*, (one volume plus two technical reports), London: Sports Council.

Sports Council (1993) *Planning and Provision for Sport* (Facilities Factfile 2), London: Sports Council.

Spretnik, C. and Capra, F. (1985) *Green Politics*, London: Paladin.

Springborg, P. (1981) *The Problem of Human Needs and the Critique of Civilization*, London: Allen and Unwin.

Stabler, M. and Ravenscroft, N. (1993) *The Economic Evaluation of Output in Leisure Services*, Discussion Papers in Urban and Regional Economics No. 80, Department of Economics, Reading: University of Reading.

Stansfield, C.A. and Rickert, J.E. (1970) 'The recreational business district', *Journal of Leisure Research*, Vol. 2, No. 4, pp. 213–25.

Stein, T.A. and Sessoms, H.D. (1977) *Recreation and Special Populations*, Boston: Holbrook.

Stynes, D.J. (1983) 'Time series and structural models for forecasting recreation participation', in Lieber and Fesenmaier, *op. cit.*, pp. 105–19.

Syme, G.J., Shaw, B.J., Fenton, D.M. and Mueller, W.S. (eds) *The Planning and Evaluation of Hallmark Events*, Aldershot: Avebury.

Taylor, J.N. and Johnson, I.M. (1973) *Public Libraries and Their Use*, London: HMSO.

Taylor, P.W. (1959) '"Need" statements', *Analysis*, Vol. 19, pp. 106–11.

Theobald, W.F. (1979) *Evaluation of Recreation and Parks Programs*, New York: John Wiley.

Thorpe Committee (1969) *Report of the Departmental Committee of Enquiry into Allotments*, Ministry of Housing and Local Government, London: HMSO.

Throsby, C.D. and O'Shea, M. (1980) *The Regional Economic Impact of the Mildura Arts Centre*, Sydney: Macquarie University, School of Economic and Social Studies.

Tinsley, H.E., Barrett T.C. and Kass, R.A. (1977) 'Leisure activities and need satisfaction', *Journal of Leisure Research*, Vol. 9, No. 2, pp. 110–20.

Tomlinson, A. (ed.) (1990) *Consumption, Identity and Style*, London: Comedia/Routledge.

Torkildsen, G. (1986) *Leisure and Recreation Management*, 2nd edn, London: Spon.

Torkildsen, G. (1993) *Torkildsen's Guides to Leisure Management*, Harlow: Longman.

Touche Ross (1985) *Michigan: State of the Arts – An Economic Impact Study: Independent Non-Profit Arts Organizations*, Detroit: Touche Ross.

Tourism and Recreation Research Unit (1982) *Priority Groups and Access to Leisure Opportunity*, Edinburgh: Dept. of Leisure Services, Lothian Regional Council.

TRRU – *see* Tourism and Recreation Research Unit.

Veal, A.J. (1975) *Recreation Planning in New Communities: A Review of British Experience*, Research Memo. 46, Birmingham: Centre for Urban and Regional Studies, University of Birmingham.

Veal, A.J. (1979) *New Swimming Pool for Old*; Study 18, London: Sports Council.

Veal, A.J. (1979a) *Six Low Cost Indoor Sports Facilities*, Study 20, London: Sports Council.

Veal, A.J. (1980) *Trends in Leisure Participation and Problems of Forecasting*, London: Sports Council/SSRC.

Veal, A.J. (1982) 'The future of leisure', *International Journal of Tourism Management*, Vol. 1, No. 1, pp. 42–55.

Veal, A.J. (1982a) *Planning for Leisure: Alternative Approaches*, Papers in Leisure Studies No. 5, London: Polytechnic of North London.

Veal, A.J. (1984) 'Planning for leisure: alternative approaches', *World Leisure and Recreation*, Vol. 26, No. 5, December, pp. 17–24.

Veal, A.J. (1986) 'Planning for leisure: alternative approaches', *The Planner*, Vol. 72, No. 6, June, pp. 9–12.

Veal, A.J. (1987) *Leisure and the Future*, London: Allen and Unwin.

Veal, A.J. (1988) *The Concept of Recreational Need Re–considered*, paper to the World Leisure and Recreation Association Congress, Lake Louise, Canada, July.

Veal, A.J. (1991) *Lifestyle, Leisure and Neighbourhood*, paper to World Leisure and Recreation Association, World Congress: 'Leisure and Tourism: Social and Environmental Change, Sydney, 16–19 July.

Veal, A.J. (1991a) *Australian Leisure Futures*, Publication 13, Sydney: Centre for Leisure and Tourism Studies, University of Technology, Sydney.

Veal, A.J. (1993) 'Planning for leisure: past, present and future', in Glyptis, *op. cit.*, pp. 85–95.

Veal, A.J., Jonson, P. and Cushman, G. (eds) (1993) *Leisure and Tourism: Social and Environmental Change* (WLRA 1991 Congress Proceedings), Sydney: Centre for Leisure and Tourism Studies, University of Technology, Sydney.

Vickerman, R. (1983) 'The contribution of economics to the study of leisure', *Leisure Studies*, Vol. 2, No. 3, pp. 345–64.

Vickerman, R. (1989) 'Economic models of leisure and its impact', in Jackson and Burton (eds), *op. cit.*, pp. 331–57.

Wall, G. (1983) 'The economic value of cultural facilities: tourism in Toronto', in Lieber and Fesenmaier, *op. cit.*, pp. 15–25.

Waters, I. (1989) *Entertainment, Arts and Cultural Services*, Harlow: Longman.

Wearing, B. (1990) 'Beyond the ideology of motherhood: leisure as resistance', *Australia and New Zealand Journal of Sociology*, Vol. 26, No. 1, pp. 36–58.

Welch, D. (1991) *The Management of Urban Parks*, Harlow: Longman.

Wheelen, T.L. and Hunger, J.D. (1989) *Strategic Management and Business Policy*, Reading, Mass.: Addison–Wesley.

Williams, E.A., Jenkins, C. and Nevill, A.M. (1988) 'Social area influences on leisure activity – an exploration of the ACORN classification with reference to sport', *Leisure Studies*, Vol. 7, pp. 81–94.

Willis, M. (1968) 'The provision of sports pitches', *Town Planning Review*, Vol. 38, pp. 293–303.

Wilson, J. (1988) *Politics and Leisure*, London: Unwin Hyman.

Wimbush, E. and Talbot, M. (eds) (1988) *Relative Freedoms: Women and Leisure*, Milton Keynes: Open University Press.

Witt, S.F. and C.W. (1992) *Modelling and Forecasting Demand in Tourism*, London: Academic Press.

Wortman, M.S. (1979) 'Strategic management: not-for-profit organizations', in D.E. Schendel and C.W. Hofer (eds) *Strategic Management*, Boston: Little, Brown, pp. 353–381.

Young, S. (1980) 'Children's play in residential settings', in Mercer and Hamilton-Smith (eds), *op. cit.*, Victoria: Sorrett, pp. 85–95.

Young, M. and Willmott, P. (1973) *The Symmetrical Family*, London: Routledge.

AUTHOR INDEX

SUBJECT INDEX